Korea Betrayed

Also by Donald Kirk

Korea Witness: 135 Years of War, Crisis and News in the Land of the Morning Calm
  (co-editor, with Choe Sang Hun)
Korean Crisis: Unraveling of the Miracle in the IMF Era
Looted: The Philippines After the Bases
Philippines in Crisis: U.S. Power versus Local Revolt
The Business Guide to the Philippines
  (general editor)
Tell It to the Dead: Stories of a War
Korean Dynasty: Hyundai and Chung Ju Yung
Tell It to the Dead: Memories of a War
Wider War: The Struggle for Cambodia, Thailand and Laos

Korea Betrayed

Kim Dae Jung and Sunshine

Donald Kirk

KOREA BETRAYED
Copyright © Donald Kirk, 2009.

All rights reserved.

First published in hardcover in 2009 by
PALGRAVE MACMILLAN®
in the United States—a division of St. Martin's Press LLC,
175 Fifth Avenue, New York, NY 10010.

Where this book is distributed in the UK, Europe and the rest of the world, this is by Palgrave Macmillan, a division of Macmillan Publishers Limited, registered in England, company number 785998, of Houndmills, Basingstoke, Hampshire RG21 6XS.

Palgrave Macmillan is the global academic imprint of the above companies and has companies and representatives throughout the world.

Palgrave® and Macmillan® are registered trademarks in the United States, the United Kingdom, Europe and other countries.

ISBN: 978–0–312–24017–2

Library of Congress Cataloging-in-Publication Data

Kirk, Donald, 1938–
 Korea betrayed : Kim Dae Jung and sunshine / Donald Kirk.
   p. cm.
   ISBN 978–0–230–62048–3 (alk. paper)
 1. Kim, Dae Jung, 1925– 2. Presidents—Korea (South)—Biography. 3. Korea (South)—Politics and government—1988–2002. 4. Korean reunification question (1945–) 5. Korea (South)—Relations—Korea (North) 6. Korea (North)—Relations—Korea (South) I. Title.

DS922.4642.K514K57 2010
951.9505092—dc22
[B]   2009013781

A catalogue record of the book is available from the British Library.

Design by Newgen Imaging Systems (P) Ltd., Chennai, India.

First PALGRAVE MACMILLAN paperback edition: December 2010

10 9 8 7 6 5 4 3 2 1

Transferred to Digital Printing in 2010

For Sunny

CONTENTS

Foreword		ix
One	Man from Mokpo	1
Two	People's Choice	17
Three	Matador Politics	33
Four	Time of Violence	51
Five	On Trial for Democracy	67
Six	From Prison to Exile	85
Seven	Birth of Democracy	103
Eight	In Democratic Opposition	119
Nine	Dawn of Sunshine	137
Ten	Sunshine at Its Zenith	155
Eleven	Sunshine under Fire	173
Twelve	Time of Corruption	191
Epilogue	Nobel *Oblige*	209
Notes		217
Bibliography		233
Index		239

FOREWORD
━━━━━━━

Kim Dae Jung's loyal followers and fiercest critics turned out by the tens of thousands to mourn his passing on August 18, 2009, at memorials around South Korea. No other Korean leader had inspired such hope yet encountered such disappointment in fulfilling his vision for a peaceful, reunited country.

This book evolved over more than a decade, from Kim Dae Jung's election campaign during the 1997 economic crisis, through his five-year presidency from February 25, 1998, to February 25, 2003, to its aftermath of revelations, denials, and explanations. I first interviewed him in his home in Seoul's Mapo district in 1972 and saw him many more times over the years. My view of the man has changed with the history of modern Korea. From the idealism of the democracy movement sprang the fervor and tragedy of Gwangju followed by imprisonment and exile in America. Then came the presidency, triumph on a global stage, the corruption inherent in the quest for an inter-Korean summit and Nobel Peace Prize—and the paradox of nonconcern about the suffering above the line between the two Koreas.

Throughout, I refer to Kim Dae Jung either by his full name or by the initials "DJ" by which he is widely known. The repeated use of the initials is a sign of neither disrespect nor informality but a device to distinguish him from the many other Koreans named Kim without having constantly to spell out the entire name. Shorthand is also used for the other two of "the three Kims," Kim "YS" Young Sam and Kim "JP" Jong Pil. (Similarly, DPRK stands for Democratic People's Republic of Korea, North Korea, and ROK is the Republic of Korea, South Korea.)

The transliteration or romanization of the Hangul spelling of Korean names is another issue since the Korean government in DJ's presidency revised the Western spellings to conform more closely to the spoken language than did the classic "McCune-Reischauer" system in use since 1939. Thus I refer to the city of "Gwangju" rather than "Kwangju" except when the name appears as "Kwangju" in titles or quotations from other sources. Similarly, "Pusan" becomes "Busan," "Inchon" is "Incheon," "Taegu" is "Daegu," and "Taejon" is "Daejeon." I have not, however, revised names of South Korean provinces or the North Korean enclaves of Kaesong and Kumkang since the revised spellings in those cases may do more to confuse rather than assist the reader. (Thankfully the names of South Korea's capital, Seoul, and the North Korean capital of Pyongyang are the same in both the "old" and "new" systems.)

For her kindness, patience, and understanding in the process of research and writing, I wish to express my deepest thanks to Sung Hee along with her sister, Sung Eun, and their parents, Lee Nam Bok and Chang Ki Tak. I am also grateful to numerous colleagues, notably journalist Choe Sang Hun for reading the manuscript and for frequent comments and cups of coffee. International human rights specialist David Hawk, Professor Kim Choong Nam of the East-West Center in Honolulu, Professor William Stueck of the University of Georgia, and correspondent and editor Hal Piper also read the manuscript and offered comments and corrections. And thanks to the staff of the Kim Dae Jung Presidential Library and Museum for providing much useful material, to the library of Yonsei University for letting me see its Kim Dae Jung collection, to the Korea Democracy Foundation for access to its library, and to the keepers of Kim Dae Jung's restored boyhood home and the Museum of the Peasants Movement in Haui 3 Islands on Haui-do for their hospitality during several visits.

In addition, I should thank editors on papers ranging from the *Chicago Tribune*, for which I visited Korea from 1972 to 1974 while based in Tokyo as far east correspondent, to *USA Today*, for which I wrote about Korea in Washington and traveled to Seoul for the 1986 Asia Games and the 1988 Olympics, to the *International Herald Tribune*, which I served as Korea correspondent from 1997 to 2003, and to the *Christian Science Monitor*, for which I filed from Seoul and Washington from 2004. Thanks also to John Barry Kotch, "the doctor," for having me write the Sunshine chapter for *Korea Confronts the Future* and to an intrepid translator who desires to remain anonymous.

Numerous contacts gave insights into Kim Dae Jung's politicking and presidency, the road to the North-South summit of June 2000 and the campaign for the Nobel. Among these are Cho Gab Je, former editor-in-chief of *Monthly Chosun*; Lee Chang Choon, former ambassador and writer; commentator Shim Jae Hoon; consultant and Rotarian Jang Song Hyon; analyst Choi Won Ki, aka Brent Choi, and scholar Victor Fic. Finally, I am grateful for interviews with Kim Ki Sam, now living in asylum in the United States.

As some of these names suggest, I became convinced while reporting, researching, and writing this book and hundreds of newspaper and magazine articles that Kim Dae Jung represents a special brand of protest in Korean society. His life was dedicated to a view of justice and equality informed by his origins in southwestern Korea and his protest against the dictators who dominated the South for much of his political career. On the basis of this experience DJ was willing to yield on other principles, to compromise on South Korea's struggle against North Korea and, finally, to provide the North with the resources to survive not just as an isolated dictatorship but as a nascent nuclear power that posed a threat to regional if not global security.

This book, then, traces the evolution of this process in the life and times of a leader who battled dictators in the South before appealing to the one in the North. In the spirit of a faux reconciliation, the South unwittingly promoted the ambitions of a mortal foe that relied on the largesse of others to achieve its ambitions as exemplified by periodic tests of ballistic missiles—and explosions of nuclear "devices." If the policy failed, Sunshine remains the dream that Kim Dae Jung held before the world as the goal for his nation and people.

SEOUL AND WASHINGTON, 2009

Map of North and South Korea

CHAPTER ONE

Man from Mokpo

From the southwestern fishing port of Mokpo, an aging commuter ferry carries passengers at a leisurely pace through a cluster of islands, dropping off and taking on people, vehicles, and light cargo. Shielded by outer islands from the sometimes rough waters of the West or Yellow Sea, the boat generally moves unmolested by strong currents and winds though occasionally service is suspended on stormy days. After three hours, the boat arrives at Haui-do, Haui Island, 20 miles southwest of Mokpo, placid if somewhat remote, 4 miles from one winding side to the other, big enough for a central market village, rice paddies, salt flats and small harbors and inlets for fishing boats from which most of the inhabitants make at least a portion of their living.

Here, on this island, Kim Dae Jung was born and lived for the first few years of schooling, after which, at nine or ten, he moved to Mokpo, the major town on the Korean peninsula's southwestern coast and the largest city in South Cholla Province. (The province surrounds Gwangju, by far the leading city of the Cholla region but an independent unit, not formally part of South Cholla.) It wasn't until 2000, when DJ, the western initials of his given names, by which he is widely known in Korea as well as abroad, had been president for two years that restoration began from the remnants of his old family dwelling to make it seem just as it was in his childhood. "Nobody was living here," says an inscription in Hangul, the Korean script. "The house disappeared, but the frame remained, and we were able to rebuild this one using the same frame."[1]

The inscription gives some clue as to the early circumstances of Kim Dae Jung's life. He was born on January 6, 1923, but DJ in the course of his political career changed his birth year variously to 1924 and 1925.

One reason was to present a somewhat more youthful image. Another was that his father, Kim Yun Sik, was apparently not married to his mother at the time of his birth, and the couple may have wanted the record to show their son was born after their marriage. (Official biographies years later gave DJ's birthdate as December 3, 1925.[2]) DJ's father cultivated rice as well as a "salt field" from which he made enough to build a modest frame-and-thatched house, a comfortable home in a poor environment. "But after the fifth grade, he transferred to primary school in Mokpo," says the inscription. "This is a small area. His father wanted a good education for him."

More details dispel speculation as to DJ's origins. His father lived until his son was over 50, the inscription goes on, and "the rumor he was a stepfather is completely wrong." Very early, before entering primary school, DJ was tutored by a scholarly uncle. From the ages of five to nine, he had to walk an hour to get to a local *Sodang*, a Confucian school found in many villages, two miles from home. "He was quite smart, and he also liked to learn," says the inscription, "so his parents decided to send him to Mokpo." An official in the local island office enlarges on the mystique: "DJ's mother was quite strict with her son. Most people take three or four years to master the class at Sodang. He mastered the class in six months." DJ in one account romanticized the lessons taught by his "very strict" mother, saying, "I could learn the right and the wrong and the good and the evil from my parents."[3]

One of Kim Dae Jung's teachers was a local Confucian scholar who died in 1959, six years after the end of the Korean War, in which North Korean troops had overrun the Cholla provinces after invading the South in June 1950. After the Americans drove them out several months later, the remnants hid in the mountains of South Cholla, often with local support, as South Korean forces methodically slaughtered North Koreans and North Korean sympathizers. If the majority of Cholla people did not support the Communists, they were well schooled in reasons for hating distant rulers in the capital. A 91-year-old man, DJ's cousin, said DJ's uncle had a library filled with 2,000 books. "He was sure he would be a great man," said the cousin. "He told other people, 'Look at the future of this boy.' Every day I saw him. When he was quite young he had leadership." In primary school DJ played "a leading role in harassing Japanese people," the cousin remembered. "When the Japanese teacher orders his pupils, 'Do this, do that,' or tells them to keep things the Japanese way, DJ told other pupils not to obey."[4]

Over centuries, the tradition of dissent, sometimes revolt, was imbued in the subconscious of the Cholla region, nowhere so deeply as on these islands. During the Yi or Chosun dynasty, which held sway over the Korean peninsula for more than 500 years until the Japanese arrived in force in the early 1900s, the kings in Seoul regarded the islands as their rightful fiefdom, their personal property to dispense or exploit as they wished, with if anything more high-handed arrogance than they dared display in more populated cities and regions. A Yi dynasty king is said to have bequeathed Haui-do as a gift to a man who married a princess. A "Museum of the Peasants Movement in Haui 3 Islands," including Haui-do and two nearby islets, portrays the story of suffering in scenes and descriptions. "So the people living here did not own the land," a local history explains. "Instead, they cultivated the land. They paid taxes to the nation. Then when the Japanese ruled, the people did not have the right to cultivate."[5]

Peasants protested periodically, against the Japanese in the 1920s, then against the government in Seoul that replaced the Japanese below the 38th parallel after the Japanese surrender on August 15, 1945. The U.S. military government two months later renamed the hated Oriental Development Company of Japanese rule the New Korea Corporation, ordering rent not to exceed one-third of the value of the crop, but restive peasants on July 7, 1946, staged another uprising over excessive rents. Like tobacco, salt was a government monopoly. DJ's father scraped up the salt and sold it to the government—a viable arrangement under dynastic rule but difficult under the Japanese. "The Japanese wanted more taxes, the people refused," said one account. "DJ took the lead in protest against Japan. DJ's father was richer. He had the salt field so he initiated the movement."[6]

Life in the best of times was tough even for a middle-class family that still had the means to educate its children. The inscription outside DJ's family home, presumably approved by DJ to answer questions about his origins, suggests the suffering typical of a rural Korean family. His father "had two wives, but the first wife died," the inscription notes. "The second wife was his mother." The marital status of DJ's parents remains uncertain. His mother may have been his father's concubine, a woman named Jang Su Geum, and she may have left his father, giving him from childhood a sense of wrong on which was grafted the historic resentment, the *hahn* shared by everyone in the region if not by Koreans everywhere.[7]

In any case, DJ has venerated the influence of his family, both father and mother. From childhood "I was attracted to politics," he wrote. His father was village chief, eligible to receive a free newspaper. At the age of only eight or nine, "I quickly became an avid newspaper reader.

I would devour the front page which carried the political news. Politics clearly was exciting to me"—though how much news he could really absorb was doubtful considering that colonial Korea was under stern Japanese control, there were no local "politics" in Korea, and newspapers would not always have been available on DJ's remote island. "I raised uncomfortably sharp political questions and enjoyed talking about politics, interspersed with my own analyses," said DJ's romanticized account. "Often I was told, 'Kim Dae Jung, you will become an excellent politician!' "[8]

DJ honored his mother's role regardless of whether she was a second wife—a label that hardly demanded explanation considering how many men had them. His parents' influence, but "particularly my mother's, made me a politician," he has written. His father "was artistic and receptive" while his mother "was an iron-willed lady and yet magnanimous when the occasion called for it." She was "clear about what was right and what [was] wrong, and when she felt something was wrong, she took a firm stand against it." DJ has built on the mystique with a tale of snatching, at the age of five, a long-stemmed bamboo tobacco pipe from an itinerant taffy peddler who had fallen asleep in a drunken stupor. The story, like that of George Washington and the cherry tree, assumes the air of legend in the telling: "I took it home and gave it to my father. When my mother learned where I got the pipe, she spanked me dearly, took me to the peddler, and had me return the pipe." Above all, he added, to his mother, "education was most important."[9]

Kim Dae Jung chose not to mention the existence of siblings, three brothers and two sisters. One of them, the son of his father's first wife, is believed to have died when he was ten. The sisters married farmers, but they and their husbands had also died years before DJ's election as president in December 1997. A second brother died after his election. A third brother, retired from the air force, was imprisoned several times under the same military-led governments that forced DJ to spend years in prison, prison hospitals and under house arrest. This brother, DJ's only surviving sibling, living in obscurity, was said to have been in a hospital when DJ was inaugurated president in February 1998.

If the facts of DJ's family relationships are sketchy, the story of his beginnings is flimsier still. If Haui-do seems picturesque, rustic and pleasantly tranquil to a visitor, its historic role was that of a place of exile where life was harsh. DJ's forebears, like many who tilled the land and fished the embracing waters, were not indigenous to the island. Most people in this area were expelled from their original homes by the government. DJ's ancestors were reputedly members of the Yangban class, the privileged elite, who had fallen out of favor with the authorities in their native town of Gimhae, near the sprawling port city of Busan, and were sent to Haui-do as punishment, to survive or fail. All told, members of about 400 households have claimed family ties to DJ's relatives or in-laws, meaning a majority of Haui-do's 2,000 inhabitants are vaguely related to DJ, 25 or so counting as close relatives, cousins, nieces, or nephews.

The flames of revolt were fanned over centuries from the period of rivalry between the Silla kingdom in the southeast and the Baekje in the southwest, culminating in Silla domination before the rise of Koryo, with its capital in Kaesong, north of Seoul, in the tenth century. The Yi dynasty, coming to power in the late fourteenth century, imposed ever harsher rule, provoking eventually a farmers' uprising, the Tonghak peasant revolt, that spread through the country in the early 1890s, got as far as Seoul, was suppressed and then broke out again in much more virulent form in the Cholla region in 1894. During and after this revolt thousands of adjudged troublemakers and their relatives and sympathizers—those who avoided execution, imprisonment, and torture—were banished to the islands off the coast, trapped in new lives from which escape or relief was quite difficult if not impossible.

The revolt assumed anti-Japanese implications when Japanese troops arrived at the port of Incheon, west of Seoul, in May 1894 on the pretext of rescuing Japanese citizens, entered the palace in Seoul, arrested King Kojong, holding him hostage in his own palace, and set up a new government. Japan then opened war against China with an attack on Chinese ships that had arrived at Asan Bay southwest of Seoul in a vain attempt at easing tensions. China failed to reassert Chinese hegemony in a vassal state, finally succumbing to Japan in a foretaste of the much worse wars of the next century.

The complexes of history, recent and ancient, weighed heavily on the people of Haui-do, caught up in the revolt a generation before DJ was born. A sense of recent history, of terrible wrong, of *hahn*, was inculcated in the young by teachers such as DJ's uncle as well as his father. While DJ was in school in Mokpo, his father, once well off, spent much of his time battling Japanese bureaucrats in a vain effort to recover the property the Japanese had confiscated. "Father's anti-Japan activity and tenancy dispute also affected my starting political life," DJ has written.[10] DJ remembers his parents as self-sacrificing, pooling resources for the sake of their family. After taking his case to authorities from Mokpo to Gwangju, the regional center, and finally to Seoul, his father went into business in Mokpo, running a low-priced *yogwan* that rented rooms to discount travelers and boarders.

From listening to tales of woe, and sharing in them too, Kim Dae Jung absorbed lifelong lessons. He graduated at the top of his class from Bukgyo elementary school but ranked second as a result of misbehavior in the form of protests against rules imposed by the Japanese whose troops had easily gained control of Korea in the Russo-Japanese War of 1904–5. Entering the locally prestigious Mokpo Commercial Public High School, DJ was drawn to lectures about Korea, Japan, and the world but seethed when forced to go by a Japanese name. Although initially a top student, "his grades began to fall in his senior year due to troubles with the Japanese."[11]

Still, DJ displayed a brilliance that annoyed the Japanese faculty. Schoolmate Jeong Jin Tae has described an episode in which a Japanese teacher gave an assignment that was "too much to memorize and told us to recite it by the next day in order to harass Korean students." DJ dispelled his classmates' worries. When the Japanese teacher asked about the assignment, he said, 'I'll do it.'" With that, "he stood reciting" until, two-thirds of the way through, "the teacher became embarrassed and stopped him," thinking DJ's performance "might get him in trouble."[12]

In high school DJ's resentment of the Japanese matured into an abiding sense of wrong, the basis for a crusading spirit that contributed to his rise as a political leader—to his undying opposition to central authority in Seoul and, ultimately, to providing funds, economic aid, and diplomatic and moral support to a North Korean regime that represented the antithesis of all that he professed to believe. The turning point came in 1938 when talking and writing in Korean, including use of Korean names, was outlawed. "We could not even speak at school," DJ wrote in an autobiographical account. "We were punished if we broke the rule." When his father came to visit, they could not communicate, fearful that his father's ignorance of Japanese would get both of them into trouble. "He never tried to learn it," the account goes on. "Since I was not allowed to speak Korean at school, I could not say anything to him, either." The memory was deeply saddening. His father "had a perplexed expression on his face and tried to say something, but he could not open his mouth, and neither could I," says the account. "So he turned around and left without uttering a word." When DJ got home, his father could not bear to say what he had gone to the school to discuss. "In the end, I was not able to ever ask my father what it was about, and because I could not, the memory of the incident remains all the more heartbreaking to me."[13]

Appointed a class leader, DJ was proudest of report cards offering incontrovertible evidence of his rebellious, patriotic spirit. The report for the first year describes him as "simple, precise, active, excellent to think and understand, smart, excellent in abacus calculations, enjoys swimming." His report for his fifth and final year offers a different perspective: "enjoys reading books, needs to be watched because he views everything critically."[14]

Despite his increasingly outspoken attitude, DJ might have gone on to a Japanese college, as did thousands of other young Koreans at the time regardless of their anti-Japanese sentiment, but he was unable physically to get to Japan after the Americans blockaded the Japanese islands in World War II. He then considered going to a Japanese university in Manchuria, part of Manchoukuo, as the Japanese named the "nation" they had carved out of northeastern China, but abandoned that idea as war spread. He might also have been drafted into the Japanese army, the fate of thousands of young Koreans, some of whom fought valiantly for the Japanese while others, viewed as unreliable, were relegated to noncombat roles, including duty at prisoner-of-war camps.

DJ got out of the Japanese draft by going to work for a marine transport company in great need of help in wartime. He won the admiration of local people both for finding a job with a company after high school and for enduring beatings by Japanese supervisors. Japanese rule was harsh, especially in the final months of the war when Japanese forces were in dire need of food and supplies from Korea, but DJ was still able in April 1945, four months before the Japanese surrender, to marry the well-to-do daughter of a local family, Cha Yong Ae, sister of one of his classmates and a student at a school for women.

Kim Dae Jung, 22 when the Japanese surrendered on August 15, 1945, and the colonial occupation of the Korean peninsula ended, was just starting out as an entrepreneur in bustling Mokpo. Born, reared, and schooled in the depths of the Cholla region, he instinctively shared the age-old sense of oppression at the hands of higher authority. Now his life was about to enter a dramatic new chapter that would shape his career, and his outlook, in family, business, politics, and, most importantly, war and peace—vis-à-vis the North and the world at large.[15]

With the transfer of rule from Japanese to Koreans, DJ shifted his focus to a new target, the entrenched elite in Seoul whose forebears had dominated the Cholla region for centuries. The new rulers, he discovered, were if anything worse than their Japanese predecessors, or so it sometimes seemed as the center in Seoul attempted to exert control. In the vacuum created by the departure of the Japanese after "liberation," that is, the Japanese surrender, DJ won his first election—workers at the factory, having taken it over after the departure of the Japanese, voted him the company manager after he had organized a union. He also joined the local chapter of Gunkukjunbi, the Committee for Founding the New Government, sometimes translated as the Nation Founding Preparations Committee. When U.S. forces arrived in Korea several weeks after the Japanese surrender, the Gunkukjunbi and the Mokpo Youth League were banned as leftist if not Communist.

The transition from Japanese colonialism to independence was filled with turmoil as DJ maneuvered through a maze of conflict and competition in business, politics, and ideas. His wife's family was essential, providing the funds for him to take over a shipping company and then a local newspaper, the base from which he forged bonds with figures caught up in the great issue of the country's emergence as a single, independent, democratic state. In the maelstrom of local politics, a micro-image of the political wars raging elsewhere after the arbitrary division of the peninsula at the 38th parallel by the Soviet Union and the United States, DJ was attracted to men and ideas with an affinity for the nationalist, socially appealing views emanating from Pyongyang where the Communists were fast expanding their influence through shrewd organizational and propaganda tactics.[16]

For Koreans, the greatest disillusionment was the realization that surrender of the hated colonialists did not mean unification of the country under one respected if not revered government. Nor did it mean an end to political imprisonment, torture, and executions, standard punishments inflicted in both Koreas. The new South Korean leader, Rhee Syngman, commanded little respect in the Cholla region. Rhee had carried the banner of Korean democracy in the United States for the better part of 40 years as a student, then as an activist before returning on the strength of the Japanese surrender and the American occupation in 1945, suppressing his foes and having himself voted president of the nascent Republic of Korea in July 1948 in an assembly election boycotted by leftists.

Rhee's opposite number in North Korea, Kim Il Sung, appeared to dedicated leftists in the South to have far greater revolutionary credentials even though he too was beholden to a foreign power, in his case the Soviet Union. After years as an anti-Japanese guerrilla fighter in Manchuria and then as an officer in the Soviet army, Kim Il Sung after the Japanese surrender returned to his native land in 1945, setting foot at Wonson from a Russian ship. Installed as Moscow's man in Pyongyang, he became prime minister of the first government of the Democratic People's Republic of Korea after its founding on September 9, 1948, three and a half weeks after the founding of South Korea as the Republic of Korea on August 15, 1948, third anniversary of "liberation" from Japan.

In the rivalry between surrogates of the two superpowers, real independence was a chimera that led in a few short years to the bloodiest war in Northeast Asian history, the Korean War, a sequel both to revolution on the Chinese mainland and to World War II, in which the Korean peninsula, while cruelly ruled by Japan, was largely untouched militarily. The Communist victory in China, on October 1, 1949, came just a year and a few weeks before the first Chinese "volunteers," many of them dragooned from the defeated Kuomintang, Nationalist Chinese, forces, entered North Korea to rescue Kim Il Sung and his land from advancing Americans and South Koreans.

Instinctively, if not deliberately, Kim Dae Jung sought out the most likely base from which to operate as a nationalist with intense regional and family loyalties. A leadership position in Shinmin-dang, the New Democratic Party, a leftist party organized by Communists, offered a path to power and influence. The Shinmin-dang had absorbed the Namro-dang, the South Workers' Party, with strong ties to the North, in accordance with Vladimir Lenin's principle of one party, one state. "Why did he take his first step in Communist organizations," one writer has asked. "By his friends' persuasion? Voluntarily with his faith in communism? Or were there no other parties to accept him except for these newly established leftist parties or the Namro-dang when he wanted to be a politician?" DJ, as a student, had "no chance of studying Communist ideology under strict Japanese rule with a strong anticommunist policy."[17]

Socialism in that period had an intrinsic appeal among Korean intellectuals and politicians. Many were attracted to socialist ideals. DJ appears to have been caught between antithetical forces, compromising where expedient, playing one side against the other, weighing the odds in a turbulent transition whose outcome was uncertain at best. "I did not know the exact concepts and aims of communism and nationalism," he wrote. "I was just eager to be the one who helps the establishment of the new country." Then too, he has admitted to having been "slightly positive to communism at first." No sooner had one of the new leaders announced the make-up of a leftist government, however, than the American forces, a month after the Japanese surrender, arrived and refused to accept it: "The urgent problem for them was the confrontation of leftists and rightists." Besides writing "propaganda for newspapers," DJ pursued the highly capitalist aim of building up his own shipping company, from which he was to acquire three vessels and earn more money than had ever been possible under the Japanese.[18]

In the conflict between communism and capitalism, DJ, the young husband, was influenced by his conservative father-in-law, Cha Bo Ryun, a businessman who ran a printing shop and was a leader of the conservative Hankuk Minju-dang, the Korea Democratic Party. It was his father-in-law, the source of much of the money that DJ needed to establish himself in business, who "ordered" him to give up connections with clearly Communist fronts in league with leftists influenced by the new regime in Pyongyang. "He called me many times to point out the anti-nationality of communism" and the movement's relationship to the Soviet Union "as their real country," DJ testified years later.[19]

For all his protestations, however, DJ was often suspected of supporting if not involving himself in leftist activities and was at pains to deny a role. One example was rioting that broke out on October 1, 1946, in Daegu, an important southeastern city, a bastion of conservatism, as complaints mounted over the paltry size of rice rations. Spurred on by leftist organizers, rioters attacked a police station in Mokpo. DJ as leader of the militant Democratic Youth League was accused of orchestrating the mayhem. He blamed a rival who he said had kidnapped him and hauled him to the police. Held for ten days, DJ endured severe beatings but had an alibi. A midwife and others swore that he was at his wife's house while she was giving birth to a girl who died of tuberculosis. Several months later DJ joined his father's conservative grouping and began what he said were rightist activities.[20]

DJ was forever arousing suspicions by his choice of friends and allies. Though it might be difficult to label him, an analysis by the Korean Central Intelligence Agency, obviously not unbiased, concluded that he had "no sense of loyalty or strong beliefs," was "hungry for power," was "an opportunist and a genius in betraying trust," was "a politico who gets in bed with anyone for political gains" and "was adept at changing situations."[21] If those views appear extreme, they avoided the temptation of accusing him, as did his foes, of selling out to Communists and leftists. Rather, they acknowledged the difficulty of pinning down the bedrock views of a man who defied facile definition through all his years in and out of office and power.

Already disliked by leftists for staying on good terms with coast guard officers for the sake of his shipping business, Kim Dae Jung managed to provoke the authorities in 1949 after loaning money to a friend's brother who turned out to have been associated with the left. DJ was able, however, to convince a young navy guard officer and a policeman that he had contributed the money to help cover his travel expenses to Seoul and was not donating to local leftists. A Communist friend, Jung Tae Muk, who had been with DJ in the banned Communist Youth League in 1945, was not so adept at double-talk. Jailed until the Communists arrived, he was freed by the North Koreans. Then, several months after the war was over, a South Korean court sentenced him to seven years in prison.

At about the same time, Kim Dae Jung also gave money when solicited by the management of the shady Bodo Yeonmaeng, National Guidance Alliance, a "league for rehabilitation" that the government compelled leftists to join before the Korean War as a means of following their activities. By contributing to a quasi-government front set up to control and monitor leftists, DJ may have been motivated by a desire for self-promotion, of camaraderie, more than ideology or belief in anything other than Korean nationalism and the need for social reform.[22] As a member of leftist groups, DJ acknowledged donating "as a standing member." He also became deputy chief of a chapter of the Mokpo marine league, Mokpo-haesang-dan. Everyone "knew that I was cooperating very closely with the navy guard in Mokpo because of my business, shipping," he has written.[23]

Questions swirl around what Kim Dae Jung did in the Korean War. He was in Seoul on business when the North Koreans crossed the North-South dividing line at the 38th parallel north of Kaesong on June 25, 1950, captured the capital four days later and pressed relentlessly southward. Witnessing the takeover of Seoul, DJ maintained years later, he got to know the evils of communism. "I came to dislike them unconsciously, and I set my mind right against them," he testified. A single event, as he told the story, convinced him. On his way to a Catholic church in Seoul, he saw three North Korean soldiers, along with ten local leftists, grab a young man. As a crowd gathered, the soldiers recounted the man's crimes and shouted, "Execution by shooting"—a sentence he assumed was carried out, as were thousands of others by both sides, soon after they dragged the man away. "This event helped me have firm anticommunism," he said. "I felt the danger of communism more directly than by reading 1,000 books about anticommunism."[24]

After North Korean troops took the capital, Seoul was not a safe place. North Koreans roamed the streets, knocking on doors, picking up those who seemed at all fit and sending them north for training, military service and, for those who survived and displayed requisite loyalty, indoctrination into work for government agencies. Elderly South Koreans, having managed to hide out during this harrowing period, told years later of eluding the North Koreans, cowering in cellars, fleeing into mountainous woodland or, in some fortunate cases, bribing South Korean doctors, whom the North Koreans had ordered to examine them, to sign papers that exempted them for some dread communicable disease like tuberculosis.

A number of leftists did volunteer, but thousands more were forced to serve a regime they feared or knew little about except that it was remote and dangerous. As many as 100,000 South Koreans went North, forced or voluntarily, during the Korean War, 40 percent of the 250,000 who migrated there between liberation in August 1945 and the signing of the truce in July 1953, a figure that compares with 1.6 million who fled to the South during those eight fearful years.[25]

Why had Kim Dae Jung gone to Seoul, what was he really doing, and how did he elude the round-up? His critics believe he was curious about the nature of Communism, that he had contacts among leftists who were providing information and assistance to the North Koreans.[26] DJ has gone to great lengths to allay suspicions about leftist proclivities accounting for his presence in Seoul at the outset of the Korean War. His version was that he found safe haven with a brother-in-law, then encountered a businessman visiting from Mokpo. He was heartened by South Korean broadcasts telling the citizenry to await the destruction of "the Red army" in the city of Daejeon, about 100 miles to the south. The fact was, however, that U.S. and South Korean troops clung to Daejeon only briefly before they were sent into precipitous retreat in the third week of July.

By then DJ was already on his way to Mokpo on foot, walking along the west coast with four others, including his brother-in-law and the businessman. En route, they heard the North Koreans had reached Mokpo while forcing the Americans and South Koreans into the enclave behind what came to be known as the Busan perimeter, shielding Busan and Daegu within the opposite southeast corner of South Korea. They pressed ahead, "without thinking of life or death," DJ was to say much later.[27] He was rewarded on arriving with one piece of happy news—his wife, Cha Yong Ae, had given birth 12 days earlier, on July 29, to their second son, Kim Hong Up, born safe and sound in a bomb shelter.

Soon, as DJ has told it, in a spirit of heroic adventure, he endured some of the worst experiences of his life, all at the hands of the North Koreans. Learning his father-in-law and younger brother had been arrested, he lost his home and other property and was then imprisoned, interrogated, and beaten. Asked by a North Korean officer, "How many patriots did you inform against," he responded, "I don't remember." There was also another explanation for why DJ was in trouble, that he had courted Communists by taking charge of a local people's committee but was picked up for embezzling property, including a Buddha statue. For more than a month, cut off from the outside, forbidden from talking, he survived on a starvation diet. His father-in-law was taken to be executed with several others but survived after the bullet glanced off him. A younger brother, forced to join the invaders' "volunteer" army, fled during a break in training.[28]

North Korean control diminished sharply and then vanished after the landing of U.S. Marines in the dangerously tidal waters of Wolmido off the port city Incheon, west of Seoul, on September 15, 1950. The bold plan of General Douglas MacArthur, from his headquarters in Tokyo, for liberating the capital, entrapping the North Koreans or forcing them to flee, also led to the liberation of Kim Dae Jung. Tied and handcuffed in prison in Mokpo, seeing the Communist guards had disappeared, "I urged people to escape at that moment," he wrote. "I persuaded them and broke the door with them. We helped all prisoners escape.... We could save ourselves thanks to the Incheon landing of American forces."[29]

Already a known dissident, reputed to have leftist connections, DJ was also viewed as suspect by government officials in authority after the North Korean retreat. Held in a warehouse in Mokpo, he and other suspects were to be herded onto a ship, then shot and thrown overboard. A local teacher, hearing of the fate that awaited DJ, went to the warehouse on the night before the execution and slipped him his own identification tag. He told DJ, when his name was called, not to answer and, when pressed, to say there had been a mistake and show his friend's name tag. Thus, DJ for the second time avoided the ultimate punishment—this time by South rather than North Koreans.[30]

Kim Dae Jung's appreciation of the U.S. military role in the liberation of Seoul and the South was not enough to motivate him to join the South Korean armed forces. How he got out of the military—first by dodging the North Koreans during the relatively brief period in which they held sway over Seoul and most of the South, including Mokpo, then by escaping induction by the South Koreans who quickly returned to Mokpo after the North Korean departure—remains a mystery. A reserve officer, refuting speculation that DJ was fostering ties with Communist loyalists, told a sympathetic politician that DJ "cooperated with the military" and was not "involved in leftist activities before and after the Korean War at all."[31] A more reasonable explanation is that, as an opportunistic entrepreneur, DJ convinced authorities that he might contribute more effectively as a businessman than as a soldier. Then too, he publicized news and commentary through the newspaper, *Mokpo Ilbo*, run by a Japanese concern until liberation and acquired by him with relatives' money after getting out of prison even though, in depressed times, the newspaper could not have been profitable.

Perhaps Kim Dae Jung's affiliation with the local defense guard, under the navy, also helped. He rose to vice commander of this nonofficial group, which had the status of a nongovernmental organization, an unofficial militia, not a bona fide military unit. Used mainly for spotting remnants of the guerrillas, inspecting vessels suspected of transporting Communist recruits, the unit broke up due to corruption. The government of Rhee Syngman was riddled with graft. (Rhee, known in the west as "Syngman Rhee," had reversed his name during his long years abroad as a student and activist.) For most people, day-to-day survival, not high-level corruption, was the main issue. Was DJ too valuable for his talents and resources to be wasted fighting the North Koreans? Did he receive a waiver, an exemption?

The answers are not clear, but who would not appreciate DJ's desire, as a young father, to want to avoid a cruel war?[32] DJ's lack of military service has never been held against him politically, even by his foes. Many young men pulled strings, fled, or deserted in the struggle to stay alive. Now owner of ten ships, transporting crops and fertilizer, DJ began living primarily in the port of Busan, South Korea's second biggest city after Seoul, swarming with refugees from regions overrun by the North Koreans and the heart of a rapidly expanding U.S. force, the center of logistics and also of Rhee's government. There has been no evidence to suggest that DJ was dedicating a portion of his profits to pay off those who could keep him from having to join the armed forces when other healthy young men had to serve.

Wartime adventurism, not military service, compelled DJ to enter public life. Away from the suffering of allied soldiers defending the Busan perimeter in the summer of 1950 and then advancing north, DJ became familiar with the machinations of a regime that he realized was as corrupt as it was inept. This outlook was sharpened by Rhee's refusal to tolerate a vote for president by the National Assembly, as required under the 1948 constitution, before his term was to end in July 1952.

DJ, reading widely and discussing war and politics in the sanctuary of Busan, was far more indignant about Rhee's megalomania, to judge from what he has written and said, than he was about far-off battles fought by armies in whose ranks he would never serve. One of those with whom he shared conversations and ideas was Lee Hee Ho, an activist in South Korea's budding women's movement, a decade later to become his second wife. In the hothouse of emotions and ideas and politicking of wartime Busan, DJ formed the worldview that was to infuse his career—and turn his crusade for democracy into a campaign of apology for the North Korean regime that his political enemies were fighting.

CHAPTER TWO

People's Choice

Chinese "volunteers" entered the war in October and November 1950, saving North Korea, the Democratic People's Republic of Korea, the DPRK, from takeover by South Korea, the Republic of Korea, the ROK. Chinese battled Americans, South Koreans and troops from fifteen other allied countries above and below the 38th parallel for another two years and eight months until the signing of the Korean War armistice in "the truce village" of Panmunjom on July 27, 1953.

In a time of vicious seesaw warfare, as negotiations bogged down in Panmunjom, 40 miles north of Seoul on the line between opposing armies, domestic Korean politics to most of the world was an irrelevant sideshow. The only politics that mattered to Americans in mid- and late 1952 revolved around the politicking for a successor to Harry S. Truman, the president who had ordered the United States to war, under the banner of the United Nations Command, and then to enter peace talks. The Republican Party would nominate Dwight D. Eisenhower, victorious commander of U.S. forces in Europe in World War II, who campaigned on the simple pledge, "I will go to Korea"—a promise that helped the popular "Ike" defeat the "egghead" Adlai Stevenson in November 1952.

To Kim Dae Jung, protest in Busan against Rhee Syngman's rule was clearly far more important than American politics though DJ may not have been politically active in the infighting between pro-Rhee and anti-Rhee factions. The protest reached a climax in May 1952 with Rhee's declaration of martial law, the arrest of obstreperous National Assembly members who opposed him for another term, and imposition of a constitutional amendment calling for a "popular" vote that Rhee under martial law would have the tools to manipulate in his favor. The charade confirmed DJ's suspicions about South Korean leadership—and convinced him of the legitimacy of protest against the conservatives who dominated the political machinery.

DJ's leftist tendencies resurfaced after generals from the United States, China, and North Korea had done negotiations, boycotted by Rhee, and had reached an agreement opposed by a majority of South Koreans for legitimizing the division of the peninsula. The South remained in the depths of economic hardship, dependent on foreign aid for survival while people scrounged for food. Nowhere was deprivation greater than in the Cholla region. DJ saw the opportunity to crusade for social justice—a cause that again led the police to interrogate him.

"Although there are many different opinions, it is difficult to deny that Kim Dae Jung was a member of the leftist party in Mokpo right after Korea's liberation," said a lengthy study in the conservative *Monthly Chosun* many years later. "According to his statements, he was arrested by Korean police twice and was released after investigation. He was also arrested by the Red Army, which had taken over Mokpo as soon as the Korean War broke out, and he escaped from them just before his death. This means that he suffered from both the right and the left, which anticipated the storms in his future life."[1] If DJ wavered in his beliefs, he was quite certain of one thing: he yearned for success as a political figure, not as a businessman.

The legacy of the Korean War was an era of repression that had begun during the presidency of Rhee, not deposed until the student-led revolution of April 1960. Kim Dae Jung's deepest instincts at this early stage were those of a populist figure to whom leftist contacts provided the avenue to votes and social reform with the interests of Mokpo, and Cholla, at heart. DJ did not, as many foreigners believed, owe his political prominence to his vision of a united Korea, his understanding of the North or his charismatic appeal among the mass of South Koreans. The source of his strength, from the time of his early upbringing on a far-off island off Mokpo, would be Cholla, a distant agricultural region, isolated from the rest of the country, exploited by kings, then humiliated by latter-day leaders and the men they relied on to consolidate their rule.

"It seems that the background of his birth and the circumstances in his family induced him to communism," one author has written. "However, more important than ideology might have been his political ambition. It is possible that DJ thought leftist parties as a more proper base from which to grow."[2] While DJ had profited in business around the southern reaches of the peninsula during the war, he had grown up attuned to the inferior position, and inferiority complex, of those who lived and worked in the southwestern provinces. As one who had avoided military service, for whatever reason, he could not be expected to share the same patriotic fervor, or war-like nationalism, or sense of superiority, of some people from other regions. Rather, he was in competition with them as he sought to lead his people, the people of Cholla, in combatting an historical legacy of oppression by all those who had come to exploit them.

Immediately after the war, DJ remained under suspicion, and investigation, as a result of his long record of off-and-on leftist contacts and, just as important, his outspoken criticism of Rhee, an increasingly unpopular figure. "With the end of the Korean War, I came to know about corrupt politics," DJ has written. "I had the strong thought that people cannot live happily under the government with deception and corruption."

From his vantage on the southern coasts, DJ shared the awareness that Rhee and his commanders had evacuated Seoul after having pledged to defend it. He was also aware that South Korean forces had been responsible for massacres. "After the war, they executed even the civilians who helped Communists reluctantly to survive." He concluded that "all these tragedies were the result of the corruption of politics." In refutation of charges that he was a leftist, he argued the need to improve conditions in order "to defend South Korea from the Communists." He had, he wrote, "decided to enter the political field" after seeing "the corruption of the Rhee Syngman government in Busan."[3]

Early on, DJ experienced failures that would have led most people to abandon dreams of political power in favor of the prosaic need for making money. His initial failure at the polls happened right in his home town. After getting out of the shipping company, he ran in May 1954 to represent Mokpo in the National Assembly. Backed by port workers, journalists, and young people, he believed that he had a reasonable chance of defeating the candidate of the ruling, and woefully ill-named, Jayu-dang or Liberal Party. "I have come to the conclusion," he said, "that the real well-being of the people could not be attained unless a genuine democratic political system is firmly established by ending the dictatorship which ignores the will of the people and downgrades the National Assembly."[4]

As an independent, however, Kim Dae Jung had no chance against the political machinery that saw his candidacy as a left-wing conspiracy against law, order—and Rhee's personal power. "Something unbelievable happened," DJ wrote. "The prosecution arrested all members of the labor union for supporting an independent member"—and did not free them until they promised to support the Liberal Party candidate. Under the circumstances, DJ placed fourth or fifth among eight candidates while Liberals won two-thirds of the assembly seats.[5]

Humiliated in defeat, DJ moved to Seoul, the seat of the nation's power brokers, in search of funding and alliances. In an appeal for popularity, he based his pleas on the need for democratic reforms. The despotism of President Rhee deepened his determination to oppose his rule—and that of the central government. The turning point came in 1956 after the presidential candidate of the Minju-dang, or Democratic Party, died before the election of May 3, 1956, giving Rhee an easy victory in his bid for a third four-year term.

Rhee, however, faced trouble from the victorious vice presidential candidate, Chang Myun, from the Minju-dang. After Chang was wounded in an assassination attempt in 1957, DJ joined his party—and also his religion. He asked Chang, a Catholic, to be his godfather for his baptism as a Catholic, a faith inculcated among dissident martyrs in the late Yi dynasty. The priest, the Reverend Kim Chol Gyu, gave DJ the Christian name Thomas More, the English statesman who died fighting persecution of priests by Henry VIII, implying "I should become a politician who does not spare his life at the cost of a proper faith."[6]

DJ's hopes for the Minju-dang's nomination for the National Assembly seat from Mokpo were blocked, however, when the party, divided between "old" and "new" members, nominated a man from the rival faction. It was a measure of DJ's ambition, courage, and dedication that he entered his name as the candidate from a district in another region, Kangwon Province, the only province divided between North and South, first at the 38th parallel at the end of World War II in August 1945 and then in a jagged line that gave more territory to the South where the shooting stopped nearly eight years later at the end of the Korean War. Kangwon on the southern side covered the mountains of northeastern South Korea; Kangwon in the North included the Mount Kumkang region of southeastern North Korea. Inje County, deep in a valley in (South) Kangwon Province, had been the scene of some of the heaviest fighting against Chinese troops in 1951 and 1952. DJ was no doubt moved by the history of the blood shed in those mountains, but to him Inje was his residence of opportunity.

Kim Dae Jung's strategy made sense. Although far from Cholla, about one-third of the voters in the county were soldiers, many from Cholla, on lonely duty against North Korean soldiers massed among forbidding peaks and valleys on the other side of the demilitarized zone, the "DMZ," the band, 2.6 miles or 4 kilometers wide, that stretches 155 miles, 248 kilometers, across the peninsula. Tension was high. Shots were fired from time to time, and the North Koreans staged intermittent raids. Many of the South Korean soldiers were homesick, not happy to have to endure harsh discipline worsened by freezing winters and sweltering summers in daily danger that alternated with bouts of terminal boredom. Here was a region to which few other politicians paid attention—a place to which DJ, with nowhere else to go, could turn in a bid for entry into the national power sweepstakes.

DJ's motives were political, not military. In an atmosphere of dubious military morale, he counted on the votes of the soldiers, eligible to cast their ballots in those days from wherever they were stationed, not their native districts. He invested his savings, all he had made from his shipping business, and money from his wife's family, in a bid to register and then campaign tirelessly as the Minju-dang's candidate from Inje. Again, however, he lost—initially when government goons blocked the registration process, stealing the seals needed to certify enough signatures for him to register his name. Charging cheating, DJ actually got the Supreme Court to rule in his favor, invalidate the election and order another election. This time, in a special election in June 1959, DJ seemed to have a realistic shot at success. The government spared no effort to block his election, intimidating the young soldiers on whom he counted for support to stay away from the polls. Having lost all his money, his job and, it seemed, any chance of a career in business, DJ lost to the Liberal Party candidate.

Kim Dae Jung's strength and resilience now faced their most severe test since his darkest moments as a prisoner in the early phase of the Korean War. With two small sons in school and little money, DJ sensed opportunity in the national mood of political ferment. Nowhere was the spirit more intense than in the Cholla region. Rhee easily won election to yet another term, his fourth, on March 15, 1960, capturing 90 percent of the votes after his opponent again had conveniently died, but his days were numbered. Students took to the streets, charging wholesale corruption in the election of Rhee's man as vice president. Finally, on May 29, Rhee was forced to board an American plane, owned by Civil Air Transport, under contract with the U.S. Central Intelligence Agency, for a flight into exile in Hawaii with his Austrian wife. Too old to join the student uprising, DJ applauded on the sidelines. Suddenly he found himself a member of the ruling party—the

Minju-dang controlled the interim government, and another National Assembly election was set for July 29.

Tragedy, though, was about to strike. Cha Yong Ae, Kim Dae Jung's wife, now working as a hairdresser, attempting pitifully to make enough to cover daily living expenses, scrimping and saving to get their two sons through elementary school in Mokpo, suffered a nervous breakdown. While DJ was excitedly preparing for his next run at the assembly, she died on May 27, 1960. DJ attributed her passing to emotional and physical fatigue. How she really felt about his obsession with political success is not known. DJ would like her remembered as a noble figure who "never complained even a bit under the most painful circumstances and inspired me with her courage." She would tell him, he wrote, that "even if you are arrested, don't worry about our household matters" and "fight like a man should do."[7] Tragically, she had taken her own life.[8] Now DJ's fortunes were at their lowest ebb. His funding, his family, all that he had hoped for, personally, politically, professionally, seemed to have vanished.

Yet Kim Dae Jung soldiered on, convinced, this time, after all his campaigning in Inje County, that he could get elected from there. He miscalculated. Although the Minju-dang won 73 percent of the seats in the National Assembly, the party was divided between old and new factions and did not give DJ, as a member of the youth faction, the support he needed. At the moment at which he expected to ride the crest of the wave into the assembly, he was caught in the undertow, dragged down, in danger of drowning, the loser by 1,000 votes—not a small margin in that remote district.

Again DJ challenged the results, charging that the winner, a former police superintendent, was a stooge of the old Rhee regime, a member of Rhee's discredited party. DJ's cohorts were not above strong-arm tactics, raiding the office where the votes were counted, destroying ballot boxes and burning ballots. As a spokesman for Minju-dang leader Chang, DJ mounted a campaign of denunciation of the former police supervisor who was declared the winner. The man, who may have been doing his share of vote-rigging, was eventually ruled ineligible for the seat under a law proscribing antidemocratic activists.[9] On his next attempt, DJ was not to be denied, winning easily in a special election on May 13, 1961, as the representative from Inje, where the soldiers from Cholla who were stationed there insured his victory.

DJ had no idea as he railed against the militarists of the plot by the man who would be his nemesis for the next 18 1/2 years. Park Chung Hee, a young general who viewed him as another troublemaker blocking his vision of Korea as a strong, independent power, staged his bloodless coup on May 16, 1961, overthrowing the civilian government of Prime Minister Chang Myun and the titular president, Yun Po Sun. Three days later Park disbanded the assembly, the best way, as far as he was concerned, to silence noisy leftist students and other dissenters who would use it as a forum to pillory his policies. In the process, he would, like the kings who had ruled for centuries before the Japanese colonial era, reward friends and allies from his native Daegu and the surrounding Kyongsang provinces while his police arrested zealots stigmatized as "Communist" or Communist sympathizers.

Park and the coterie around him looked down on Cholla—and in particular on the young man who would become the region's favorite son. Having gone from Inje to Seoul to sit in the National Assembly, DJ was banned from political activities—and then accused of scheming to set up a nonmilitary government in place of those who had seized power on May 16. The plot allegedly called for mobilizing students, assassinating officials, and forming an interim regime with the support of colonels who opposed Park. The plotters contacted the U.S. command, asking for help in toppling those who had illegally seized power. DJ, however, was too clever to commit himself to a wild idea that was sure to fail—and ruin the careers, and lives, of anyone implicated. Finding nothing with which to charge DJ after a month of questioning him and others, the police let him go on May 20, 1962, a year and four days after Park's coup. Both DJ and Park moved on—DJ as Park's worst foe, Park as head of a government that had survived a plot that never went beyond planning.[10]

From his roots in Mokpo, Kim Dae Jung would expand his political influence over all Cholla. Under Park, DJ emerged as a champion not only of the interests of the downtrodden of his region but also of millions of other Koreans who objected to increasingly heavy-handed one-man rule. In the first two years, Park had to fend off mounting pressure, from home and abroad, to restore a measure of democratic freedom. At the same time, the Minju-dang was wracked by internal strife. Freed from prison, DJ was able to go back to politics. Close to Chang Myun, he again surfaced as party spokesman, a tribute to his growing reputation for eloquence. Able to enter the fray more openly—and more eagerly—than ever before, he zeroed in on a target that was if anything more challenging, more controversial, and more guilty, if that were possible, of repression and violation of human rights than Rhee.

Park, moreover, bore the added burden of having gone to a military academy in Japan and then having served as a junior Japanese officer—in Manchuria, not Korea, but still clear evidence of his alienation from those whose interests he so patriotically claimed to serve. Imprisoned for joining Communist rebels in the mountains of South Cholla, not far from where DJ was in ferment in Mokpo, and then released after betraying his Communist cohorts to investigators and given a dishonorable discharge, Park returned to the ranks at the outbreak of the Korean War when the army was falling apart in flight.

Try as he might to claim security concerns as the rationale for going after foes, Park could not follow Rhee's example and use the Korean War as an excuse for abuses since the war was well over at the time of his power grab. Moreover, his record as a one-time Communist was more dubious than DJ's association with leftist groupings. Now a zealous anticommunist, Park dreamed of consolidating power. At the same time, he was under terrific pressure to demonstrate to the world, notably his American ally, that Korea was a free country with stable leadership, capable of sustained economic growth.

Kim Dae Jung was joined at about this time by a powerful new companion, his second wife, Lee Hee Ho. They had first met in 1951 in Busan where she, like so many others, had taken refuge. In charge of external affairs for the Korean Young Women's Group, she was introduced to DJ at a dinner of youth leaders. Soon DJ was attending monthly gatherings of a fraternal society to which she belonged. Unlike DJ, Lee came from a professional background with links to the Yi dynasty. Fourth of eight children of a doctor, Lee had been educated at two of Korea's most prestigious institutions for women, Ewha Girls' School in central Seoul and Ewha Woman's University in a nearby university district, and then at top-ranked Seoul National University.

Lee Hee Ho came from a Methodist background, a denomination that had steadily increased in numbers and influence since the arrival of Methodist missionaries in the late nineteenth century. Her education interrupted by the Korean War, Lee continued her studies in the American Bible belt, first on a scholarship at small Methodist-affiliated Lambuth College in Jackson, Tennessee, and then at Scarritt College for Christian Workers in Nashville, from which she received a master's in social studies in 1958.[11]

Back in Seoul, a dedicated church person, living with an activist foe of the regime, Lee Hee Ho became executive director of the Korea branch of the Young Women's Christian Association. "One day after my return from the United States, I had a chance meeting with Kim Dae Jung on the street," Lee wrote nearly 30 years later. "Until then we had had no communication." The relationship blossomed in the fall of 1959 while Lee's former partner was caught up in his own causes and DJ's wife, Cha Yong Ae, was in Mokpo. "Sometime in late or early autumn," Lee wrote, "I began to have chances to meet with him sort of naturally." Lee professed, "I do not exactly recall the nature of our meetings," asking, "Shall I call it kharma, or the divine will of God?" She never hinted the timing had anything to do with Cha's unhappiness, writing that Cha, who did not pass away until May 1960, had died in August 1959, the month before she left for a YWCA conference in Mexico.[12]

Korean Christians at that time were beginning to mobilize, as they had in the bloody, short-lived revolt that broke out against Japanese rule on March 1, 1919. Lee was the idealist, the high-born woman who saw in this man of the people, with his oratorical skills and lifelong opposition to dictatorship, the fulfillment of her own beliefs, her dreams, for her country, herself. In a society riven by class and regional distinctions, with a dual emphasis on educational attainment and financial success, the idea of marriage to a man with no higher education, no solid source of income, with two sons from a previous marriage, from a region looked on with disdain by people in Seoul, was nothing short of scandalous. Lee battled "tremendous opposition from my family as well as among my friends to the very thought of my marriage to him." Nonetheless, "Gradually but surely, I began to believe or feel deep down in my consciousness that one day his dreams would become reality," she wrote. "I finally decided that this was the man that I had to help."[13]

Socially and politically, Lee Hee Ho was altogether different from DJ's first wife, the daughter of a quintessentially middle-class mercantile background, with no education beyond high school, consigned to work as a hairdresser when times were tough and driven to desperation by the constant need for money while her husband pursued political ambitions. The fact that Lee was now around 40, born on September 21, 1922, nearly four months before DJ, may have tipped the balance on family approval. She was not only strong-willed but far beyond an age when she would slip into traditional marriage with a young man looking for a conventional wife with whom to build a respectable career.

Rising above proper society's objections, Lee Hee Ho and Kim Dae Jung were married on May 10, 1962, by a pastor at the home of an uncle who, ironically, had once worked for Rhee Syngman. A photograph shows her in a long white dress, looking pleasant but serious, wearing heavy glasses—a sign of her determination to present herself as a committed professional who would not discard her spectacles for the sake of the usual wedding portrait. Lee would treat DJ's and Cha's two sons as her own, the elder brothers of the third son that she and DJ were to have together.

Forty years later, receiving an award at the place where she had studied in Nashville, she would hark back to the hardship that she and DJ faced together. "Words cannot express how much my husband had to suffer," she was to say, "but no less unendurable was the suffering I experienced as his wife."[14] DJ's marriage to this energetic, capable and wholly dedicated woman had much to do with propelling him beyond the level of a local dissident to a national figure. The presidential campaign of 1963 offered DJ, his bride often at his side or waiting patiently nearby, ready to advise on everything from tactics to speech to dress, the perfect opportunity to revive broken dreams.

Eager to legitimize himself as a democratic leader, Park had to countenance political activities by all sorts of undesirable people before running for president for the first time. DJ was among 4,000 banned for seven years from political activity. His offence was that he was an "old politician," having served if only for three days in the National Assembly that Park had disbanded. Park would have preferred to annihilate the whole cantankerous lot, but he also had to legitimize his "democratic" rule in the eyes of his American ally, on whom he relied for aid and military security while battling to elevate the Korean economy from the doldrums in which it languished nearly a decade after the Korean War. On February 27, 1963, DJ's name was listed along with more than 2,000 others who could return to politics. In the presidential election of October 15, 1963, in which Park firmly expected popular endorsement, he got 4.7 million votes, defeating Yun Po Sun, the man whom he had overthrown two years and five months earlier, by the embarrassingly narrow margin of 150,000 votes.

The fact that Park did rather badly despite having the full panoply of the government security, propaganda, and political apparatus at his command showed how unpopular he was in some quarters, notably the southwest. The next step for DJ was to run again for the National Assembly, this time not from Inje but from the city where he already had an entrenched machine, Mokpo. So much power and influence, so many contacts, had DJ nurtured in his own bailiwick that he had no trouble getting a sympathetic policeman to reveal to him the government's plot to block the voting so its candidate would win. DJ could counter the government's tactics in Mokpo even as government agents elsewhere used them with impunity. Government-backed politicos wound up with 110 seats in the assembly elections on November 26, and DJ's Minju-dang won only 65. In the minority party, however, DJ was one of the winners. DJ had another blessing for which to be thankful. Lee Hee Ho, two weeks before the election, and two and a half years after the death of DJ's first wife, gave birth on November 12 to a son, her husband's third son, Hong Gul.

Kim Dae Jung's ascent to the National Assembly gave him the forum from which to emerge as a national figure. He soon distinguished himself as an orator who could mesmerize a small audience in an influential chamber as easily as thousands at a rally. On April 20, 1964, nearly three years after Park's seizure of power, he carried on for five hours and nineteen minutes, crusading against the arrest of a fellow lawmaker and party member—a display that earned him recognition by the Guinness Book of Records for having set "the longest speaking record in the National Assembly."[15] Although predisposed first against Rhee and then against Park, DJ was not necessarily a foe of everything he wanted. He opposed the extremists battling relations with Japan, arguing that national interests called for diplomatic ties with the former colonial power.

The issue was intensely emotional for those to whom memories of the Japanese era remained fresh. The signing of the Korea-Japan treaty on June 22, 1965, was a milestone event that DJ refrained from exploiting. Might DJ have spoken out, as did those loyal to the fiery Yun Po Sun? Possibly so. Secret documents accompanying the treaty, as revealed 40 years later, showed that South Korea might have been more forceful in demanding compensation for more than one million Koreans forced to work under onerous conditions in Japan and to serve in the Japanese armed forces.

Kim Dae Jung was equally circumspect on the explosive issue of sending troops to Vietnam after U.S. forces had begun arriving there in large numbers later in the same year. He doubted if Seoul's commitment would affect the outcome. Rather, it could become another irritant in attempts at rapprochement with North Korea. Why not, he suggested, in response to complaints from Yun Po Sun and others, fill Korean units in Vietnam with reservists and retirees? Cooperation with the Americans would be profitable for sale of munitions, for remittances and for favorable terms for trade and aid. DJ's advice was not heeded—Korea sent the White Horse and Tiger divisions to the central coastal region of South Vietnam, where they earned a reputation for ruthless efficiency. DJ, while not supporting a combat role, skillfully stayed away from shrill opposition to the U.S. alliance or to Korea's military establishment.

This seemingly rather moderate position, however, was deceptive. DJ had long since sensed his role as a rabble-rouser, a defender of the downtrodden, a battler for the farmers who dominated the economy in the rice-rich Cholla provinces. His language during this period reflected the radicalism to which he had grown accustomed after World War II when he was flirting with communism. He did not hesitate to attack the central planning that Park imposed as the foundation of a visionary program for beginning to turn South Korea into one of the world's great industrial powers. Addressing the National Assembly, DJ declared, "The five-year plan of economic growth is based on the corpses of the public's sacrifice." In fact, "It has nothing to do with the public even though it makes skyscrapers and highways." DJ veered toward recommending armed revolution of the sort he had read and heard so much about in China. "In seeing the wreck of farmers," he told the assembly, "we can say that this is the right time to apply the theory of a farmers' revolution in Asia."[16]

What was DJ trying to say or do? As in his formative years as an opinionated student and then a political activist, he bounced between extremes, feeling out where and how to gain the best political advantage. Strident opposition to opening relations with Japan, or to sending Korean troops to Vietnam, would not have much long-range impact. Twenty years after the Japanese surrender, Korea had to form ties with Japan for the sake of burgeoning commercial dealings and for constant interaction between people in both countries—friends, loved ones, and relatives in Korea and ethnic Koreans in Japan, whether forced to go there or willing servants of the former Japanese empire. As long as both Japan and South Korea relied on separate alliances with the United States in a trilateral relationship engineered and presided over by American diplomats and military leaders, there was no chance of a revanchist Japan attempting to regain imperial supremacy. Similarly, Koreans could view support for U.S. forces in Vietnam as another opportunity for expanding commercial relations.

In the suffering of Korean workers and farmers, however, Kim Dae Jung found an issue that had great popular appeal. Park would be remembered many years later for the economic achievements of his often dictatorial rule. To accomplish them, he made business leaders pursue his whims, ordering them to take over specific industries rather than compete. He set goals and deadlines, pointing at maps and charts to specify what he wanted done and where. Under his heavy hand, Korea began a long, almost unbroken rise to economic power, but workers and farmers paid a high price. While Americans preached "the right to strike" for realistic minimum wages, fair pay, overtime and other benefits, Korean workers had few of the perquisites of an advanced democratic society. Strikes were illegal, hours long, pay was low, job security minimal. Labor actions were brutally suppressed by beatings and jail terms.

The opposition to Park—the democratic movement—was divided and in turmoil, probably more so in this period than at any other time previously. As a son of Cholla, DJ was not going to ally with Yun Po Sun, who made one final run at the presidency in 1967 after his party and the Minju-dang reluctantly settled on him as the lone candidate. DJ, however, was not above working with known Communists, and spies, for his ends. His old friend Jung Tae Muk had gone to North Korea on a North Korean vessel in 1965, five years after his release from jail for pro-Communist activities, had undergone some training and returned to promote the election of Yun as well as DJ. Jung met DJ in Mokpo and offered election advice but spurned DJ's request to assist in his campaign, not that of Yun.[17] No matter whether DJ knew that Jung was actually a spy, the lesson was clear: DJ would work with whoever would support him but not for an extremist who had little chance of victory.

In his lack of revolutionary fervor for Yun, who had shown himself as a firebrand on major issues, DJ undoubtedly reflected the regional differences intrinsic to his success. Yun was from the west coast of South Chungcheong Province, north of the Cholla region. People there might share many of the same problems as those from Cholla, but they spoke with different accents, and they gravitated, politically, professionally, vocationally, to Daejeon, an independent municipality surrounded by the province, as well as to the capital of Seoul. Although the Chungcheong region would produce its share of activists and dissidents, people there were more conservative and less likely than those from Cholla to think in terms of revolt. Income levels were higher and governments in Seoul disposed to dispense greater benefits. With DJ and his allies unwilling to advance Yun's cause, Yun suffered his worst defeat, losing to Park by more than one million votes in the election on May 3, 1967.

Yun's loss freed DJ to campaign ever more fiercely as the voice of the dispossessed—mostly the dispossessed of Cholla but those from elsewhere too. Park by this time saw him as a threat that had to be suppressed. DJ's rabble-rousing in the National Assembly had become a nuisance that Park felt the need to silence. With no ready pretext for arresting him, Park had one of his ministers run against him in Mokpo for the sole purpose of eliminating this irritant. DJ fought back with mounting passion. He charged that the candidate was a stooge of the government, that the election would be rigged, and he organized demonstrations as the ballots were counted on January 3, 1968. Again he emerged as an easy winner from a minority party that fared far worse overall this time than in the previous assembly election. The Minju-dang held a mere 45 of the 175 assembly seats, and the number fell when some opposition members refused to attend amid charges of fraud at the ballot boxes.

Tensions on the Korean peninsula were rising. A second Korean War seemed possible when 31 armed guerrillas from the North penetrated the sprawling grounds of the Blue House, the center of presidential power, at the foot of the wooded mountains of northern Seoul, early on January 21, 1968. Twenty-eight of them were killed, one was captured and two never found in a chase through surrounding forests in which 68 South Koreans and three American soldiers died. The idea that North Korea could come so close to their goal of assassinating the president was deeply disturbing. Nor was the U.S. alliance all that certain.

Two days later, on January 23, the *USS Pueblo*, a one-time small cargo vessel outfitted as a U.S. Navy ship with electronic surveillance gear for the extraordinarily boring routine of monitoring military signals and radio traffic in North Korea and eavesdropping on Soviet vessels between the Korean peninsula and Japan, was hijacked after the North Koreans fired on it in international waters off the North Korean port of Wonsan. The inability of the American military machine to defend the *Pueblo* and its 83 crew members, including 1 killed in the shooting, the failure of U.S. warplanes to get there nearly in time to drive off the North Korean MiG fighters, torpedo boats and sub chasers that hunted it down, was extremely troubling to South Korean as well as American leaders.

The attack on the Blue House and the capture of the *Pueblo* raised searching questions about the stability of South Korea and the U.S. commitment. The Vietnam War dominated the headlines in the United States, pushing the "forgotten" Korean War and its long aftermath ever deeper into the miasma of history. On January 30 and January 31, 1968, North Vietnamese and Viet Cong troops attacked nearly every city and major town in South Vietnam at the beginning of the Tet or lunar new year holidays. Most of the attacks were turned back within a few days or a week, but fighting raged on in the walled citadel of the ancient imperial capital of Hue for four weeks, and American marines at the Khe Sanh combat base, in jungly northwestern South Vietnam, near the Laotian border, were under siege for 77 days. Although U.S. and South Vietnamese forces recovered most of the losses, the North Vietnamese achieved an enormous propaganda victory by showing their capacity for seizing critical ground if only temporarily.

Shockingly, President Lyndon Baines Johnson on March 31, 1968, stopped the bombing of North Vietnamese military targets above the 20th parallel and announced he would not run for election that November. Three days later, on April 3, North Vietnam called for negotiations, and peace talks opened in Paris on May 10, the beginning of a fitful process that ended with the Paris Peace Accords of January 27, 1973, the prelude to another two years and three months of fighting before the Saigon government, bereft of American support, surrendered. The conflux of the attack on the Blue House, the seizure of the Pueblo and a succession of offensives in Vietnam sparked fears about the American commitment to South Korea. Did North Korea's leader Kim Il Sung believe now was the time, while U.S. troops were bogged down in South Vietnam, for a second invasion of South Korea?

Park and his generals had to contend with such questions even as Kim Dae Jung and other politicians raised a hue and cry about democratic rights on the home front. DJ, as in the Korean War, was not likely to focus on defense requirements. If he had no desire for the Communists to conquer the South, he would leave that worry to others. Just as he had not fought in the Korean War, he was not going to wave a rhetorical fist at the North. The people of Cholla, wellspring of his support, had their own struggle against a central government that had repressed them for centuries, and DJ needed to harness that sentiment as he built up his political machine and base of power.

CHAPTER THREE

Matador Politics

Bullfights in Korea are between two bulls, not between a red-cape-waving matador and a charging bull as in Spain, Portugal, and Latin America. Nor do bulls die in Korean bullfights. They butt heads for a few minutes until one gives up and trots off to lick his wounds. The matador in politics deliberately incites a powerful figure, a government or corporate leader, inducing him to charge like a bull before he turns tail and runs. More specifically, said one observer, "Matador is a tactic in which people circulate or manipulate false facts to denounce rivals in electioneering."[1]

Matador tactics often relied on deception. A canvasser might introduce himself to an old man as a canvasser of a rival, handing him rubber shoes, then returning and saying he had made a mistake, giving them to the man beside him, bumming a cigarette and bowing impolitely. Or campaign workers might drive cars—emblazoned with signs urging people to vote for a rival—across wheat fields as farmers were about to harvest their crops. Or a rival's supporters might mark houses with small circles, triangles, and X's to denote which favored the ruling party, which was neutral and which the opposition, then switch the marks around. After the rival's people dropped off campaign gifts at the wrong houses, the rival lost votes.[2] Enduring losses in four campaigns before learning how to win, Kim Dae Jung, a master matador, now had to survive his greatest challenge, a neophyte run at the presidency. The first hurdle was to defeat the man who would become his arch-rival and conservative opponent for the next generation, Kim Young Sam. Both were dissidents, impassioned critics of authoritarian rule, but there was a difference. "YS," known like DJ by his Western initials in the headlines and in ordinary conversation, was from pivotal

Busan, Korea's second city, generally much more supportive of central government rule than was DJ's Cholla region. YS was an outspoken critic of Park Chung Hee and the generals around him, but many of them were also from the same Kyongsang region that included the two Kyongsang provinces and the independent cities of Busan and Daegu. Park was born near Daegu, the heart of conservative support, on the rail and road network to Busan. The region was historically hostile toward Cholla though YS and DJ shared common cause in their view of the military-dominated regime.

Like DJ, YS had made his mark as a member of the National Assembly. Both competed for the nomination of the Shinmin-dang, the New Democratic Party. Their rivalry, which had begun when they were angling for power over the party's minority grouping in the assembly, turned into hatred when DJ bargained for the support of another faction within the party as YS was about to win the nomination. Kim Jong Pil, aka "JP," a former army colonel from the central Chungcheong region between Daegu and Seoul and an in-law of Park, had founded the KCIA on June 13, 1961, four weeks after assisting in Park's coup of May 16. Park and JP's KCIA believed they had a better chance of defeating the upstart from Cholla than a more popular figure from the Kyongsang region whose outlook and record did not seem so antithetical to national interests. YS by this logic might cut into the votes that would otherwise go to Park. Nominated by a narrow margin at the party's convention in September 1970, DJ campaigned relentlessly in the weeks up to the election on April 27, 1971, on a populist platform that had little heartfelt support from the YS faction.

In the first of his four presidential campaigns, DJ came out with utopian pledges that anticipated the dreams he would pursue for the rest of his career. He would, for one thing, get rid of a newly established local defense force. Set up after the Blue House attack, the force was barely operational, but already there were complaints about its intrusive tactics and suppression of rights. DJ's own image, however, was less than perfect. Young people hoped that DJ would end the draft, something he never tried to do, but those with memories of the Korean War were concerned about President Richard Nixon's "Nixon doctrine" rationalizing U.S. withdrawal from Vietnam. After the United States early in 1971 pulled 20,000 troops from Korea, including the entire Seventh Division, reducing the U.S. contingent to 43,000, Park and his aides had to ask if the United States might leave the South defenseless. The North Korean military build-up, consuming one-fourth of the North's economy, was always cause for alarm. As long as North Korea had several million reservists, in addition to 1.1 million regulars, a local defense force seemed like a sensible deterrent.

Kim Dae Jung, if elected, promised to focus on getting security guarantees from the four major nations with the biggest stake in the Korean peninsula, the United States and Japan as well as the two Communist countries that had bailed out the North in the Korean War, China and the Soviet Union. But how, in the midst of the Cold War, could those four powers "guarantee" South Korea's security? Such recommendations were controversial if not traitorous in the eyes of hard-liners who saw North Korea, and its Communist allies, as mortal enemies. The Korean War had ended less than 18 years earlier, North Korea had staged bloody incidents, infiltrating spies and saboteurs, and leaders of the government and armed forces were insecure. A statement on Park's behalf, summarizing the conservative view, accused DJ of "blurring the reality of national security" for the sake of "attracting people."[3]

On a practical level, DJ campaigned for president with the fury, and meticulous planning, that had characterized his campaigns for the National Assembly. The goal was to surround a beleaguered Park presidency and inner circle, including his Republican Party, Kongwha-dang, with massed public opinion. A great issue was the need to invalidate a constitutional amendment giving Park the right to run for a third term. Shouts of "knock down the dictatorship" and "make the third-term presidency invalid" rang out at rallies. Kim Jong Pil, the former KCIA chief, campaigned for Park. He and DJ fired and counterfired accusations of corruption and cheating. DJ attacked Park and his party for exploiting their ruling power to rig the election, drawing up lists of ghost voters and bribing witnesses. The Kongwha-dang fired back with charges of false cheering by the same followers at every rally, of attempting to get public officials to rig the voting and of hiring gangsters and DJ's private organizations to demonstrate on the day before the election.

The campaigning accentuated regional differences with DJ gaining ever more support in the Cholla region while Park focused on the southeastern Kyongsang region and Seoul. In a speech in Busan, DJ berated the Park administration for promoting national divisions "between the rich and the poor, the city and the countryside and, in particular, regions." Consumed by "anger and unbearable grief after seeing the actions of propaganda politics trying to promote regional conflicts," he promised "to eliminate causes for regionalism by fairly regrouping the administrative districts, especially the leftover provinces and districts from the Yi dynasty and the imperialist Japanese, and change their names to fit the times."

Talking in Incheon, DJ promoted "municipalism"—that is, the rights of municipalities, including elections of leaders and other officials, all of whom were then appointed by the central government. "Municipalism is necessary to improve the ability to self-govern, develop each region, prevent abuse and corruption of government authorities and enhance participation for national unity," he said, charging the government with "carrying out illegal elections and using executive agencies as a political tool."[4]

DJ reserved his greatest passion for denunciations of the government's flaying of foes in the name of national security. "We are well aware under the Article Four of the Act (National Security Law), those who do not have the slightest intention to support anti-state organizations can be punished," he said in a speech at Jeonju, capital of North Cholla Province. "It is such an evil law that cannot exist in a democratic state. We also know that it has been arbitrarily misused by those in power, not for anticommunist purposes but for a political aim to suppress scholars, reporters, literati and students." Foreigners, critical of the National Security Law, tended to forget that North Korea had made numerous attempts to destabilize the South in hopes of achieving a socialist revolution. Although the government had undoubtedly abused the law, adopted by the Rhee regime in 1948, it provided a tool to combat North Korean espionage and political activities as long as Communist revolution remained a top priority for Pyongyang. Was it that DJ was naïve—or just not concerned about national security?

DJ, however, was far from alone in his distaste for the National Security Law, often denounced by human rights groups. He did not promise if elected to repeal it, as demanded by leftists, but he did say the notorious Article Four would "be applied to only those who have explicit anti-state purposes," and he promised to "protect all citizens who criticize the administration with patriotic intentions and engage in creative activities, in particular, intellectuals...." Lest conservatives fear a vengeful witchhunt akin to conservative roundups of leftists if he were elected, he vowed not to "take political revenge on any people ranging from former presidents to middle ranking public officials, neither on those in economic circles nor societal organizations." His "objective," he told an audience in Daejeon, was "not to punish people but to reform the misrule of past governments."[5]

In the voting on April 27, Park won handily, picking up 6,342,828 votes as opposed to 5,395,900 for DJ. The margin of nearly one million,

53.2 percent of the 11,923,218 valid votes cast for Park, 45.2 percent for DJ, was almost as wide as Park's last victory over Yun Po Sun four years earlier.[6] The victory, however, was less than the ringing endorsement that Park believed he deserved for all he had done for the economy and defense. Seen as personally incorruptible in a society accustomed routinely to corruption, Park believed he had gotten the economy moving in the right direction. He had directed industrialists to move quickly as global competitors and had watched proudly as favored tycoons such as Chung Ju Yung, founder of the Hyundai empire; Lee Byung Chul, the Samsung founder, and Daewoo founder Kim Woo Choong built factories spewing out cars, heavy machinery, merchant ships, and other wonders of Korea's "economic miracle." The vote might have been still closer had Park not had the power of his intelligence and security forces ranged behind him.

Kim Dae Jung exacerbated tensions by exercising his oratorical skills in wild accusations, largely not provable, and by rejecting the outcome. Almost immediately, he plunged into a struggle for control of his party. The in-fighting was highly divisive, and embarrassing, in the run-up to the next National Assembly election on May 25. On the day before the voting, the car that was to carry him on the eight-hour drive to address a rally in Seoul was struck from behind by a truck in Muan district north of Mokpo. Two men in a taxi that had cut in front of his car were killed. DJ and two of his aides were injured, DJ so severely that he suffered from aches and pains in his leg and hip and walked with a permanent limp.

Ever afterward DJ portrayed the accident as an assassination attempt, but that was highly improbable. The fatality rate on Korean highways was one of the world's highest. The road north between Mokpo and Gwangju, about an hour's drive, was narrow and winding, not the expressway that DJ, as president, saw to building to his home district. DJ was in a rush after bad weather grounded commercial flights, and he had to move quickly to get to a campaign appearance. No matter whether the accident was an attempt on his life, Kim Dae Jung had reason to capitalize on its value.

The next day, candidates of DJ's New Democratic Party captured 89 seats, a solid showing that gave them a strong position to battle the 113 members from Park's Kongwha-dang, Republican Party.[7] Park was incensed not just by DJ's strong showing but also by his defiance. DJ was the most visible of numerous foes whom Park's regime wanted to silence. Fast losing patience, Park was plotting how to get rid of them, and the 1971 presidential election was the final "open" campaign of his rule. The KCIA and other arms of the government had begun compiling their longest and worst record of abuse, torture and, in some cases, killing. The poet Kim Chi Ha, arrested in 1970 as a result of circulation of his mordant satire on the rich and powerful, "Five Thieves," and another biting satire, "Rumours," was sentenced to life in prison. Thousands were jailed under the National Security Law, increasingly used as a device for interrogating and jailing opponents of the regime.

Park on December 6, 1971, issued an "emergency declaration," and the National Assembly two weeks later passed an "emergency powers" bill at a post–midnight session attended only by members of Park's party. Under the bill, Park had the authority to issue decrees controlling wages, trade, production, collective bargaining—and, of course, the press. Rarely, however, did Park find it necessary to invoke these powers. "The CIA operates without any legal sanction at all," an American diplomat told me. "It has so much extra-legal power that it's not necessary to issue decrees. It can just threaten and intimidate people legally." Since its founding in 1961, the KCIA had inveigled its way into leading industries, banks, trading companies, and real estate firms. The purpose was often not to inform but to earn much needed funds. "The problem was the [K]CIA needed more money to carry out its activities," said one informant. "It was modeled originally after the American CIA, but it assumed an internal security function that made it entirely different. CIA officials needed much more money than was allocated under the national budget"—and the KCIA grew into the richest agency and biggest employer after the defense ministry with operatives in every major private business and every government office.[8]

The international atmosphere, meanwhile, was changing in ways to which Park was acutely attuned. Nixon's program of "Vietnamization" meant the United States would turn over prosecution of war in Vietnam to the RVNAF, Republic of Vietnam Armed Forces, a policy that was certain to lead to their defeat and Communist takeover of the South, the Republic of Vietnam, by the North, North Vietnam, the Democratic Republic of Vietnam. The nomenclature, "South" and "North," was alarming to the leaders of "South" Korea, the Republic of Korea, fearful of U.S. betrayal. Comparisons between the two wars, however different, were invidious.

Then, as if the flagging U.S. effort in South Vietnam were not enough of an ill omen, Nixon's national security adviser, Henry Kissinger, in July 1971, nearly three months after the South Korean presidential election, made a top-secret trip to Beijing to lay the groundwork for relations between China and the United States. The KCIA knew about the Kissinger mission from American briefings as well as its own sources and saw the reversal in U.S. policy as complete when Nixon in February 1972 made his breakthrough trip to Beijing, meeting Mao Zedong, Chou En Lai, and other Chinese leaders. Reading the Shanghai Communiqué in which the United States and China pledged to work toward normal relations, Park decided on some fence-mending of his own. Incredibly, considering Park's crackdown on anyone suspected of colluding with Communists on any level, he ordered the KCIA director, Lee Hu Rak, to open contacts with the North Koreans.

The second most powerful man in South Korea after Park, Lee visited Pyongyang from May 2 to May 5, 1972, slightly more than a year after the 1971 presidential election, got a meeting with Kim Il Sung and also met other top officials. Back in Seoul, he described Kim Il Sung as "quite a guy, very strong, one-man rule!"[9] A North Korean delegation paid a return visit from May 29 to June 1, and on July 4 Lee and Kim Yong Ju, his counterpart in Pyongyang as director of the organizational and guidance department and, more importantly, Kim Il Sung's younger brother, put their names on a communiqué proclaiming "principles" for "achieving unification...independently, without depending on foreign powers and without foreign interference." North and South would accomplish that goal "through peaceful means...transcending differences in ideas, ideologies and systems."[10]

The communiqué was a prelude to "the Red Cross talks," that is, highly publicized visits of delegations from both countries under the wing of the Red Cross organizations of North and South functioning as agencies of their governments. "In September 1972 North Koreans once again poured across the DMZ, but this time in peace," wrote Don Oberdorfer of the *Washington Post*. "They were met by embraces and bouquets of flowers at Panmunjom and by close to a million people lining the streets of Seoul, waving or simply looking on in curiosity as their motorcade slowly passed." For Oberdorfer, "The high point" was a "glittering party" that he described as "the reception of a lifetime"— "the beginning of the elaborate gambits that the KCIA and the rest of the ROK government intended to impress the North Koreans."[11]

While making overtures to Pyongyang, whatever lingering patience or tolerance Park might have had for dissent ran out as he perceived a gathering threat to his own designs. These included not only his plans for economic development but also an approach toward North Korea that was not altogether different from that advocated by Kim Dae Jung. The interaction with North Korea stole the thunder from one of DJ's central demands, namely that the dictatorial Park open dialogue with the North.

More than ever before, DJ and Park shared mutual frustration and outrage. The animosity was fueled as DJ cultivated contacts in the United States, Japan, and elsewhere in pursuit of international sympathy and funding. He began in February 1971, when he might have been expected to be campaigning in Korea for the April election, by calling on two sympathetic Democratic Party figures in Washington, Senator Edward M. Kennedy of Massachusetts and Senator J. William Fulbright of Arkansas, chairman of the Senate Foreign Relations Committee, both opponents of the U.S. role in Vietnam and sure to sympathize with a foe of a South Korean government led by a general.

DJ had been in close touch with American missionaries and ideologues as they sided with him in their zeal for American-style democracy and their revulsion over the excesses first of Rhee Syngman and then, worse, of Park Chung Hee. "SAVE Kim Dae Jung" was the title of a brochure published in the United States that typified the feverish support he was engendering in certain circles. "For the restoration of democracy in Korea, I stand up against the dictatorship of anti-people regime," read the quotation ascribed to DJ, "1971 presidential candidate of Korea." Inside, the brochure promised "Material on the Movement to Save Kim Dae Jung."[12] In his meeting with liberal antiwar senators, he enlisted American legislative support at a time when they and their colleagues were at the forefront of a national peace movement and against domination of policy by the White House, the Pentagon and the "military-industrial complex" that Eisenhower had warned against before stepping down from the presidency in January 1961.

The Washington visit gave Kim Dae Jung an excuse to stop off in Japan on the way back to Korea. A meeting with Japan's Prime Minister Kakuei Tanaka was on the itinerary, but DJ's mission was to round up funds and set up an organization there. His trip was financed by Koreans living in Japan, banded together in the pro-Pyongyang Federation of Korean Residents, on which North Korea counted for two-way commerce as well as remittances. *Monthly Chosun*, published by the conservative *Chosun Ilbo* and edited by Cho Gab Je, an inveterate critic of DJ and the Sunshine policy, 30 years later obtained the record of the investigation that showed the cooperation DJ had received from pro-North Koreans in founding Hanmintong, the acronym for Hankuk Minju Hoebok Tongil Chokjin Kukmin Hoei, literally "Korea National Committee to Restore Democracy and Promote Reunification." If one could believe the KCIA investigation, the chief operative in the Hanmintong had financed DJ's trip to Japan and then "became more intimate" with him after he got there.[13]

The consequences for DJ were severe. "Now none of the papers may report on my speeches," he told me on one of my first visits to his Mapo residence, built in the style of a traditional home of a high-born person, rooms fronting on a courtyard behind a tall wall beyond which plainclothed agents lurked in the alley. "The [K]CIA is paying off spies in my own party and arresting people for supporting me. There is no more democracy in Korea."[14] The next time DJ arrived in Japan, on October 11, 1972, the ostensible reason was the need for treatment for sciatica, a nervous disease that probably resulted from his motor vehicle accident. "For political reasons, I was afraid of the treatment I would receive in a Korean hospital," he said in an interview with Christian missionary journalists, "so I have been coming to Japan for treatment." He had had "no warning," he claimed, when Park, less than one week later, on October 17, set in motion the machinery that would make him a dictator by law, not just by deed and repute.[15]

Dissolving the National Assembly, Park imposed martial law in the name of "national emergency." More importantly, he fortified and sanctified his one-man rule by ramming through the Yushin—"revitalizing"—Constitution, duly approved by 91.5 percent of the voters in a referendum on November 21, 1972. Scarcely a month later, Park again was elected president, this time by a vote in which he would never risk the humiliation of a narrow victory. The several thousand handpicked members of the newly formed National Council for Unification on December 23 cast their ballots for Park, the lone candidate, and he was inaugurated again—at a closed ceremony on December 27.

The Republic of Korea by now had descended into true dictatorship, untrammeled by the fetishes of democratic reform. The constitution, insuring that Park would always have a wide majority in the Assembly, put in place procedures under which he could never be voted out of office. Under the rubric of the Yushin Constitution, Park devised a menu of legal measures—legal, that is, within the context of that constitution. Abuses extended through a system in which newspapers were censored and shut down and professors, journalists, students, and numerous others were watched, interrogated, and detained routinely. The KCIA divided suspects into categories—A, B, C, D—with active support for anyone demanding the downfall of the government at the top of the list. As discontent smoldered and simmered, Park was increasingly determined to snuff out opposition. Armed with such power, he turned up the degree of repression, abusing human rights as never before since the Korean War.

Kim Dae Jung was clearly not happy that Park, not he, had made the first overtures to North Korea. Some of his remarks gave credence to the suspicion among hard-liners that he really did want to overthrow the government—with no apparent concern for exposing the country to hostile forces from the North. "If Park tries to stay in power, it will be a tragedy for him and for our country," he warned in an interview with me in his Mapo home. "Some unhappy thing may take place. In fact, he may follow the same fate as Mr. Syngman Rhee."[16]

DJ ruthlessly debunked Park's efforts at reconciliation with North Korea, accusing Park of "misusing the (North-South) joint communiqué" of July 4 "for the tightening of his dictatorial rule and the perpetuation of his political power." Park's "real objective is not to win over communism in the political confrontation or to improve relations between the two parts of the divided land but to misuse it," said DJ, inveighing against "adversities taking place in every field in politics, economy, diplomacy." DJ believed revolution was possible: "The Korean people are resistance-minded. Japan ruled us for 36 years... but we did not lose the characteristics of our nation. The spirit of resistance still rules the heart of our people. At present Park's government is strong and almighty, but when it tries to propitiate power, then a strong reaction might occur. Our people will be valiant—and will rise up."[17]

DJ had on his side the weight of religious figures, Catholic and Protestant, although many were conservative. The fiery prelate of the Roman Catholic Church in Korea, Stephen Cardinal Kim Sou Hwan, was outspoken in denouncing martial law. It was "time for the government to return to the proper attitude of seeking unity of national opinion and national consensus through frank and unreserved exchanges of views between the government and the people"—that is, he added bitterly, "assuming the government of this country is not a dictatorship but a government built on democratic order."[18]

Clearly, the government fit the former, not the latter, category. Many Koreans in all walks of life found themselves under surveillance, under arrest, undergoing torture and jail sentences for activities against the regime. Most of the charges rested on the National Security Law. The National Intelligence Service, as the former KCIA was renamed in 1999, had to apologize after Kim Dae Jung had become president for acts of torture that resulted in the deaths of as many as 100 people during the presidencies of Park and Chun Doo Hwan, the general who replaced him after a bloody interregnum. The National Police and the army counterintelligence could also arrest, interrogate, detain, and bring charges against suspects. Besides imposing martial law three times for a total of two years and seven months, Park also employed such devices as emergency and garrison decrees that remained in place for five years and nine months.

In much of what he did, Park saw DJ as the chief villain, the most visible figure in a cast of culprits, the target that Park most wanted to destroy. The reason for Park's animus toward Kim Dae Jung was obvious. DJ had decided to stay in Japan, and also to visit the United States, after hearing about the declaration of the Yushin Constitution on the radio and then from his wife by telephone. "The shock and indignation I experienced at that time was indeed enormous," DJ has written. "I knew immediately what a terrible thing this was. I also knew that it could last almost indefinitely. I therefore felt a strong sense of mission to fight, alone if necessary, this Yushin dictatorship that Park Chung Hee had declared."[19] Having had to learn Japanese as a schoolboy, DJ felt comfortable communicating with Japanese. From his base there, he castigated Park and his Yushin Constitution as never before. He also set about studying English, learning enough to answer questions from journalists and to make speeches, haltingly but understandably.

DJ, uninhibited and unrestrained, with no agents to watch his residence, as they did in Seoul's Mapo district, to tap his telephone, to intercept his mail or to tail him wherever he went without arousing the suspicions of the Japanese police, presented a graver menace abroad than under guard in Korea. As reports of DJ's crusade got back to Seoul, DJ, the matador, aroused the fury of the Blue House and the KCIA bulls who would charge blindly to disembowel him.

Kim Dae Jung knew full well the treatment that awaited him if he were to go back. Although he had said after the Yushin Constitution was adopted that he would return in January despite the risks, he had changed his mind. "It became clear that I would be either jailed or put under house arrest," he told interviewers. "Even if I could work, there is little chance to do anything.... So rather than return and be arrested, I presently think it's more important to keep channels open to the rest of the world."[20] DJ, however, had another agenda. Just as Park had proclaimed the Yushin Constitution, so DJ proclaimed a battle against the Park regime. He was not plotting an armed uprising, but he did in July 1972 go again to the United States, call upon sympathizers in academe, politics, and religions groups—and, most importantly, open Hanmintong's Washington headquarters.

Returning to Japan, he opened the Hanmintong office there with the financial and moral support of the pro-North residents' federation. "I gave up returning to South Korea after Yushin and began to fight against it," DJ said later. "I organized Hanmintong to proceed more effectively, and that means that I used part of the money through this organization." An inscription in the Kim Dae Jung Library in Seoul summarizes the origin and purpose of the Hanmintong. Established in 1973, the Hanmintong "was one of the major groups that supported the democratization movement organized by Koreans in the United States and Japan." DJ, "then in exile," said the inscription, "made critical contributions for the establishment of the group, which spurred efforts for the democratization of Korea by promoting solidarity and peaceful unification efforts and raising tensions on pending issues."[21] This justification for Hanmintong overlooked, however, the organization's purpose as a vehicle for reunification through compromise with North Korean dictatorship. Pro-Pyongyang elements joined Hanmintong with strong support from pro-North residents in Japan. Their priority, driven by Pyongyang, was socialist revolution.

Through the pro-North federation DJ and members of the group received regular infusions of funds covering hotel, living, and traveling expenses, including those incurred in the United States. Those who provided DJ with the money "were all spies from North Korea," the *Monthly Chosun* wrote of the investigation.[22] DJ's contacts in Japan were the source for much of what he did outside Korea in the coming years as he marshaled worldwide sympathy. As in his early years in politics in Mokpo, however, he distanced himself from radicals who seemed overly close to North Korea. He was "discontented," according to testimony revealed by *Monthly Chosun*, by the "antigovernment" stand of the pro-North newspaper published in Japan.

Kim Dae Jung claimed to have been receiving donations from relatives and in-laws, including members of his wife's extended family, business people, and one anonymous donor who contacted him through a mutual friend, and he said he had a complete accounting of how the money was spent.[23] His pro-North contacts had assured him at the opening of the Hanmintong in Tokyo's sumptuous Keio Plaza Hotel on July 13, 1973, that "many wealthy people" would "be willing to support" the group.

If DJ himself was not "pro-North," the nomenclature of some of the organizers suggested their leanings. They were members of "Viet Cong factions"—the term from the Viet Cong guerrillas who had been fighting the American and South Vietnamese forces, as well as the South

Koreans, in South Vietnam. The war in South Vietnam had entered a new phase after Kissinger and Le Duc Tho had signed the Paris Peace Treaty in January 1973. The gathering at the Keio Plaza included representatives "from six Viet Cong factions."

The term *Viet Cong* connoted inspiration from the long struggle for South Vietnam by North Vietnam—and, by inference, South Korea by North Korea. All those at the meeting agreed on the need to bury factional differences behind the single goal of ridding the South of dictatorship. DJ was glad to accept contributions from the pro-North Korea federation regardless of the Viet Cong name, but he stopped short of commitment to the North. When members of the group suggested the Hanmintong hold a joint celebration of the anniversary coming up in two days of liberation from Japan on August 15, 1945, DJ reminded them "our purpose was to fight against dictatorial government." As the debate went on, "I told them that I would not be together with you for Hanmintong and got out of the meeting room."[24]

One of DJ's regular contacts in Japan was a man with whom he had gone to primary school on Haui-do, Kim Jong Choong, who had befriended DJ after his election to the National Assembly in 1967. Kim had become his "political ally and close aide" when DJ left Korea for Japan five years later and "eventually joined the democratic movement against the dictatorship in Korea."

Over the years DJ and Kim Jong Choong corresponded "to discuss the operation and action plans of democratic organizations in Japan and the U.S.," said a brochure on the exchange. "Through Kim Jong Choong, he continuously provided direction and instructions for democratic movements in Japan, including Hanmintong." In a letter from Korea addressed to "Mr. Satou Numada," Kim Jong Choong's Japanese name, DJ reminded him that "Hanmintong should support the Republic of Korea and draw a clear line against communism." DJ warned, "If our efforts in Japan are branded as anti-Korea by Koreans against our will, all time and efforts will be in vain." At the same time, he called on him to "make your utmost efforts in editing *Minjoksibo*," a paper that would promote his Minju-dang in Japan.[25]

While Hanmintong was getting organized in Japan, Kim Dae Jung was planning a lengthy visit to the United States, including a fellowship at Harvard. "However," DJ promised in an interview, "if any opportunity arises, I will return despite any dangers."[26] The "opportunity" came with shocking swiftness when the KCIA under Park and Kim Jong Pil, presumably hoping to snuff out DJ's life, made him an international hero. DJ on August 8, 1973, was on the twenty-second floor of the Grand Palace Hotel in Tokyo after lunching with the local head of the Hanmintong when he was seized and bound. The plan may have been to kill him then and there. Possibly his captors shifted to a backup plan when they were about to be discovered. In any event, DJ was drugged and spirited off.[27]

The episode was the single most terrifying event of DJ's life—so brazenly heavy-handed as to play into the hands of the very people, domestic dissidents, antiwar activists, foreign critics, and sympathizers, that Park had hoped to shut up. Much later, DJ put it all in the context of his decision in 1957 to become a Christian, baptized as a Catholic. The story had elements of a violent film, surely not from real life. With no independent corroboration, we have to rely on DJ's account for the colorful details:

> At first they planned to kill me and cut up my body into small pieces in the bathtub of the apartment where they first got hold of me and then stuff the pieces into knapsacks, which could be conveniently discarded.... It turned out that conditions did not allow them to kill me in that room, so they forced me into a car and drove for five or six hours. They took me to a small two-story house in a small port, taped my face and bound my hands and feet. Then they drove another hour or so and moved me to a large vessel off the coast and headed out to sea. The following morning they tied my arms behind my back, placed me on a wooden plank and bound me like a corpse to be placed in a coffin. Then they hung thirty to forty kilograms of weight on each of my arms, making me ready to be thrown into the sea.[28]

In his terror, DJ may not have known exactly what was happening. His story of what happened next has become the stuff of mythology.

> Then there seemed to be a flash and the sound of an explosion.... Four or five young men in the cabin shouted, 'It's a plane!' Then they dashed out on the deck. The ship accelerated maddeningly at top speed. The cacophony of sounds continued.
>
> This tense situation continued for about half an hour, and then the ship started slowing down. At that point I heard a young man's voice close at hand. "Aren't you Mr. Kim Dae Jung?" he asked. I detected a Kyeongsang [sic] Province accent. All I could do was nod my head.

"I voted for you in the election two years ago," he continued.... Again he whispered in my ear. "You seem to be saved now."[29]

Some details, however, differed in the telling. No sailor on the KCIA ship, the *Golden Dragon*, acknowledged saying that he had voted for DJ. Sailors did report, however, that DJ, held next to the engine room, had confused the sound of the engine revving up, shifting gears or speeds, with that of an airplane. "If a plane was overhead, questions arise as to how the U.S. knew and dispatched a plane," historian Lee Wan Bom has written. U.S. forces were not ready for a rapid response to anything short of a full-scale attack, and it was unlikely the U.S. command would have "thought the issue so important as to scramble an aircraft." The notion that the United States would send a plane to hover over a small craft on an uncertain course at night was all the more far-fetched considering the failure to get any aircraft to the scene during the Pueblo hijacking five and one half years earlier. If "what saved Kim from a burial at sea was pressure on President Park by the U.S.," said Lee, "it means that the U.S. CIA came to know about the KCIA's plan via a spy." Lee speculated the Americans "decided to exaggerate their roles and influence" to promulgate the view that "the United States' strong pressure saved Kim from the jaws of death."[30]

According to a former U.S. official in Seoul, the Americans "got wind of the kidnapping almost immediately, as did the Japanese, of course, since it was a public (and very clumsy) abduction." The Japanese "were in the lead on the ground, and I think they were the ones who tracked Kim's whereabouts." The U.S. CIA could have intercepted communications between KCIA operatives in Japan and the KCIA in Seoul as well as calls from Japanese officials or could have had informants within the KCIA or another Korean agency with information on what the KCIA was doing. As the former U.S. official put it, "Bottom line: it was a botched operation, which is what saved KDJ."[31]

The American ambassador, Philip Habib, the ex-official noted, "would not have been in position or authority to directly order military operations, this would have been done in Japan, but was certainly involved diplomatically at the highest level." The American CIA station chief in Korea, Donald Gregg, "was in direct contact with Lee Hu Rak, the KCIA chief, telling them to cease and desist in no uncertain terms."[32] Gregg then went to Habib with what he had. "I know how things work here," Habib told him. "They're going to wait twenty-four hours, and if we don't say anything, Kim will be killed."[33] Habib called on Park, demanding DJ's release, reminding him that DJ's killing would be "a stain on Korea's escutcheon," said one account.[34]

Also critical was the response of the chief of the State Department's Korea desk, Donald L. Ranard, who had gotten some believed overly close to DJ while political counselor in the embassy in Seoul at the time of the student revolution against Rhee. Ranard was instrumental in getting the United States to recognize the "grievances" of the student revolutionaries and send Rhee into exile. A committed advocate for South Korean human rights, which he equated with DJ's survival, he now saw himself as an unofficial adviser to DJ. After calling Habib in Seoul, Ranard worked with his deputy, Wes Kriebel, on a statement in the name of the State Department blasting the kidnapping as "an act of terrorism" and demanding DJ's "imminent release." One of Ranard's sons, Donald A. Ranard, recounting talks with his father, has written, "The message was clear, and it reiterated what Habib was telling Park: Hands off Kim Dae Jung, or else."[35]

The *Golden Dragon* dumped DJ near Busan, and on August 13, five days after his disappearance, DJ, bruised and battered, was back in Seoul. "Some strange man told me, 'We belong to the Young Men's Group for Saving Our Country' and said they had abducted me from Japan to Korea because I conducted anti-nation activities," he said in an interview several months later. "I replied I did not do anything against the nation, only against the government. He said it was the same thing."[36] He was dropped off in front of his house in Mapo, blindfolded, and told not to remove the blindfold for three minutes as the car sped off.

DJ's wife Lee Hee Ho and sons were inside. Lee has written that "U.S. intelligence services could have easily cracked the communications secrets" between the KCIA headquarters in Seoul and the kidnappers and that "the identity of the plane is still unknown." Whatever, "my husband and I sang a prayer of thanks to God," wrote Lee. "Surrounded by reporters, my husband didn't have a wink of sleep that night." The next morning "a veritable mob of people showed up." The day after that, on August 15, the Mapo police commander ordered all visitors to leave, including relatives and secretaries. Three policemen occupied one room of the house, "there to stay indefinitely on an official police assignment."

DJ survived, but his ordeal was far from over. "A grave-like quiet had set in around us once more," Lee Hee Ho recalled. "The police had disconnected all the phones in the house, except the one in their room. They did everything and anything they wished in our house, and we didn't count in our own home. It was truly an Orwellian world of illegal brutality. Whenever a call came in for us, the policemen simply but rudely replied: 'They are not here. They are sleeping. Tell the story, and we will give them the message.' "[37]

The kidnapping and its aftermath, however, did not deter the opening on August 19, one week after DJ was deposited in Mapo-Gu, of Hanmintong's Washington office with DJ as chairman in absentia. For the next decade the Korean Congress for Democracy and Unification, as the Hanmintong was known in the United States, spread the word about DJ's plight, his program and his policies. "*Hanmintong*'s branch office in the U.S., based in Washington, D.C., had a wide network with regional committees in major cities," according to a summary of its history. "Since October of 1975, it started to publish the *Hanmintong Newsletter* and carried out organized activities, taking immediate countermeasures whenever important events occurred in Korea." The next sentence—"The organization was maintained through membership fees and contributions from sponsors"—revealed its primary mission, to raise funds and begin a program of investment that would enrich the democratization movement in DJ's looming struggle for power.[38]

CHAPTER FOUR

Time of Violence

Japanese officials were indignant about the kidnapping if only because the KCIA had grossly violated Japanese sovereignty. The Koreans had intended no harm to Japan, but by carrying out such an outrageous plot on Japanese soil they had made the efficient Japanese police look like fools and besmirched Japanese integrity. Japan had suffered the worst indignity, a grievous loss of face.

After the police found the fingerprints of a KCIA agent, holder of a diplomatic passport, on the bottle containing the chloroform used for drugging Kim Dae Jung, the Korean ambassador stoutly responded, "No Korean government organization is involved."[1] The United States had to intercede for DJ's sake as well as relations between Japan and South Korea. Both countries were bound to the United States in military alliances that made an outburst of ill will over one unimaginable incident a security concern. President Park Chung Hee freed DJ from house arrest on October 26, 1974, then dispatched Prime Minister Kim Jong Pil to Japan to apologize since "both the victim and the culprit turned out to be Koreans." The Korean ambassador said the KCIA diplomat was "under investigation." It was all an exercise in face-saving that avoided blaming the KCIA or the Korean government. The sole purpose, not very successful, was to assuage Japanese anger over a rude offense perpetrated by a country that the Japanese looked down on as a former colony now ruled by difficult upstarts.[2]

If Kim Dae Jung the matador had goaded Park and his KCIA into uncontrollable rage, he remained in grave danger of getting gored himself. As protest flared and authorities wreaked vengeance, Korea projected the image of an historic culture of violence, the latter-day incarnation of dynasties in which justice was inflicted cruelly by death by the sword, by beatings and torture unto death in an authoritarian society unaccustomed to criticism by prying foreigners. As DJ rose in influence abroad and at home, he found a crusade against dictatorship a sure way to gain international approbation—and also win the popularity of downtrodden people, notably those from his own Cholla region, long deprived of a significant voice. Government officials found themselves having to explain and justify acts of violent repression that they viewed as none of the world's business—except that Korea depended on the United States for military survival and on the United States and the rest of the world to buy its products.

After Park on January 8, 1974, imposed another set of emergency decrees, Kim Jong Pil, the KCIA founder, now prime minister, was in the unenviable position of trying to explain to me the government's position. It was the kind of interview that he was delegated to give for international appearances while Park spurned meetings with the media as an unwelcome intrusion. "We cannot stand for these dissidents creating problems particularly with the Communists infiltrating the South from the North and economic difficulties," said Kim Jong Pil, "JP" in the headlines, a powerful man in his own right, a presidential aspirant. He seemed supremely confident of how to deal with the threat from the North—a topic that DJ and other activists avoided—as well as pressure for democratic reform. "The problem spreads rapidly, like a contagious disease," JP elaborated. "We feel we must maintain strict discipline." Later, a dissident told how "discipline" was imposed when warnings and instructions were unheeded: "If anyone refuses to obey, they take them individually and beat them. They have tortured professors until they write notes saying they won't write any more."[3]

Park's program, however, was more refined than such reports suggested. In the anxiety to come to terms with his foes, he dropped the scheming Lee Hu Rak as KCIA director as an easy way to eliminate a rival and appease his foes, including the U.S. CIA station chief, Donald Gregg, who did not want to have to deal with him. As a government source explained, the KCIA hoped "to try to convince people they must pull together." By such techniques, the government would sideline DJ. From his home base, under house arrest, however, DJ was soon able to rally supporters and give interviews while under 24-hour surveillance, unable to get a passport to leave the country and unable to participate directly in politics.

"They don't prevent me from going out, but I do not leave here," DJ said in a lengthy lunchtime conversation in March 1974, seven months after the kidnapping. "I know if I go out and meet somebody, then that person will get in some difficulty." DJ called the situation "very serious" and demanded Park acquiesce to the demands of student demonstrators. "He and his opponents must make a compromise to seek a solution," he said. "This kind of suppression will bring unhappiness not only to the Korean people but to Park himself."[4] DJ said he wanted to leave the country again soon, but there was no doubt that Park and the KCIA would hold him where he was if only to keep him from pillorying the regime abroad. In the meanwhile, his door was open to visitors to whom he freely expressed his views while presenting them with samples of his own calligraphy. "If we do not have freedom, there is no reason to be against communism, there is no way to enjoy our lives," he observed in a typical conversation, intimating that South Koreans might just as well yield to North Korea as long as Park remained in power.

DJ believed, however, the end for Park was near. "I am solidly convinced our people will enjoy democracy in the near future," he told me. "I am convinced South Koreans are still strongly anticommunist, but we cannot accept totalitarian rule in the name of anticommunism. No country is safe from communism if it does not guarantee freedom for its people." As for his own ambitions, he said, "Basically, I want to do something for my people, for their freedom, but I am limited very much."[5]

Idealistic and altruistic though he may have sounded, DJ spoke as one hardly committed to fighting communism as spread by the country that had invaded the South less than a quarter of a century before. He never mentioned North Korea's massed forces above the DMZ, much less their repeated forays across the line. He showed no awareness of the discovery for the first time, in November 1974, of a North Korean infiltration tunnel. Nor did he and other dissidents express concern when a second tunnel was found in March 1975, and they never criticized the activists who seemed to take their cue from the North on core beliefs.

In this culture of violence, no one was safe, definitely not the leaders who meted out the violence. If Park had any inclination to temporize in the months after DJ had settled against his will into his Mapo home, he lost it entirely on August 15, 1974, the anniversary of "liberation" from Japan. On that morning a young man rushed down the center aisle of Seoul's National Theater, charging the podium, waving a pistol at Park as he was delivering his annual liberation day address. When Park's security guards drew their pistols and sprang into action from the wings of the stage, the man, now close to the well of the theater, fired wildly. The president's wife, Yook Young Soo, was mortally wounded—whether by Park's would-be assassin or by one of the security guards firing back at him has never been clarified.

"Down by the well, men from the audience pounced on the assassin, threw him to the floor and pummeled him as they disarmed him," as *New York Times* correspondent Richard Halloran, who was there, described the scene. "One of the president's security guards shouted from the stage [in Korean]: 'Don't kill him, don't kill him.'" In the melee, a bodyguard shot and killed a teen-aged girl who had been in the chorus for the occasion. The intruder was Mun Se Gwang, a Korean living in Japan, who Halloran reported "had stolen a pistol from a Japanese police station, entered Korea with a false passport, and somehow eluded security to get into the National Theater." It was never clear whether he was a lone activist who wanted to kill Park for promulgating the Yushin Constitution or was a North Korean agent. Halloran believed both theories might be true.[6]

The killing of Park's wife, a popular woman who was, wrote Halloran, "considered to have had a leavening influence on Park, persuading him to ease up on some of his more authoritarian and repressive measures," confirmed Park's worst fears about the dark forces that he believed were out to destroy him and his vision of a mighty industrialized Korea. Nearly eight months later, on April 8, 1975, Korea University was closed by decree as a breeding ground of revolt. On April 9, eight people were hanged for plotting to rejuvenate the "People's Revolutionary Party," a name fabricated by the KCIA from leftist movements in other countries to help frame them on capital charges under the National Security Law.[7]

Next, in May 1975, Park came up with his draconian Emergency Decree Number Nine that gave the government limitless powers to arrest critics for sedition. Any political speech against the regime was viewed as an inflammatory act of rebellion. Although never a radical threat comparable to Kim Dae Jung, that other influential foe, Kim Young Sam, was also placed under house arrest and expelled from the National Assembly. Park was free to carry out deeds that were unjustifiable even under his Yushin Constitution but made possible by the powers he held under the cover of that document.

There were two rationales for much of what Park did. Most obviously, he and his aides accused their critics, particularly any discerned to harbor liberal or leftist tendencies, notably Kim Dae Jung, of acting on behalf of North Korea. While there was no doubt North Korean agents and sympathizers were in South Korea, Park used the

Communist threat for stifling all forms of dissent. The second rationale for suppression was Park's perception of the need for stern discipline and central planning to lift Korea from the devastation of the Korean War and put Korean industry into competition against the biggest and best manufacturers in the United States, Japan and Europe. Park instituted a series of five-year plans while setting specific goals for production and exports. He told leaders of the multitentacle family-controlled conglomerates, the *chaebol*, whose Chinese characters mean "fortune cluster" or "rich clans," what industries to enter, blocking what he saw as needless competition. For those *chaebol* chieftains who toed the line, the reward was the rise of their own industrial empires, passed on to their heirs, that continue to hold sway over the economy.

As Park pursued his foes ever more relentlessly, pressure arose in inverse proportion at home and abroad to inhibit his extraordinary transgressions against basic rights in a land defended by the United States as an outpost of democracy against Communist dictatorship. Christians, theological descendants of the missionaries who had transformed educational institutions and implanted new ideas and invention in a nation stultified by a rigid class structure in which royalty reigned supreme and slaves clung tenuously to the bottom rung, had much to do with inculcating the revolutionary spirit.

"There were a couple of things those activists, Korean and non-Korean alike, had in common," according to Donald Baker, historian and former Peace Corps volunteer. "They were both dedicated to promoting democracy and respect for human rights in Korea. And most of them were Christian."[8] The closest missionary connection to Kim Dae Jung was probably Pharis Harvey, whose wife, Jane, had known DJ's wife, Lee Hee Ho, when they were both college students in Tennessee. Baker described Harvey as "relentless" in his efforts to promote more respect for human rights" in Korea. Park saw foreign missionaries as enemies, ordering the expulsion of two for service in the teeming port of Incheon and for campaigning on behalf of the eight doomed members of the "People's Revolutionary Party." George Ogle, a Methodist who had worked with the Urban Industrial Mission organizing female textile workers, and the Maryknoll priest James Sinnott, who had ministered to the poor, both testified before congressional committees about what they had endured—"another way," Baker wrote, of how "Christians overseas helped the struggle for democracy and human rights inside Korea."[9]

Park, however, had other grounds for fear of dissent—defeat of the U.S.-backed governments in Vietnam, Cambodia and Laos. He and the

KCIA were acutely aware of the relationship between enormous political opposition abroad to the U.S. role in Vietnam and the downfall of the Saigon government on April 30, 1975. South Korea had deployed more than 300,000 troops to Vietnam between 1965 and 1973 when the last of them pulled out simultaneously with American forces. More than 5,000 South Koreans had died—nearly 10 percent of the number of Americans killed in the Vietnam War and far more than those from any other foreign country—but the world was largely unaware of their role. "In those days, all major Korea-related news revolved around Kim Dae Jung as he was repeatedly imprisoned, released or put under house arrest," wrote Paul Shin, a longtime correspondent in Korea for American news agencies.[10]

On March 1, 1976, 57th anniversary of the 1919 uprising against Japan and ten months after Hanoi's victory in Vietnam, Kim Dae Jung and a number of other dissidents angered Park with a "declaration for democracy and national salvation" for which all of them were put on trial and imprisoned. The declaration, issued at Myongdong Cathedral, was an appeal for democracy and a blanket attack on every aspect of government policy, including the economy. There must, it stated, "be a fundamental assessment of the plan for economic development." "National unification," it said, was "the most important task," and the way to achieve it was "to promote our national capability for democracy." The declaration was not exactly fair about the economy, which Park was making a Herculean effort to build. While talking of "our intense conflict with the Communist regime in the North," it also betrayed little comprehension of how to deal with North Korea other than to note that "military defense and economic power" would collapse in the South "without the support of the democratic ability...."[11]

Imprisoned for this declaration, Kim Dae Jung had unreserved sympathy from American liberals. Senator Kennedy, in response to an appeal from DJ's wife, Lee Hee Ho, addressing her as "Dear Mrs. Kim," wrote that he had been "deeply distressed to learn of the arrest of your husband and the charges that have subsequently been leveled at him by the Government of Mr. Park." Having "followed closely the serious events of past weeks in your country," he said he had been "extraordinarily impressed by the courage and determination shown by yourselves and other brave Koreans in signing the Declaration of Democracy" and assured her of "my continuing respect and support for the goals for which you have so long fought." It had, he said, "long been clear that the steady and systematic erosion of liberties in your country are undermining the basis of cohesion...."[12]

Such outpourings translated into what Park saw as a dastardly betrayal, Jimmy Carter's proposal to withdraw American ground forces from South Korea. Carter as a potential Democratic Party presidential candidate had begun talking about pulling U.S. troops from Korea even as the North Vietnamese were staging their final campaign in early 1975 for the takeover of all South Vietnam. The American public was fed up with war in Asia. A total of 58,209 Americans had died in Vietnam, 33,686 in Korea, far fewer than the millions of Vietnamese and Koreans who had perished but far too many for Americans to accept when "Make love, not war," was a slogan and "peaceniks" and "hippies" a subculture.

Reminders of the dangers never ceased. On August 18, 1976, two U.S. Army officers, a captain and a lieutenant, and four South Korean soldiers were hacked to death by North Korean soldiers in the Joint Security Area, the enclave on the line between the two Koreas at the site in Panmunjom of the signing of the Korean War armistice. The fracas broke out when the North Koreans tried to stop them from cutting down a tree that was blocking the line of sight from the South Korean side of the line. American soldiers in the uproar did cut down the tree as U.S. warplanes flew overhead; the "axe murder incident" was another reminder of the horrors of the "forgotten war" years earlier. To the American public, and to Carter, now the Democratic presidential candidate, feeding on emotions after President Gerald Ford had abandoned the U.S.-backed Saigon regime the year before, the incident dramatized the futility of confrontation in a country that most voters preferred to forget.

After his inauguration in January 1977, Carter decided to make good on his campaign promise, summoning up plans for pulling out U.S. troops, now down to 40,000 since withdrawal of the Seventh Division during the Nixon presidency. The fact that Park was a sometimes cruel dictator undoubtedly steeled Carter in his determination to end the commitment. After 3,400 troops had left, however, pressure from Japan, as the U.S. ally that saw South Korea as a buffer against North Korea and China, and from the State Department and the Pentagon, armed with estimates of growing North Korean strength, forced Carter to give up the idea of more withdrawals. When Carter visited Seoul for the first time on June 29, 1979, he was ready, like every other American president, to conclude the summit with a joint communiqué reaffirming the U.S. commitment. Putting to rest "the question of further withdrawal of American ground combat forces," he assured Park the United States would "maintain an

American military presence in the Republic of Korea to ensure peace and security."[13]

Carter would never forsake his liberal views on Korea, but it was difficult for any American leader to get away from the reality of the North Korean threat. Radical activists and dissidents, egged on by foreign missionaries and courted for quotes by foreign correspondents who saw "protest" and "reform" as the story, refused to acknowledge North Korea as a threat against which the South had to defend itself. DJ reveled in foreign media attention but skipped this reality while tearing into Park for just about all his policies, including his hard line against the North. Even as DJ was under constant guard in Korea, his Hanmintong organization in Japan was raising funds, mobilizing demonstrations, expenses paid by the pro-North Korean residents' federation. DJ believed North and South Korea should join the United Nations simultaneously and pursue South-North federation under which they would retain separate governing structures but present a common front on defense and foreign policy. It was an impossible dream that distracted from the need for dialogue.[14] Vilified at the time, the federation idea was raised over the years by North Korea though most people in the South viewed it as a theoretical abstraction.

In constructing the economy, Park was as blind to the suffering of his people as DJ was to the dangers posed by North Korea. Snuffing out dissent as an obstacle to both economic planning and defense, Park believed he had to stifle a labor movement outside the context of a single government-sponsored national labor federation. He had no idea that labor in an industrializing economy had to organize, as in the United States and Europe during the industrial revolution of the nineteenth century and into the twentieth. Huge new factories were springing to life out of fields, forests and swamps, and apartment complexes were rising around them. In the tight-knit environment of assembly-line production and regimented lives, at the mercy of owners who were getting very rich, workers formed sub rosa unions that would defy the harshest attempts of police and corporate goons to destroy them.

As the domestic industry that Park had fostered, coddled and planned began to compete internationally in such heavy-duty products as motor vehicles, ships, and eventually electronic gadgets and gizmos, each advance was cheered as a triumph for the nation. As Korea became a leader in construction projects around the world, especially in the Middle East, Park saw the country as an emerging international power. As the economy marched onward and upward, he was convinced that workers, like soldiers, had to respond to orders. Oblivious to the need for workers' rights, Park believed industry would grow bigger, faster, if run like an army with a chain of command from the top, from him.

Park's inability to deal with a burgeoning, if underground, labor movement formed the background to his murder—not at the hands of one of the radical activists whom he most loathed and feared but by a trusted lieutenant from his tightest inner circle. In a drawn-out crackdown on a spreading outbreak of labor turmoil in metropolitan Busan and nearby Masan, on the southeastern coast, senior officials clashed over what to do. Park, intensely aware of the dangers he faced, of the likelihood of another assassination attempt, never would have imagined how he would come to his own violent end.

At a dinner party on October 26, 1979, attended by two hostesses in a KCIA "safe house" near the Blue House, Park's security chief, Cha Chi Chul, berated the chief of the Korean Central Intelligence Agency, Kim Jae Kyu, his longtime rival for influence, for failing to stop the protests. Outraged at affronts to his competence from one whom he regarded as beneath him, Kim pulled out his pistol, shouted, "You dirty dog," fired and mortally wounded Cha. As the dying Cha crawled off, Kim fired at Park, killing him with bullets in the head and spine. Other KCIA people, in cahoots with Kim, rushed in and killed four of Park's bodyguards before soldiers swarmed over the scene. Kim left in the melee, contacted the army chief of staff, General Chung Seung Hwa, in a nearby building and told him the president was shot. They rushed to the Ministry of National Defense, where Kim hours later was revealed as the assassin. Chung took over as martial law commander, and the prime minister, Choi Kyu Hah, became acting president.

Park's death inspired grief among a fundamentally conservative people to whom economic achievement outweighed infringement on human rights. In a Confucian society, the death of Park, dictator or not, was mourned like the loss of a father. More than two million lined the broad avenue, Sejong-ro, from Kwangwhamun, the imposing gate in front of another Japanese-built edifice, the former Japanese governor-general's building, later the central government building, then the National Museum and finally torn down, condemned as a Japanese plot to obstruct the view of Kyongbok Palace, seat of Yi dynasty kings. What counted more, democratic reform as envisioned by religious reformers and student activists, or jobs, money and food on the table? People wept as the stately procession wended slowly by to the stentorian tones of Buddhist chants and funeral dirges.[15]

There was no doubt that life in the Park era had become measurably more bearable than before. In 18 years and 5 months in power, from the time of the launching of his first economic plan in 1962 through the end of 1978, the last full year before the assassination, the gross national product on a per capita basis had soared from $87 to $1,242. Exports, on which Park firmly believed the economy would rely for full recovery, leapt from $55 million in 1962 to $12.4 billion in 1978. Park had given the country "a positive alternative to communism or the colonial past," wrote Japanese scholar Fuji Kamiya, borrowing from Japan's experience "as the explicit model" and adopting "an economic strategy of creating heavy and chemical industries and paying for imports by increasing exports."[16] For all his mistakes, Park was a successful nation-builder—remembered by many Koreans years later as their greatest president.

With Park's passing, the country teetered shakily on the edge of a new era. Was democratic reform possible—and did it have to conflict with the requirements for economic advancement? Park's undoubted economic success was lost on his foes, including Kim Dae Jung, who saw it as achieved at the expense of workers existing on subsistence wages. The future was highly uncertain, especially to DJ, Kim Young Sam, and other contenders. When Park was assassinated, DJ was under house arrest, having been freed in December 1978 from the prison hospital in which he was held after serving part of his sentence for the 1976 democracy declaration.

Chun Doo Hwan, a major general, was in charge of the defense security command at the time of Park's assassination. That position gave him the authority to round up the usual suspects, as well as some unusual ones. His drive for power put him in conflict with Choi, who promised as one of his first acts as president to do away with the Yushin Constitution. Chun had another agenda. He publicized himself at a press conference after flights to Seoul, suspended for two days after the assassination, resumed and correspondents arrived. If his tone was bureaucratic, his words conveyed the message. He would capture those behind the assassination and bring them to justice.[17]

President Choi to superficial appearances was in control when on December 8 1979, six weeks after Park's assassination, he freed a number of dissidents, including DJ, from prison and house arrest. Four days later, on December 12, Chun engineered the arrest of his superior, General Chung Seung Hwa, in a shoot-out in which more than a score of soldiers were killed. Chung was charged with complicity in the assassination, the principal evidence for which was his failure to arrest KCIA director Kim right away rather than go with him to the defense ministry headquarters. Although Chun would not assume complete power for several months, the arrest of Chung was a mini-coup d'etat in which Chun took over de facto authority from Choi and all military people loyal to Chung. Koreans would refer to the mini-coup by the date, "12/12."

Chun's military ally in his takeover was his Class of 1955 Korea Military Academy classmate, Roh Tae Woo, also a general and commander of a division based along the DMZ. Together they would tighten controls even as Kim Dae Jung, his civil rights restored, was giving interviews and talking to political friends. DJ gave an impression of supporting Kim Young Sam, long since freed from house arrest and elected to the National Assembly, only to be expelled from the assembly in August 1979 for protesting the "dictatorial regime" after a crackdown on young female workers staging a protest in the sanctuary of his party offices.

The clouds of dictatorship were lifting in the months after Park's assassination. As the winter of 1980 ended, and trees and grass turned green and flowers bloomed, this interlude came to be known as "Seoul Spring." People were thinking politically in terms of "three Kims"— the leftist DJ, the moderate liberal YS, and the conservative JP, Kim Jong Pil, KCIA founder and prime minister under Park—as if all three were running for president even though no election was scheduled. From its office on Washington's K Street, the avenue of lobbyists, law firms, and brokerages, the American branch of the Hanmintong, Korean Congress for Democracy and Unification, announced its "eighth annual meeting" to run "August 8–10 1980" at the Mayflower Hotel.[18]

Like the buds that blossom on the cherry and lilac trees for two or three weeks and then die, Seoul Spring faded fast. Dissidents and opposition politicians had a source of support that Chun had no idea how to handle peacefully or diplomatically. That was the student movement that boiled over in the first week of May in protests on campuses and then, in the second week, erupted in central Seoul in front of those two edifices of the Japanese era, the glowering grey city hall and Seoul Station, modeled on Tokyo Station, a pinnacled brick derivative of nineteenth-century Dutch architecture. Several hundred thousand jammed those vast spaces and the broad avenue between them, dominated by Namdaemun, the ancient South Gate portal to the capital. The protest raised the specter of a bloody civil war. "Revolution! Revolution! Revolution!" and "Final judgment" and "Let's win victory with blood," were some of the battle cries cited by the government to justify a strong response.[19]

The outpouring to many was unexpected. President Choi, on a mission befitting the title that he had acquired, was on a state visit to Saudi Arabia and Kuwait. Accompanied by the minister of energy and resources and the construction minister, Choi sought to promote national interests in a critical region. South Korea relied almost entirely on oil imports to fuel its growing economy, and Korean builders, notably Hyundai Engineering and Construction, the biggest, had enormous contracts to build ports, refineries, apartment blocks, hospitals, and expressways traversing the urban complexes and deserts of both countries.

As the protest grew, Choi rushed back a day early from the Middle East, arriving on the night of May 16 to take charge. Choi, though, would never be in charge. A former diplomat and professor, he was an outsider as far as Chun and Roh were concerned. Like Park, these two generals were also from Daegu and North Kyongsang province. Like-minded friends and allies, sharing the same regional prejudices, accents, friends, teachers, and often near and distant relatives and in-laws, they were known as "the TK mafia"—Daegu and Kyongsang. (The term *TK mafia* lingered in the media even after spellings were changed from Taegu to Daegu and Kyongsang to Gyeongsang in the revision in the late 1990s of the transliteration from the Hangul script.)

Chun moved quickly against all foes, including President Choi and dissident DJ. Having already been forced to appoint Chun as KCIA director, Choi was shunted aside with nothing to do but hang on as a symbol as Chun staged the "palace coup" of May 17–18 in which he had the cabinet expand existing martial law decrees under "Decree Number Ten" and established a military committee to lord it over the governing structure. DJ and YS were both on an arrest list that included everyone suspected of instigating or organizing student protest, labor walkouts or the democracy movement that Chun, his military clique and the KCIA held responsible for unrest in all forms. Others, including Kim Jong Pil, were arrested for corruption as the government demonstrated its high moral tone. DJ's wife recalled him telling her, "Don't panic! They have come to arrest me." She saw "some thirty heavily armed soldiers pointing their guns at my husband's throat and neck before the soldiers searched the house, taking "all sorts of things" and demanding she turn over blank checks found in a drawer.[20]

Almost at once, revolt broke out in Gwangju, the central city of the region to which DJ owed his political strength and popularity. A minor protest, characterized early by rock-throwing clashes with policemen, escalated into an uprising in which class warfare and regional prejudices boiled into violence. The two other Kims, YS and JP, would not be held for long; Chun saw DJ as his worst enemy. Investigators were certain that DJ while free from prison had spurred on the protesters. Well before the students rampaged through the city on May 19, taking over the central government buildings, DJ had expressed concerns that "extra-political forces" might invite armed intervention. Chun's decision to divert the twentieth infantry division from duty near the DMZ with orders to retake Gwangju precipitated brutality captured on TV worldwide—though not in Korea, where the government clamped down on reports in both the broadcast and print media.

The Martial Law Command on May 22 claimed to have firm evidence of DJ's role in inciting nationwide student demonstrations through his own organizations, including the Fraternity for Democratic Constitutional Rule, the Hankuk Political and Research Institute, and the League of Democratic Youth associations. DJ's first son, Hong Il, was named as "an intermediary," said an unsigned newspaper report that appeared to have been written by the command for distribution to all the media. DJ was alleged to have given money to one of the leaders of the street demonstrations when he visited DJ's home in mid-May. Another student leader, a law major, was said to have received money from son Hong Il. A third student leader, from Busan, was alleged to have come away with a somewhat lesser sum from a visit to DJ's home. A member of DJ's Fraternity for Democratic Constitutional Rule was said to have picked up a book about Kim Dae Jung entitled *National Seoul* along with a copy of the plea that assassin Kim Jae Kyu offered to justify killing Park Chung Hee.[21]

Kim Dae Jung, in solitary confinement, unable to receive visitors, did not know what was going on, much less the charges against him. He has written that he was interrogated at KCIA headquarters for nearly two months before a Martial Law Command officer, his first visitor, made him an offer: "Cooperate with us, and we will give you anything you ask," DJ quoted him as saying. "Should you decline, we will have to mete out capital punishment." The officer left behind newspapers in which DJ learned "for the first time that a series of demonstrations had broken out in Kwangju on May 18." The demonstrators "had demanded my release and called for an end to martial law." In the ensuing ten days, as the army, led by the special forces, put down the struggle, he heard that 200 or more people had died. "Thus I learned about the 'Kwangju Democratization Movement,' as we called it later, from newspapers that carried only incomplete, warped reports...." He fainted, he wrote, in shock. "Obliged to accept the fact of my powerlessness in the face of events, I was weighed down with shame."[22]

The dawning realization of what had happened had the opposite effect from that intended by the officer from the Martial Law Command. After the officer's visit, "I wept in my cell at the KCIA," DJ wrote. "I had been weakened physically and emotionally in the course of my forty days of imprisonment. However, the example of the victims of this outrage in Kwangju gave me the strength to refuse the generals' enticing offer of mercy in return for my cooperation. I preferred to die in the name of democracy and for the sake of the Korean people." As a result of such intransigence, "I was accused of being the chief instigator of the Kwangju 'rebellion'—of plotting the violent overthrow of the government."[23]

The near-total loyalty that Kim Dae Jung inspired in the Cholla region was beyond the imagination of the military leaders who wanted him eliminated. He had come to represent the deepest aspirations of a regional grouping that also defied the understanding of American officials, who yearned to bring Koreans together for the sake of the alliance, and of missionaries, scholars, teachers, and journalists who saw the Gwangu revolt as a crusade in microcosm. The depth of the sentiment for DJ transcended any vision of nationalism, of unification of the two Koreas. It was born of an emotion that visitors found difficult to comprehend in its scope and enormity. Kim Chung Keun, a reporter for *Dong A Ilbo*, in those days a leading newspaper with an eye for wrongs committed by the government, has described what he saw and heard the day after the round-up of all foes and critics of the Chun regime:

> All the .... people were gathering in groups.... I saw tension, resolve and determination, and of these three, tension was the strongest. Someone shouted,
> "End martial law!"
> It was like a gunshot.
> People poured out of shops, side streets and buildings. They had been waiting for the word, and a demonstration was forming. Leaders shouted slogans.
> "Let the prisoners go. Let them go."
> "Let Kim Dae Jung go!"
> "Announce the nation's political timetable. ANNOUNCE!"
> That was not all. The people demanded to know who was responsible for the violence at Chonnam University the day before

(when the military had broken in on students studying for their exams and beaten them indiscriminately).

"Apologize, Apologize!"

That was how the demonstrations began in downtown Kwangju that morning. Out came the riot police, of course. They chased after the demonstrators, doing their best to catch them, but still numbers were limited. It was close on lunchtime when the whole streetview changed. People in business suits came out for lunch and mingled with the demonstrators as they came.

[The violence escalated]

Military trucks crammed with heavily armed paratroopers with fixed bayonets lurched into sight.... The paras jumped out and waded into the crowd from both ends of the street, working toward the middle—striking with heavy-duty clubs, left, right, left right....

It was terribly one-sided. Some bold spirits threw stones. Others had bottles full of petrol—Molotov cocktails—prepared. But the soldiers reacted quickly....

The outcome? Kwangju citizens' idea—to demonstrate peacefully against martial law and to protest violence—was blown away. The exorbitant violence of the troops was what did it. The reaction was: What the hell is the military up to?: "How could a (Korean) national army do this to fellow Koreans?" Rank incomprehension was overtaken by a sense of outrage.[24]

That day was just the beginning, the first. The worst lay ahead. There was no way that DJ, in jail, could have masterminded the revolt. Nor was he in a position before his latest and final incarceration to have advised or planned what the demonstrators were doing. In a culture of violence, however, the example of DJ, the favorite son and hope of Cholla, inspired a level of defiance that had the potential for tearing the country apart as surely as had the North Koreans, eager to harass the South with spies and saboteurs and rhetoric. Years later, DJ preferred to see the Gwangju revolt in terms of the spirit and principles displayed by the people. "The outcome was a victory for democracy," he wrote. "The name of Kwangju stands as a symbol of justice for the oppressed." If there was "an international aspect," DJ believed, it was that the "spirit of Kwangju is not a monopoly of Koreans, something we keep to ourselves," but was "cherished by mankind at large—wherever democracy and human rights are respected."[25]

Thus Gwangju was not only the symbol but the foundation of DJ's outlook as he dreamed of appealing to that other Korean society above the DMZ as a partner with which to reconcile. In a culture where violence was the norm for regime survival, it did not seem necessary for DJ to mention that repression in North Korea could be far worse than anything he had experienced or seen in his own society. What would be the point of vilifying the North when the South had problems of its own? It was as though people had heard enough about the evils of North Korea. Here in Kim Dae Jung was a political figure willing to defend them and their interests against historic oppressors.

CHAPTER FIVE

On Trial for Democracy

Chun Doo Hwan vastly enhanced Kim Dae Jung's reputation as Korea's bravest dissident by having him tried, convicted and sentenced to death for the Gwangju revolt. DJ was charged not only with treasonous "antistate" activities, aiding and abetting rebellion, but also with staging a campaign of heavy-handed repression.[1] His trial in August and September 1980 was a show open to limited coverage by journalists for foreign news agencies on a pool basis. On the day of DJ's indictment, August 1, 1980, 23 others, professors, pastors, politicians, writers and student activists, all linked to DJ, were also indicted. A dozen were charged with planning the Gwangju revolt, the others with violating martial law decrees.

The judicial process was reserved for the worst cases. The government on the same day said it had purged 611 primary, middle school and high school principals, teachers and school administrators, all part of its drive for "social purification," and was shutting down 172 magazines and newspapers, 12 percent of all those registered. Political parties were disbanded, hundreds of opposition politicos were banned from politics, journalists and broadcasters lost their jobs, private broadcast facilities fell into government hands, and news agencies were forced to form one national news agency, Yonhap, "alliance." Chun believed he could expunge the memory of Gwangju, wiping it out by tight control over the media. At the same time, attempts at strikes against major manufacturers, especially the motor vehicle and ship-building plants under the Hyundai group in the southeastern industrial enclave of Ulsan, were more fiercely suppressed than ever before with the arrests of scores of members of "illegal" labor groups.

The trial of Kim Dae Jung was also a trial for democracy. On the day it began, August 14, 1980, Kim Young Sam, as president of the opposition Shinmin-dang, New Democratic Party, still under house arrest, said he was giving up politics since he was no longer able to fulfill his responsibilities. Kim Jong Pil, as leader of the late Park Chung Hee's Kongwha-dang, Republican Party, had already resigned from politics and been freed from prison after promising to donate his ill-got wealth to the state. Chun Doo Hwan, as acting director of the KCIA and chairman of the standing committee of the military-led special committee for national security measures, still nominally led by President Choi, was putting all the pieces into position to remove Choi and install himself as president.

The image of DJ, in white prison garb, handcuffed, with helmeted military policemen on either side as he was led into a courtroom filled with journalists, diplomats, and relatives of some of the other 23 defendants but no members of his own family, symbolized Chun's complete domination of the scene—and the government. Visibly angry, DJ was seated beside two other well known dissidents, the Reverend Moon Ik Hwan, a Presbyterian pastor, and Lee Mun Yong, a Korea University professor.[2]

The list of charges before the five-judge military panel was long. One of them was that DJ had sought to form public opinion by conducting anti-Korean activities in Japan and the United States from the time he went to Japan in October 1972 for medical treatment until August 1973 when he was kidnapped from his hotel room in Tokyo. A second charge was that he had had his followers set up the headquarters in Japan of Hanmintong, the Korean Congress for Democracy and Unification, arranging for him to become chairman, and had received cash from a Japanese political figure. He was also charged with plotting a nationwide antigovernment campaign in the weeks before the Gwangju revolt, inciting student riots and seditious acts in order to overthrow the government, handing a large amount of cash to students in Gwangju when they had visited his home and distributing pamphlets to demonstrators stating that South Koreans would unite to challenge the government and fight for the lifting of martial law if the military authorities did not do so on May 19, the day after its imposition. The grounds for imposing the death penalty would be sedition and conspiracy to overthrow the government.[3]

From day one, democracy was on trial. Two reporters for foreign news agencies—foreigners and Koreans—were permitted to cover each session, also witnessed by small numbers of foreign diplomats and members of the defendants' families. The journalists' reports, distributed on a pool basis to all correspondents, show DJ and his co-defendants in defiant mood, rejecting charges and attempting to reveal how he had been treated since his arrest on May 17.

Kim Dae Jung on the first day of questioning refused to respond, calling the whole charade "political persecution and political retaliation" and declaring, when reminded that refusal to respond would not help, "I am only protesting against the nature of this trial." DJ had a powerful ally among his co-defendants in Moon Ik Hwan, who denounced the procedure as illegal and refused to accept it as a trial. "We have worked so hard for democratization of our country," Moon said, "but now that we are trapped by the crime of sedition our feelings are confused and we think it's too unfair." The judge cut him off immediately after he declared, "This is a political trial and just a formality trying to justify the political trial."[4]

DJ in the afternoon session was in a more talkative mood though not inclined to provide the answers demanded by prosecutors. For an hour, sitting on a wooden bench, he fended off the long litany of charges against him. From the time of its launch, he said, Hanmintong had opposed the "dictatorial system of Park Chung Hee," not South Korea as a country. The platform, he explained, focused on support for South Korea rather than its dictatorial political system, placing top priority first on restoration of democracy and, second, reunification. DJ was anxious, moreover, to ward off any impression of the anti-Americanism advocated by leftist activists. Never, he said, had he favored cutting off U.S. aid and support. Nor had he called for withdrawal of U.S. troops. As for the leftist leanings of those with whom he had consorted in Japan before his abduction in 1973, he professed to know nothing of all that and did not espouse friendly relations with North Korea. He might have talked longer than an hour had the judge, in response to a prosecutor's request, not asked him to refrain from "long-winded explanations."[5]

The next day, for the first time publicly, or semipublicly, Kim Dae Jung revealed what he had endured while held in a cell underground for interrogation from nine o'clock in the morning until midnight for 60 days. "It is beyond description how I suffered mentally," he told the court. "Sometimes I was stripped of clothes and driven to the very point short of torture." DJ flatly denied all the charges. "I have never thought of resorting to violence as a means to seize power," he said. "My thinking always was to come to power through elections." He had told investigators "all the truth" but they "never tried to believe me," he went on. "They told me it would be better for me to admit all now because I would have an opportunity to deny them all at the court." He said he had "a weak heart and the situation was too much for me to stand," that he was "extremely tired, mentally as well as physically." All DJ would admit was that he had "signed some statements against my will, thinking I could deny them at the court."[6]

As for the charge that he had intended to create social unrest and overthrow the government, DJ shot back, "We never thought about overthrowing the government by violent means" but rather "tried to improve the situation by applying pressure on the government." The censor deleted that remark as well as a lengthy reply that he gave to the accusation that he had ordered one of the students to spark the uprising. "It's a lie, it's a fabrication," he said emphatically. "I haven't met him. I don't know him." The censor did not delete DJ's admission that he had earlier sent secretaries to "look and report" on demonstrations in central Seoul but excised his denial that he had given money for his party to support the protests.[7]

Prosecutors spent much of the time trying to corral DJ with testimony from some of the others on trial with him. The poet Ye Choon Ho, a former National Assembly member, denied having heard DJ tell dissidents at a meeting in a hotel on May 17, the night martial law was imposed, that nationwide demonstrations should be held simultaneously. Similarly, he denied urging young students at the meeting, attended by DJ, to "bring back April 19 uprising," a reference to the revolt that had toppled Rhee Syngman 20 years earlier. The censors deleted those remarks but left intact, "Oh yes, with all my heart," his response to whether he opposed the Yushin Constitution. The presiding judge overruled an attempt by DJ to protest that the prosecutor had not given Ye the chance to defend himself.[8]

Other defendants were also questioned, all to show how DJ plotted his rise to power. Korea University Professor Lee Mun Yong, on the stand the next day, said that DJ had signed a written draft of the plan drawn up by the Hanmintong only after "dropping the call for mass public rallies."[9] Kim Sang Hyun, DJ's secretary-general during his 1971 presidential campaign, denied that DJ had told him to build up an organization called the Research Institute of Korean Politics and Culture as a base for his drive for the presidency, insisting the institute's purpose was "solely to educate political aspirants in the spirit of patriotism." Kim Sang Hyun said he had asked the institute to conduct a survey on DJ's popularity but did not know the money for the survey had come from DJ. Nor did he know the student in Gwangju whom the prosecutors said DJ had ordered him to provide funds. "I have never met the man," he said. "I find no words to say anything about it."[10]

Students made equally recalcitrant witnesses. One of them denounced as "vicious fabrication" the claim by the prosecution that he had received money from one of the older dissidents to organize antigovernment protests. Another denied wanting to overthrow the government by violence but blurted, "My dream was to tear down the Yushin system."[11]

On the seventh day of the trial, August 25, Kim Dae Jung made what seemed like a campaign speech when asked if he had ever attempted to overthrow the government either through student protest or popular revolt. "I have openly called for dialogue with the government and made it clear that I would cooperate with the government of President Choi Kyu Hah should the government carry on democratic development as promised," he said. "I only hope the next government would be formed through elections. I did not think student violence or demonstrations should topple the government, nor did I have the intention of encouraging to that end." He was confident of victory in an open election. "I will win the election overwhelmingly," he went on, explaining why he needed no student revolt on his behalf. Like others on the stand, he denied knowing anything about a payment to a student organizer in Gwangju. "That is a total lie," he declared. "I have never urged, directly or indirectly, a single student to stage demonstrations since the assassination, and not a single man has received any funds from me to organize demonstrations."[12]

The trial provided a platform for others to speak passionately for democracy. Moon Ik Hwan waxed eloquent. "The question of who should become president of South Korea is up to the South Korean people to decide," he said when asked if the Hanmintong was a tool to promote DJ's ambitions. "A democratic society cannot function where there are only two groups—the ruler and the ruled." Asked what he thought it meant to be antigovernment, he responded, "Democracy includes the right to oppose the government" and was "a right of all democratic citizens." The pastor had an obvious explanation for why he opposed violence. "How can I ask students whom I saw for the first time to arm themselves with wooden staves and gasoline bombs as the indictment claims and seize key government offices," he asked rhetorically. "Peaceful demonstrations I recognize, but never violent demonstrations."[13]

What, then, did Reverend Moon think of a Christian pastor getting into politics? "Under the regime of Rhee Syngman, Christians were accused of supporting the government for material benefit," he said. "It's inconceivable to be a Christian and ignore what the people want." Asked if students burning police cars was "peaceful" or "violent," Moon dodged the question, blaming the government for failing to answer demands for reform and saying students had exercised "restraint."[14]

Those remarks went uncensored, but the censors excised revelations of harsh treatment at the hands of interrogators. Korea University Professor Lee Mun Yong was on safe ground when he talked airily of his belief in "loving your neighbor, love of justice and non-violence, sympathy for the poor, human rights"—even when he explained that he opposed the Yushin system "because economic growth and national security could not be served" and also "because it was beginning to produce effects that minimized democratization." The authorities did not, however, want the world to know about his claim that he was "severely beaten during the investigation" and made to "rehearse for this trial" and to say DJ's research center was his base for "seizure of power." The interrogators, it seemed, played good cop, bad cop. "People always beat you after they've been kind to you," said Lee. "At the KCIA those who beat me said I could deny my statement at the court trial."[15]

Violations of the National Security Law ranked along with aspirations to take over the government as the most serious offenses. Questioning late in the afternoon of the eighth day of the trial turned to what had long been, and would remain, one of the pet theories of DJ's foes, that he was in cahoots with North Korea for joining the two Koreas in a separate-but-equal confederation of North and South. DJ said he had broached the idea in a speech at the Foreign Correspondents' Club of Japan in March 1973, but a news clipping showed Kim Il Sung making the same proposal in 1960. When DJ said he had not known whatever the North Korean leader had said, the prosecution cited another newspaper report that had DJ commenting on the idea in his role as Minju-dang spokesman.[16]

If Kim Dae Jung's guilt was preordained, the prosecution still had to go to great lengths to prove the nature of his plotting for power. The movement of cash, however small, was a favorite topic for questioning. Kim Sang Hyun, the secretary-general of DJ's 1971 presidential campaign, again had to testify about payoffs, including a proposal for producing cassette recordings of DJ's speeches for 750 won apiece and distributing them for 1,000 won, a profit of 250 won or about half of one American dollar.[17] One student said that he had received money after a rally in front of the YMCA building in central Seoul several weeks after Park's assassination to protest the indirect election of Acting President Choi Kyu Hah as Park's successor, as called for by the Yushin Constitution.[18]

A lawyer, Han Sung Hon, said that DJ had given him considerable cash to write and publish books on "the way to save the country democratically" and a smaller sum for writing a speech that DJ gave to a journalists' group.[19] Another defendant, Kim Yoon Sik, said DJ had given him money because "I have been jobless for the last eighteen years." A former professor, Han Wan Sang, said DJ had given him money for writing speeches. The censors deleted the rationale he gave for loyalty to DJ. "I supported Mr. Kim Dae Jung not as a politician but for being a man campaigning for human rights," was his comment, deemed not fit for the general public to know about. "I am a scholar, and I set a clear line of limit in counseling Mr. Kim."[20]

The martial law authorities were incensed by a document issued before the revolt, portentously entitled a "pronunciamento on the current situation," signed by "134 intellectuals." An economics professor, Yoo In Ho, said the statement was not written to instigate students but reflected the conscience of intellectuals; he had not believed it necessary to report on a meeting in a tea room. The former managing editor of *Dong A Ilbo*, Song Kun Ho, admitted having been called on to draft the pronunciamento in view of his skills as an editorialist but said he had not expected authorities to object since the document was similar to those written by professors in the local media. The censors excised his comment that "students should not demonstrate and another April 19 affair should be avoided"—again a reference to the uprising against Rhee. He denied that he had opposed the Yushin system, saying he was too busy as a journalist covering North-South Red Cross talks and other events.[21]

Lee Ho Chul, a novelist, said that he had helped to draft the pronunciamento but was not interested in politics. DJ, he said, had asked him to participate in the same spirit as French novelist André Malraux writing on behalf of the government of Charles De Gaulle but all he had done was join DJ's research institute.[22]

The prosecution hoped to drive a final nail into DJ's coffin with a tag that never quite stuck—that he was a card-carrying Communist Party member. Lee Taek Dong, a member of the Minju-dang who had been in the National Assembly, said that he had not suspected DJ of party membership in the late 1940s when DJ had been associated with leftist organizations in Mokpo. An investigator, he said, had pulled out a card that showed DJ belonged to South Korea's Workers' Party, the equivalent of the same party in North Korea. The investigator also showed him a report by a Communist activist calling DJ "Kim Dongmu"—Comrade Kim—in the parlance of party members. Lee said he would have told the authorities had he been aware of DJ's party membership, and the investigator said that DJ's main rivals for national leadership, Kim Young Sam and Kim Jong Pil, had been informed. Lee said YS had never mentioned it to him and DJ had strongly denied previous membership in Communist organizations. The documents shown Lee were presumably fake—not for public distribution since they could be exposed as fraudulent but for purposes of interrogation, to intimidate people into confirming such claims, into saying, "Yes, I knew that."[23]

The prosecution by the second week of September began wrapping up its cases. There were, said the prosecutor, no extenuating circumstances for DJ. He should be sentenced to death. Sentences for the 23 others should range from four months to 20 years for Moon Ik Hwan. The defendants, said the prosecutor, had sought to overthrow the government when the nation faced labor disputes and the threat of North Korean Communists. Severe punishment was needed so nothing like it happened again. "Should their plot have not been shattered in advance," the prosecutor asked, "what would have happened to the nation?"[24]

The most damning evidence against DJ was testimony, picked up in harsh interrogations repeatedly denied in court, that DJ had given funds before the Gwangju revolt to the student leader in Gwangju to organize demonstrations. Second came the charge that he had led the Hanmintong after organizing it with Korean agents in Japan whom he knew to be members of the pro-North Korean residents' federation. DJ, said the prosecutor, was "an opportunist and agitator," a politician who "did not hesitate to seek the help of even a known North Korean spy" in pursuit of political goals. The evidence was his contact with Jung Tae Muk, the agent from Mokpo who had gone to the North, then returned and met with DJ before the 1967 National Assembly election. The prosecutor was most emphatic: "Such an opportunist, agitator politician must be eliminated from this land for good."[25]

The arguments of DJ's defense attorney, Huh Kyung Man, were endured for no apparent reason other than the need of the Martial Law Command, with the blessing of the court, and the court, with the blessing of the Martial Law Command, to be able to claim that he had had a fair trial. "Free democracy needs full debates to make it work," he said, "and any society devoid of confusion is not necessarily strong."[26]

Having let that one slip by, the censor deleted Huh's assertion that DJ's "confession" to prosecutors was not made with his free will, that he had been detained since May 18, far longer than the legal limit of twenty days, that the Martial Law Command did not have the authority to hold a person indefinitely and that any statement made during a prolonged detention should not be acceptable. DJ's denials of intent to stage a revolt against the state, of establishing the Hanmintong in Japan as an antistate organization, of providing funds for a student activist in Gwangju, of being pro-Communist—all those were deleted. So was Huh's statement that the death sentence, as demanded by the prosecution, would not be wise when the country under Chun Doo Hwan, inaugurated as president on September 1 after forcing Choi's resignation, was entering a new historical era.[27]

The defendants offered emotional pleas that would help their cause—but not their cases. "I want the judges to decide our guilt or innocence, not just whether our sentences should be short or long," said lawyer Han Sung Hon. "The question of whether a country has democracy or not depends on whether the people have the right to criticize the government or not. I think the recent social confusion was caused by the lack of freedom to criticize the government." As for the specific charge that he had violated censorship laws by distributing books about DJ, he said he had not needed the censors' approval since he had yet to distribute them. "As this is a political case," he told the judges, "no prejudice or emotion should be interwoven."[28]

One after another, student activists offered their pleas, some more defiantly than ever. Almost unable to speak through his tears, Kim Chong Wan sobbed, "As I am a Christian, I will never forget that I made a false witness as banned by the Ten Commandments." He had "felt fear when the prosecutor demanded death for Kim Dae Jung because of my first false witness"—that "in interrogation I was beaten without reason and the investigators forced me to confess that I was trying to incite mass uprisings at the request of Kim Dae Jung" and he had written "what they dictated." Song Ki Won said he did not "want to reveal the torture during interrogation" but apologized "to Kim Dae Jung, whom I have never met, for my false statements." The government, he said, "should apologize to the people for their fabrication of these sedition charges and should release us." Lee Sok Pyo said he was honored to be tried with famous politicians, professors and pastors.

"I was beaten overnight during interrogation, and I felt shame that I wrote a confession as it was dictated to me."[29]

Student Lee Shin Bom offered graphic testimony regarding all he had endured while jailed four times and interrogated six times by the KCIA and 19 times by other agencies during 13 years as an activist. Suffering from sleep deprivation, he was led into court, he said, after a videotaped rehearsal of what he was supposed to say. Deviating from the approved script, he said the KCIA had offered reduction of his sentence if he acknowledged the charges against him. When he refused, he was beaten for two days, his fingernails stepped on by boot heels and his legs twisted by inserting a stick between them. He asked why students would stage protests if the National Assembly and the government were truly democratic and called on the judges to understand the rage of the youth.[30]

Seoul National University student Lee Hae Chan breathed the idealism that infused Kim Dae Jung's political outlook, then and later. "The Anti-Communist Law and National Security Law exist because this nation is divided," he said. "When this nation is unified, this kind of unfortunate incident will disappear." Lee found it "very heartbreaking that I was forced to participate in a plot to kill a politician by making a false statement that was tortured out of me." While others had died "for criticizing this government," he was "ashamed that I couldn't resist making a false statement to save my life." Although "not a follower of Kim Dae Jung, Lee found it "very heartbreaking that a man, a father, a husband, should die in proceedings disguised as a legal trial."[31]

The show did not go on without a touch of the unexpected. Cho Sung Woo had gotten through claiming to have been at a restaurant with his mother on Mother's Day, May 8, the exact time the prosecution said he had been plotting a protest. Suddenly his mother, in the section for relatives, stepped into the aisle and shouted, "Go ask the lady who runs that Chinese restaurant, and then you'll know." Two military policemen hauled her into an anteroom whence her voice was audible for several more minutes. Unfazed, Cho talked on, appealing to the honor of judges who would never imagine that they, not the defendants, were the ones really on trial. "By making a just decision, let us have pride that this court was the last conscience of our army," he concluded. That said, Cho's mother was let back into the courtroom.[32]

Two of the defendants, both poets, said they did not want to make a final statement. Ko Un Tae, with some literary license, said he preferred "to be imprisoned for life," "to desert all my social desires, and, as time passes, I want to die in prison." Ye Choon Ho said he had confessed after fifteen days of interrogation and still "I have some scars on my body." Why, he asked, "won't this society accept truth as truth?" He was not going to make a final statement but changed his mind after hearing the prosecution ask the death sentence for DJ. "I don't care how long I have to stay in jail, but if a man gets a death sentence in a political trial, this should be corrected." For the new president "to unite the people together to bequeath a true image of democracy to our descendants," he asked, "please exempt Kim Dae Jung from the death penalty for this nation and for this people."[33]

Activist Sul Hoon was among the more eloquent. "The reason why the people provided the military with guns was for the military to protect their lives and property," he said. Instead "the military killed and stabbed and shot our brothers and sisters. Since then I haven't considered this government our government. But we never thought about resorting to violent means. We thought that peaceful demonstrations would bring the lifting of martial law. But the Gwangju incident escalated our anger. Already people have been killed, and we will willingly die. Although I die, the nation should be saved. For the future of the country, the current regime should resign, disclosing their misdeeds before the people and honorably stepping down like true soldiers."[34]

Pastor Moon Ik Hwan, the most dangerous of the accused after DJ in the eyes of the Martial Law Command, politely noted that Chun as president had advocated "a just society" but warned, "A just society cannot be achieved by presidential will or instructions—the people themselves have to do it." The protesters were not "trying to incite riots but rather our resolution was to democratize this country despite imprisonment or any other hardship." He questioned how DJ could have been a Communist and gone through so many election campaigns, including his run for the presidency in 1971, without someone attempting to smear him for political advantage. "If Kim Dae Jung were a Communist, would his political enemies have ignored that and left him alone," he asked.[35]

Lee Hae Dong was more damning in his riposte—so much so that his remarks were censored. "As a pastor, I am shameful to have made a false statement in the course of interrogation," he said. "At one point I told the interrogator I would rather die than to make a false statement. But I was so badly beaten for days and said yes where I should have said no." His wife, in the courtroom, started to sob as he talked about dealing with the bruises from the beatings. "To cure bruises, some raw meat was used and the beef blood was marked on my underwear. I couldn't send it back to my family because they might misunderstand it." Still, he kept the faith. "I have always prayed for the nation to become a just and democratic country," he said. "Some people argued that church people should not involve in politics, but that couldn't change my belief. I pray the God bless the nation and the people."[36]

A succession of allies of Kim Dae Jung offered arguments in vain to judges who already knew the verdicts expected of them. Lee Taek Don, who had once been an army officer, said that he had "buried many sacrificed students' bodies during the students' revolution in 1960" and had even served as an army prosecutor but had "never suggested or participated in any plot to overthrow the government." Novelist Lee Ho Chul said he had supported the pronunciamento by the 134 intellectuals because "an intellectual at that time should express his opinion." Han Wan Sang, describing himself as "a Christian and a political sociology professor," said he had returned home after a church prayer meeting on May 17, five days after his mother had died. "Having sleepless nights, I was very much tired," he said. Then, at 10:30 p.m., four investigators showed up to arrest him. "I asked them whether I could go the next morning," he said. "They said no. I didn't know why I was taken in," but after four months' detention "I have never changed my prayer for the nation to become a just, democratic and welfare state."[37]

Kim Sang Hyun, secretary-general of DJ's 1971 campaign, again swore that he had never met the key witness in the government case, the student leader in Gwangju to whom DJ was alleged to have given a large sum. "If we really intended sedition," he said, "we would have done it right after the assassination of President Park Chung Hee when Yushin followers lost their direction." He believed it was regrettable that the court had denied the request of the defense for the student leader to have to testify.[38] The prosecution, in asking the court to refuse, may have claimed the need to shield his identity, but the impression was that of a cover-up. If the judges were to be judged, this refusal would have been enough to find them guilty of failure to conduct a fair trial. The *Wall Street Journal*, after the show was over, complained that "the defense was denied the opportunity to cross-examine a key witness against Mr. Kim and that official censors blocked news reports by pool correspondents allowed into the trial—including Norman Thorpe of the *Asian Wall Street Journal*."[39]

As the central figure in the case, Kim Dae Jung, the one whom the prosecution wanted to impale, was the last to take the stand before all 23 defendants and 23 members of their families. He spoke for 1 hour and 48 minutes. Much of what he said was deleted by the censors, beginning with his view, "if there was no assassination, massive antigovernment demonstrations in Busan and Masan last October would have spread across the nation."

Similarly, the censors deleted his remark that "the government should bear the initial responsibility for student demonstrations in May across the country." First, "the government overrode students' patience by not lifting the martial law for more than six months, which has no proper reason to exist," he argued. Second, "the government's obscure political timetable gave rise to a suspicion on its pledge of democratization." As a politician, he felt "some moral responsibility for student demonstrations, but I still don't understand why students should come out to the streets."[40]

Kim Dae Jung's account of his ordeal was also deemed not fit to print or broadcast. The government did not want him arousing sympathy for himself and condemnation for the regime by letting it be known that he had been "confined in a basement for sixty days" and denied the right to a lawyer. "I have been through ordeal which seemed to make me go insane," he said. "I can hear somebody's moaning in a room next to me. I was stripped naked and was forced to wear worn-out military fatigues. I was threatened to be tortured." Those words were excised, as was his denial of relations with the Hanmintong. He had planned to organize it but "was soon spirited to Korea by the KCIA," he said. In any case, the Hanmintong was "against the Yushin system which Park introduced to bolster his power, not against South Korea itself."[41]

The censors let stand Kim's remark that his oldest son, his brother and his secretaries were sentenced to between three and four years each by other military courts. Nor did they cut his assertion that "sedition is the thing that I never imagined or thought of," his claim that he did not "want any leniency," his willingness to "take all the responsibilities," and his plea, "please do not be unfair to others." All he wanted was for Chun "to endeavor to achieve a true national unity by giving consideration to democratic forces centering around oppositionists." Finally, "as my will," he wanted "to achieve democracy, aspired by all the people in this country, as soon as possible by compromising and cooperating with each other." And "although I die, political retaliation like this incident should happen in this land never again." After the session, family members cheered and began singing, "We Shall Overcome." Security guards hustled them out of the court. The censor banned from the media record the note that the defendants shouted "Long live democracy, long live Mr. Kim Dae Jung" while blaming authorities for torturing them and "fabricating the whole story."[42]

Kim Dae Jung's final statement at his trial was one of the best performances of his life, but the effort was wasted on the five military judges. In a six-minute session on September 17, the 19th day of the trial, the chief judge, Major General Mun Ung Shi, announced the verdicts almost exactly as recommended. DJ stood motionless while the judge advocate read a four-minute explanation of his crimes. "Kim Dae Jung's activities, sympathizing (with) North Korean puppet's line, instigating students and creating national and social confusion, cannot be forgivable," he stated. The court rejected all the defense attorneys had said with one all-embracing sentence, "Their arguments had no reasons to be proven," but set a schedule. First, the martial law commander would confirm the verdicts within ten days. The defendants would be notified of the confirmation and then had seven more days in which to appeal.[43]

The censors deleted any suggestion of personal reactions, including the report by Lee Young Ho of *The Washington Post* that members of defendants' families stood up and began to sing the Korean national anthem "in excited high voices" before security men "immediately took them out of the court room in less than a minute." The public should not be told that DJ "smiled to two American State Department officials as he was led out of the courtroom by South Korean military policemen" or that wife Lee Hee Ho boycotted the final session, as she had the others, or that 80 military policemen, ward officers and plainclothed men "guarded the courtroom in a tense air." Nor should the public know that "throughout the brief session, all defendants kept quiet, occasionally exchanging smiles and nodding with each other," or that they wore "traditional Korean 'baji-chogori,' white trousers and jackets with white rubber shoes," or that, "on their left chests, they put on tags of prisoners' numbers" or that DJ's "number was 201." The censor did not object to reporting that the defendants were "immediately led out for military buses" but deleted the final words of Lee's pool report, "to be escorted to the military prison."[44]

The ordeal was not over. There were still the formalities of an appeal process, part of the show the government wanted to put on for international consumption. In an appeal hearing in October, the prosecution and defendants had to go through a reprise of the same show. The performance, though, was becoming a bore. One of the prosecutors, said the pool report, "slumped over asleep and one defense attorney was dozing as well, as were several of the relatives and the captain in charge of the MP guards." DJ "spoke in a slightly hoarse voice, but was sometimes quite animated, gesturing or raising his voice to make a point, said the report, "and he sometimes rocked from side to side as he talked." Again DJ was questioned about violations of the National Security Law. "I am a liberal democrat, not a Communist," he insisted. "If there were Communist unification, I would oppose it. I never thought of unification under communism." When the judge asked his attorney to keep the questions brief, DJ asked, "How can you ask him to cut it short when a man's life is at stake?"[45]

Much of the questioning centered on whether DJ had been a Communist Party member—or was at least pro-North. "As for the charge of praising North Korea, I have never done that," he said. As for whether his Hanmintong organization in Japan was to have been a government-in-exile, he answered, "Never." Asked whether he had once remarked, "In South Korea, there is neither bread not freedom, but in the North at least there is bread," he said he had been quoted out of context to appear pro-North. The appeals hearings gave DJ a chance to enlarge on the need for democracy. Yes, DJ admitted, he had said the United States should not support dictatorships—a remark that could be interpreted to mean the United States should not support the one in power in South Korea.[46]

Later that day, DJ expounded on democracy and nonviolence. "All my life I firmly believed that any violent methods would only bring misfortune," he said. When people spoke well of Park's assassination, he said that he had responded that "democracy could not be revived through assassination." As for whether he had wanted to overthrow the government, "I have had absolutely neither any plot nor any plan for rebellion." To the thousands who called on him when he was freed from house arrest after Park's death, "I always advocated my belief of Gandhi's style of non-violence in the movement of democratization." He believed that "politicians should play politics, the military occupies itself with national defense while students study" and it was "not a good thing for students to come out into the streets." Those remarks were fine by the censors, but they could not stand disclosures of physical mistreatment or fabrication. DJ's claim that he was told he could later deny all that he had admitted when "on the point of being tortured" was excised.[47]

The prosecution, however, sought to fortify its case against DJ with a surprise witness, a former Korean resident of Japan who had studied Marxism and Leninism, had been aligned with pro-North Korean residents, had visited Pyongyang four times and had recruited a member of the Hanmintong whom he had earlier persuaded to go to North Korea for training as a spy. Happily settled in Daegu, the witness, testifying under an assumed name, described the Hanmintong as a pro-North organization whose leaders had applauded a speech by Kim Il Sung at a party congress. Under questioning by DJ and his defense lawyers, however, the witness had to admit that he had never met DJ and could only repeat what the Hanmintong member, trained in North Korea, had told him. DJ charged that everything the witness had said was false, and Moon Ik Hwan demanded that the court arrest him since he did not seem to have switched allegiance entirely to South Korea.[48] Those remarks were censored as was Moon's protest that the witness had "insulted the court and the people and therefore the entire Republic of Korea."[49]

The procedure was beginning to degenerate into farce. In an argument over the seating of defendants' family members, two or three defendants called security officials "dogs." Another fracas broke out when a court officer interrupted the student Lee Hae Chan as he denied discussing a sedition plot. The judge ordered the 13 defendants charged with sedition to leave the courtroom for disturbing order. One asked to be tried "in absentia." Returned to the courtroom, defendants scuffled with guards as they tried to walk out again.[50]

The next morning family members protested that three were blocked from entering. Inside, other family members called to the defendants, ridiculing the proceedings. "The court suddenly plunged into chaos," wrote a pool reporter, when a legal officer threatened to remove trouble-makers. "'Let me be the first to be taken out,' the defendants shouted, raising their fists in anger." When a legal officer ordered military policemen to remove some of them, all stood and "volunteered" to walk out. "Ultimately, all of them were forced to leave the courtroom."[51]

The afternoon session was wilder still. As soon as the presiding judge stood up, Moon Ik Hwan rushed up and again challenged the former Communist spy whom the prosecution had introduced as a witness. "Since we believe we cannot be tried by such a court, we all have decided to leave the court," he said. When all the defendants got up to walk out, military policemen and prison officers held them back. Then they all broke out in the national anthem, joined in by family members—this detail censored in the pool report—after which the presiding judge announced an adjournment. Wives and mothers cried loudly as the session ended.[52]

The curtain fell on the spectacle on January 23, 1981, when the Supreme Court unanimously upheld all the sentences. The fate of the defendants was up to Chun Doo Hwan, who as president had the power of clemency. The chief justice, Lee Young Sup, took 12 minutes to affirm all the military court had decided. On DJ's sentence, he said, "The court has ruled that the appeal is rejected because it has no reason." As the trial ended, eight relatives were present. DJ's wife, Lee Hee Ho, and most of the others by now were under house arrest. The eight began to sing the Korean anthem. Lee Young Ho's pool report quoted one of them as shouting, "It's all fabricated." Paul Shin quoted the relative as shouting, "This trial is fake." Both versions, as translated by the two pool reporters, were censored.[53] The Supreme Court had confirmed its own guilt as a tool of a military leader who wanted DJ, if not quite dead and gone, at least well gone.

CHAPTER SIX

From Prison to Exile

The government of Chun Doo Hwan, by putting Kim Dae Jung and the 23 others on trial for Gwangju, was exposed not only as nondemocratic but also of dubious legitimacy. DJ had the full sympathy of the American establishment, including the U.S. Embassy and the State Department, which had sent a young diplomat to monitor every session. Had the U.S. government not taken such a strong position, first Park and then Chun would have presumably followed their instincts as military men and imposed still harsher dictatorship than the porous system in which opposition leaders were at times outspoken and demonstrators able to take to the streets in defiance of the severe punishment that many received and all risked.

The State Department made its discomfiture clear from the outset of the Gwangju revolt. Hodding Carter, assistant secretary for public affairs, at a briefing on May 19, 1980, let it be known that "we are deeply disturbed by the extension of martial law throughout the Republic of Korea, the closing of universities and the arrest of a number of political and student leaders." The State Department, he said, had conveyed "the seriousness of our concern to Korean leaders, and we have stressed our belief that progress toward constitutional reform and the election of a broadly based civilian government, as earlier outlined by President Choi, should be resumed shortly."[1] Two days later, as attacks on civilians in Gwangju were reported worldwide, Hodding Carter repeated the "urgent call" on "all parties" to "exercise restraint." Amid news that Korean troops had opened fire, he said "the reports of escalating confrontation in Korea are most disturbing" and it was "not clear at all" if "a conciliatory dialogue" was "going to be successful.[2]

Probably the most disturbed member of the U.S. government was President Carter, no relation to the State Department spokesman. The president had visited Korea the year before and, against all his liberal inclinations, instincts and beliefs, on the basis of advice and pressure from senior diplomats and military people, had assured Park Chung Hee of the enduring nature of the alliance. One puzzling aspect of the American response before the revolt, then, was why the U.S. military commander, General John Wickham, who also wore the hats of commander of the United Nations Command and the Combined Forces Command, including all South Korean forces, had rubberstamped a Korean request for transfer of the twentieth division from U.S. to Korean command for duty in Gwangju.

Neither Wickham nor the U.S. ambassador, William Gleysteen, wanted a shooting crackdown. Nor did they have any idea of the severity with which the government, using special forces that Wickham said he had not approved for deploying to Gwangju, would act. One obvious reason why Wickham and Gleysteen displayed weakness in the face of an affront to the power, dignity and integrity of the U.S. and UN commands was the priority they placed on a warm relationship with Korean leaders in the face of a persistent threat from the North. Military people felt a need to get along with their "counterparts," on whom they lavished ritualistic praise for toughness and discipline, and were not concerned with politics or protests, especially those with an anti-American edge as seen in the stoning of U.S. Information Service libraries, notably the one in Gwangju that eventually was shut down.

However Wickham might justify the chop of approval that he struck on the troop transfer, neither he nor Gleysteen was able to live down this decision. Explanations from them and the U.S. government lost credibility in light of Chun's claim that Wickham's approval meant U.S. support of the decision to put down the Gwangju revolt with military force. "That made it possible for Seoul to deploy Special Forces in Gwangju and resulted in the tragedy on May 18, 1980," said an analysis in Kim Dae Jung's library, presumably written with DJ's approval.[3]

Documents obtained by investigative journalist Tim Shorrock under the U.S. Freedom of Information Act revealed the hypocritical nature of the vacillating compromise reached by top-level U.S. officials as they debated on the afternoon of May 22 what level of support to offer the Chun government. "There was general agreement that the first priority is the restoration of order in Gwangju by the Korean authorities with the minimum use of force necessary without laying the seeds for wide disorders later," as recorded in the minutes of a meeting chaired by Secretary of State Edmund Muskie. "Once order is restored, it was agreed we must press the Korean government, and the military in particular, to allow a greater degree of political freedom to evolve."

In Seoul, Gleysteen and Wickham agreed that the twentieth division could wrest Gwangju from the rebels. "We did not want the special forces used further," Shorrock quoted Gleysteen as having said in an interview. Chun angered the Americans by publicizing the U.S. decision to release the troops but omitted Carteresque warnings against a "political crackdown." Gleysteen in another cable turned up by Shorrock's research moaned of a "deliberate effort on the part of the Chun Doo Hwan group who are determined to manipulate American public opinion."[4]

The abject weakness of the U.S. position was evident in a waffling statement by Hodding Carter. He did not mention the troop deployment but warned, "Continued unrest and an escalation of violence would risk dangerous miscalculations by external forces," the North Koreans. The United States, he promised, would "react strongly in accordance with its treaty obligations to any external attempt to exploit the situation...." Sanctimoniously, the statement vowed, "When calm has been restored, we will urge all parties to seek means to resume a program of political development as outlined by President Choi."[5] The statement was a study in diplomatic double-talk: U.S. officials in Seoul, and Washington too, knew that Choi was not in charge and that Chun did not care about the niceties of "political development."

Nonetheless, the United States did convey a level of discontent that made it difficult for Chun to act as he might have liked. A State Department official said the government "did not see anything in the charges (against Kim Dae Jung) that look to us to have much foundation" and they were "far-fetched." A South Korean government spokesman countered those and other remarks by regretting "the intemperate statements of foreign government officials." He loaded the statement with nationalist verbiage. "Premature expressions of concern are inappropriate and can be considered tantamount to an attempt to manipulate the judicial processes of a friendly country."[6]

Chun Doo Hwan, however, was never so oblivious to U.S. pressure as he would have liked to have been. His aides were aware that the State Department, in response to efforts by the Carter administration to figure out what was going on in the aftermath of Park's assassination, had turned to a secure internal State Department communications system dubbed "NODIS Cherokee" that had come to focus on the imposition of martial law and DJ's arrest on May 18 and then the Gwangju revolt. "After the [Gwangju] incident, the Kim Dae Jung case was more than a humanitarian issue," as seen from DJ's perspective in a summary in the Kim Dae Jung Library. "It was a political issue of vital importance in the relationship between the United States and Korea."[7]

Gleysteen saw Chun a number of times in the second half of 1980, reminding him of the quality of mercy—or the quality of its rewards. "With new governments in Korea and in the US in 1981, there would be a rather unique opportunity to establish a healthy relationship and a degree of rapport which had been absent in our relations because of serious strains during the 1970s," he reported having said in one such meeting while the revolt was raging. If DJ were executed, "The Korean government will find the bilateral relationship so damaged that the interests of both nations are hurt."[8] The death sentence when handed down on September 17 galvanized the State Department. Richard Holbrooke, assistant secretary for East Asia and the Pacific, wrote Gleysteen to warn that "the execution of Kim Dae Jung will have the most serious consequences to the U.S. policy toward Korea."[9]

DJ and wife Lee Hee Ho were confident of the full sympathy and support of President and Mrs. Carter, to both of whom she wrote an impassioned appeal on October 1 in which she described him as "a sincere Christian believer devoted to the cause of true democracy." Lee's letter went to the heart of her own and the Carters' deep religious and political convictions. Her husband, she said, "has consistently maintained that only a democratic system is capable of overcoming the threat from the Communist north, and has accordingly struggled in behalf of human rights and democracy."

Far from communicating with the Hanmintong in Japan after his abduction more than seven years earlier, Lee Hee Ho wrote, her husband had "met with like-minded friends" but was "accused on totally unfounded charges of the crime of plotting the violent seizure of the government." She repeated DJ's claim that he had been made chairman of the Hanmintong in Japan after the kidnapping "and without his knowledge" and there was "never any public or informal contact between him and that group." The only conversations with anyone in Japan had been "telephone contact to him from Japan from anticommunist friends there, but they were personal calls and Hanmintong was never mentioned during these contacts." The authorities, she said, "are fully aware of the contents of our conversations" since the line was constantly monitored, "and yet they have used them as a means of accusing my husband of violating the National Defense law and anticommunist law and have sentenced him to death."[10]

After the defeat of the liberal Carter by the conservative Ronald Reagan in the presidential election in November, the State Department had to bring Reagan into line behind the crusade to save DJ. Gleysteen on November 21 messaged that he had "stressed that a humane resolution would open the way for an excellent relationship between the Chun government and the new administration, while the opposite would lead to extreme difficulties, including calls for an opening toward Pyongyang."[11] In early December, Defense Secretary Harold Brown, accompanied by Donald Gregg, now on the National Security Council staff, called on Chun in Seoul. Gregg years later recalled Chun saying: "I've got a terrible problem with Kim Dae Jung. Every single Korean military official wants me to execute him. If I do, I know I have trouble with you and in Europe. I do not know what to do.'" Gregg "left the meeting thinking that we failed and Kim Dae Jung was a dead man."[12]

With Reagan's victory, Chun and his closest associates figured they would have a far more understanding friend in the White House than Carter would ever have been. At Holbrooke's suggestion in the dying days of the Carter administration, President-elect Reagan in December asked Richard Allen to negotiate commuting Kim Dae Jung's sentence. "During the secret negotiations, Allen, who headed the U.S. National Security Council from 1981 to 1982, allegedly told South Korean officials that the incoming Reagan administration had strong concerns about executing Kim," said a Japanese report. "The South Korean government can no longer expect U.S. support for the administration if it allows the penalty to be carried out, Allen told South Korean leaders."[13]

Gleysteen messaged the State Department on New Year's eve quoting Chun's foreign minister, Roh Shin Young, as assuring him "President Chun will deal with the Kim Dae Jung issue in a way he would value the honor of Ambassador Gleysteen"—a comment that Gleysteen took to mean DJ's "life would be spared."[14] The deal, however, called for a *quid pro quo*. What could be a better way for Chun to assume an aura of legitimacy than to be the first foreign leader to call on Reagan after his inauguration on January 20, 1981? Sure enough, on January 21, the White House announced plans for Chun to visit on February 2, thirteen days after Reagan's inauguration.[15] Chun had succeeded admirably in using DJ as a pawn for recognition and respect, at home and abroad.

Two days after the White House announcement, on January 23, 1981, by no coincidence the same day the Supreme Court reaffirmed all the sentences, including death for DJ, Chun commuted the death sentence to life behind bars, removing DJ from solitary confinement in the military prison where he had suffered for five months, and reduced the sentences of 11 others. Chun sought to project an image as a man of mercy and reconciliation as he convened his state council, or cabinet, an hour after the court had upheld the sentences. Describing the case of DJ and his allies as "a sad political legacy from the old era," he said the time had come "to usher in a historical era by ending the confrontation-dominated political situation of the 1970s and the national chaos" after Park's death. At the same time, he acknowledged the pressure applied by the United States and Japan to save DJ, observing that "friendly nations at home and abroad have appealed for clemency from a humanitarian standpoint."[16]

Chun prepared for his debut in Washington with the enthusiasm of a debutante primping for her coming-out party, in this instance his debut on the world stage as a statesman. One day after sparing the life of his arch political rival, Chun said he was lifting martial law, in effect since Park's assassination, claiming "the foundation for social stability has been fully restored." He also set February 11 as the day for election of a handpicked electoral college that would in turn select a president on February 23 with election for a new National Assembly a month or so later. Chun guaranteed a "free and fair atmosphere" for the elections.[17] The words appeared like a satire on the lingo that Washington wanted to hear to justify the presidential invitation—and to insure enthusiasm about the large American commitment to Korea.

Dressing up the image, aides at the Korean embassy in Washington announced Chun would address the National Press Club on February 3, the day after his summit with Reagan, before taking off for Honolulu. He would talk on a wide range of topics, including his plan for further legitimizing his rule through indirect elections of a handpicked body similar to that which Park had set up under the Yushin Constitution. He would also advance what seemed like a rather bold proposal to North Korea for an inter-Korean summit—an initiative that North Korea promptly spurned but again showed DJ was not the only influential South Korean in search of dialogue with the North.[18]

Embroidering, the minister of culture and information, Lee Kwang Pyo, talked about the commutation of sentences. Chun's idea, he enthused, was "to open an era of harmony and participation in the 1980s by ending the era of discord and conflict in the 1970s." The minister was quite the salesman. There were "no creative politics in the 1970s, but only self-aggrandizement," he confessed. There was no reason for "the politics of confrontation, tension and conflict of the 1970s" to go on into the 1980s. The country had gotten over the political climate of "resistance, criticism and struggle" of the 1970s.[19]

In the weeks after commuting DJ's sentence, Chun basked at the apex of a career that was to perpetuate the harsher aspects of Park's rule, to degenerate into thoroughgoing corruption covering his wife and extended family and to end in mass protest and disgrace. First President Reagan gave him a full-dress White House welcome on February 2, complete with 21-gun salute and then, ten days later, the 5,278 members of the newly formed National Conference for Unification, an electoral college formed under Chun's new constitution, a version of Park's Yushin Constitution, overwhelmingly elected him to a seven-year term. The power and adulation bestowed on him made him feel like one of those Yi dynasty kings, entitled to riches for him, his wife and relatives, close and distant, even as he pretended to crack down on the corruption of his predecessors.

All the while, Kim Dae Jung, tried, sentenced to death, then reprieved, languished in Cheongju Prison, about 60 miles southeast of Seoul, with no assurance of getting out. In a total of six years in prisons, DJ had learned to survive by reading and writing. His tastes varied widely, from philosophy to history to current affairs. Works by Dostoevsky, Tolstoy, Camus and Nietzsche were on his first list of requests for books while he was still in solitary confinement. He was able to send only one letter a month, confined at least initially to a single sheet the size of an aerogram, all subject to censorship, but he wrote in small script on both sides of the paper. His lengthy musings ranged from intensely personal advice to his wife, sons and grandchildren to economic theorizing, to religious and philosophical ramblings. They reflected a vast storehouse of energy, the breadth and depth of his mind and an underlying optimism as he looked to a future beyond prison life.[20]

"Despite my imprisonment and precarious future, I still feel happy that I have so few worries about my family," he wrote in one of his first letters, penned in careful Hangul script in November 1980 to his second son, Hong Up, after he had been sentenced to death. "I know that I can entrust you to God's care in everything."[21] To Hong Gul, his third son, the only son of second wife, Lee Hee Ho, he imagined how his son would feel: "While you were in grade school, you had to go through the ordeal of my abduction. In middle school, you saw my imprisonment. And during two years of high school, you have first had to suffer through my house arrest and now through this situation. When I try to imagine what a terrible shock this must have been to you in your childhood and adolescence, I feel guilty of having done this all to you, myself, even though unintentionally. And yet I cannot describe my feelings of joy and gratitude when I see how well you have come through it all, strengthened in great adversity by belief in God and by His help."[22]

DJ's most moving words were for Lee Hee Ho together with all his sons—her two stepsons, Hong Il and Hong Up, and her own son, Hong Gul. In his first letter after his transfer to Cheongju Prison, he conveyed the physical suffering he was enduring and the guilt he felt for his family. "I felt wretched when my head was shaved and I had to change my clothes immediately on arrival," he wrote. "The cell was icy cold. I hurried through my dinner and rushed under the blankets, but my body kept shivering with cold. Under the blankets I began to weep, and I kept calling out, 'My Father!'" His thoughts turned quickly to his family and friends. "Think how much pain and inconvenience I am inflicting on my children, brothers, relatives, friends and colleagues," he wrote. "Although it was unintentional, the damage has been great and of long duration."[23]

Lee Hee Ho wrote her husband almost every day. Her letters were far briefer but laden with emotion and longing along with such news as would get by the censors. "I read it as though I were seeing you in person," she wrote after receiving one letter. "I think about how a day for you must feel like a thousand years and how we sense the swift passage of time in the warm outside world." She could hardly "control my tears when I sing hymns at church," she confessed. "I can see Jesus Christ carrying the heavy cross all alone up to Golgotha. I pray for the lonely and isolated brothers of Christ. I believe you will witness, 'I am not alone, for our Father is with me,' when you meet the hero of absolute solitude, Jesus Christ."[24]

Lee Hee Ho helped in other ways, visiting monthly, with Hong Gul when he was free from school, sending or bringing shipments of books, including a Bible in Korean and a Korean-English dictionary, knitting woolen gloves with holes in the fingers so he could conveniently turn the pages during the winter. They remain on display in the Kim Dae Jung Library, a modern five-story building under the aegis of nearby Yonsei University on the site where he maintained his Seoul residence while KCIA guards in the alley in front watched his comings and goings. "He sensed the importance of informanization after reading Elvin (sic) Toffler's *The Third Wave*," according to the inscription beneath the only other book on display from his prison days, a Korean translation of futurist Alvin Toffler's famous work. "This motivated him to lead Korea into an IT power when he became president later." Also on display: the cotton clothes that DJ wore when he was sentenced and the blue prison uniform issued him in Cheongju Prison, a pair of rubber shoes and a rosary with a cross.[25]

One day Lee Hee Ho drove with DJ's second son, Hong Up, to visit DJ's brother and his oldest son, Hong Il, both imprisoned in Daejeon, the major city south of Cheongju, for helping DJ in his "sedition" against the government. "Hong Il says not to worry about him and that he prays for your health and for many other people," she wrote. Their circumstances were not quite so harsh as those suffered by DJ. "Because they are confined in groups, they don't seem to have the kind of solitude that you have," she wrote. DJ's needs were her highest priority. "The blanket that I sent today is pure wool also but may not be as warm as the one you returned," she went on. "I have requested but haven't gotten the book on Kant. I sent *Between Men, the Life of Tolstoy*, and the *History and Structure of Korean Shaminism*." And she was waiting "joyously for next week's visit" though "tormented that I am not able to say all the things I would like to say, not only when we meet, but even in my letters to you."[26]

The letters elevated spirits, DJ's, his wife's and sons,' during an imprisonment that was to last for more than two years, and DJ's reading vastly increased his storehouse of knowledge. His constant allusions to prayer, to the bible, to Jesus and God may have helped to persuade the officials who read and relayed his every word of his fervent religiosity and anti-communist credentials. DJ's record as a compromiser would lead to the assumption that he wanted the authorities to realize his opposition to their rule was posited in his Catholic faith, not communism. "Every Christian has a responsibility to proselytize," he wrote in one discourse that ranged from Plato to Toynbee to Nietzche.[27]

If the depth of DJ's faith as a Catholic were uncertain, no one doubted Lee Hee Ho's deep-seated belief as a loyal and leading member of one of Korea's largest, most powerful Protestant denominations. She never attempted to "convert" DJ from Catholicism to Methodism, choosing instead to treat his brand of Christianity with reverence. "Today marks the meaningful anniversary of your decision to believe in God as your savior," she wrote in July 1981, 24 years after his baptism. "I hope and believe that our Lord will remember this day as the great moment of your life; when the 'old' you (before you acknowledged God) was transformed into a 'new' person (your promise to serve and follow Him) and He bestowed on you His renewed blessing."[28] Her last letter of the year, the last she was to publish, exuded an understated confidence. "With faith, our prayers will come true," she wrote. "We have to pray sincerely so that our God will not turn away from us."[29]

More important for her husband's future than religious belief was his determination as revealed in his writing to steel himself for the next two decades of struggle against an entrenched regime, against a way of governance that he saw as corrupt and dictatorial, against an approach to dealing with North Korea that he believed outmoded and counterproductive, also against an economic centralism that he argued depressed productivity while oppressing creativity, not to mention the welfare of millions dragooned into serving the *chaebol*.

"The reasons for the current crisis in our morals are complex," DJ wrote in a long epistle to his wife and children in January 1982, slightly more than a year after his transfer to Cheongju Prison. With that he enumerated such problems as "continued emphasis of money as the top priority," "the colonial mentality that accepts foreign culture without reservation," "a tendency to hold our native morals in absolute contempt," "opportunism and careerism and the destruction of conscience and traditional values...." The result: "Leaders have failed to set an example of honesty, consistency between action and words, frugality, probity, diligence and service"—an attack on his foes in high places though DJ as president would fail to follow the high standards enunciated from his prison cell.[30]

When DJ expounded at length on the meaning of religion and the deity, the impression was that he was girding for his own crusade. "God neither creates nor confers evil," he wrote in a prolonged discourse on God's existence. "Most of it has been caused by human abuse of freedom." In the end, "We can believe in the eradication of evil and the triumph of justice and also in the perfection of this world and our eternal salvation only when we are one with God," he concluded. DJ was confident of prayer as a force for action. "God may be blamed or faith weakened" if one left "the solution of a problem entirely up to God." Better "to place the problem before God and ask what one should do...so long as one's efforts are according to His will."[31] DJ had no doubt of God's will in his politics and policies.

If he was certain that the Lord was on his side, however, Kim Dae Jung had to be careful in whatever he wrote not to engage in direct criticism of the Park or Chun regimes. Still, he had no trouble getting across his views about dictatorship, incompetence and corruption in high places by commentaries on the flaws of the Yi dynasty and a devastating critique of the Rhee regime. "Syngman Rhee did not hesitate to protect Japanese sympathizers," he charged, hitting at the paradox of Koreans hating yet serving the Japanese during the colonial era. "Moreover, Rhee repeatedly violated democracy, the founding framework of the republic of Korea, and stirred up political turmoil.... The result of Rhee's protection of pro-Japanese elements was to make a new beginning for Korea, in spiritual and personal terms, impossible."[32]

DJ, however, had virtually nothing to say about the Korean War. The invasion that had sent Rhee and his government and army into hasty retreat, their rescue by U.S. forces, the rescue of the Communist government up North by Chinese "volunteers," these all passed unmentioned. Nor did he talk about what he had done while sheltered in Busan. Seldom discussing the exigencies of waging a horrible armed struggle, DJ did get to the subject in words cast to show his heart was in the right place by crediting his countrymen with heroically resisting North Korean invasion. "The masses, who rose to defend freedom from Communist dictatorship, which they knew from experience, succeeded in repelling the Communist aggression," he wrote. "The power of the masses also crushed the North Korean Communists' attempt to take over the South," he went on, glossing over the need for U.S. forces to take charge under the aegis of a United Nations Command that drew troops from 16 countries.

DJ saw that same mystical power, together with the masses' "aspiration for democracy," as the dynamic behind "their enthusiastic support of the April 19 Student Revolution"—the 1960 uprising against Rhee— "and the energy they have shown in economic reconstruction"—the program led by the despised, unnamed Park Chung Hee. Overall, DJ saw "power" as evil and "masses" as good. If Rhee, Park, and Chun were terrible, in his estimation, he never mentioned the perilous times in which they ruled. As a future leader, DJ betrayed a totally negative interpretation that was in itself a problem. Still, his belief that "the energy of our populace is increasing and moving forward"— economically and socially if not militarily—was beyond dispute.[33]

Kim Dae Jung did have much to say in his prison writings on how to achieve lasting peace on the Korean peninsula. Unlike Rhee, who had fantasized uniting North and South by conquering the North, DJ called for "mutual recognition of south and north by the four great powers," that is, those with the most direct influence on the Korean peninsula, the United States, China, Japan and Russia, and "membership of south and north in the United Nations." North Korea's reluctance "to give up its mistaken yearning for the possible takeover of South Korea," he believed, was all the more reason "to stress once again the extreme importance of national conciliation and democratic unity within the Republic of Korea." DJ had long espoused reconciliation, perhaps under a North-South "confederation," a term reviled by conservatives as traitorous, but never before his imprisonment had he refined and expanded in writing on these views, a reflection of long opposition to a succession of hated conservatives beginning with Rhee.[34]

DJ had much more to say, all of it hyper-negative, about the centrally directed economic steps initiated under Park Chung Hee that were turning Korea into an economic powerhouse. DJ himself had not had a regular job since giving up the shipping business and diving into politics but unreservedly opposed policies widely seen as responsible for the "miracle" rise of the economy and the entry of Korean industry into fields far too capital-intensive for any other "developing" economy. "The most important rule in formulating new economic policy is to adhere to the basic principle of a free economy," DJ wrote in one of his last letters from prison before his release. "The mistakes of these economic policies lay in ignoring this principle, seeking excessive growth, and concentrating on trade, thereby weakening the entrepreneurial structure and making it dependent on special power. As in geometry, there is no king's way. It should be realized that safe and consistent development depends on perseverance."[35]

Kim Dae Jung's career as a democratic reformer evolved from his formative years as a son of the Cholla region and his observations of Rhee's heavy-handed rule. From this background sprung his view on how to deal with North Korea, whose forces he never had to face in combat, and then his hostility toward all that conservatives in Seoul were doing to oppress their and his people.

"The greatest mistake of the economic policy of the 1970s was its disregard of creativity and improvement of productivity," he wrote. If in the 1960s "we demonstrated substantial economic growth," it was due to "no more than the setting up of a simple economy and exporting its surplus, making use of cheap and limitless labor just as oil-producing countries tap underground oil and export it." After all that "easy moneymaking," however, "we soon were challenged intensely by other middle-tier countries...." The government "raced down the road of one-sided development in the heavy chemical industry" while neglecting "concerted efforts to stabilize prices and attract foreign money by continually stressing domestic demand and export-related light industry"—a view that denied all credit for Park's role in Korea's economic emergence.[36]

It is difficult to know what to make of DJ's sweeping evaluation of the failures of the Park era considering, in retrospect, Park's place in Korean history as the leader whose single-minded emphasis on development had much to do with the country's spectacular economic success. There was a certain obvious truth in DJ's emphasis on the need for creativity, his view that the *chaebol* had overweening power, his belief that economic indexes were not the only arbiters and that export goals, like high marks in school or the accumulation of wealth, should not be the only priority. In his unqualified denunciation of economic policy, he bypassed the deeper truth of Korea's growth under government leaders and *chaebol* chieftains whom he intensely disliked but who had a great deal more experience, and far more at stake economically, than he.

Whatever DJ wrote, however, he did so under excruciating conditions. "He is in constant pain," Lee Hee Ho told me in an interview in early 1982 a year after Chun had commuted his death sentence to life and ordered his transfer to an otherwise empty-cell block in the prison in Cheongju. After a 20-minute conversation with her husband through prison bars, the time permitted by prison authorities, she said that a doctor had visited him and recommended an operation on the hip that had suffered permanent injury in the 1971 motor vehicle "accident."

The Chun regime's treatment of DJ, as recounted by his wife, was extraordinary testimony to the fear of anything he might do if given the slightest opportunity, even from prison. He had to sleep on the floor of his tiny cell, watched by three guards in the daytime and two at night, said his wife, and could barely move when trying to get up. In addition, she said, he suffered from an ear ailment that resulted in a constant ringing—usually the only noise he heard in his special cell. A loyal aide, working dutifully in an office across the courtyard of DJ's home in Seoul, told me that DJ's family and friends prayed the United States would intervene on his behalf, perhaps on medical grounds. "We are not asking for anything," said the aide. "We are just hoping."[37]

Kim Dae Jung's days and nights of formulating views and putting them into writing in forced isolation were about to end. After holding him for two years and four months, the government on December 16, 1982, ordered his transfer to the Seoul National University Hospital for medical treatment for his injured leg and spine. American pressure, applied by friends in the U.S. Embassy, in the U.S. Congress and in

U.S. academic circles, was responsible for the transfer inside Korea and then, on December 23, to "forced" exile to the United States. Chun Doo Hwan, having commuted his sentence to life in January 1981 and then from life to 20 years on March 20, 1982, was persuaded that his government would get along better with the Reagan administration if DJ were sent to America, ostensibly for more treatment. If free to operate politically in South Korea, DJ would again pose a threat to his regime. In the United States, he would be a blast from the past, never again able to thrill the opposition as he had in the old days.

Chun's calculation was right in the sense that he managed to rid himself temporarily of a serious irritant. Once in the United States, however, DJ was as busy as he had ever been, building on the sympathy and support he had already won from political and academic figures, giving speeches and writing analyses on all the ills of Korea's leaders and policies. He became the darling of American liberals, a celebrity living up to their ideal of a democratic leader and symbol of the struggle for democracy in an ally that still depended on U.S. forces for security against communism. Americans had grown disillusioned by longstanding relationships between the United States and corrupted, military-led regimes. In the figure of Kim Dae Jung and the democratization movement, epitomized in his crusade against injustice and oppression, lay hope for reform in democratic style, beginning some day with free, open, inclusive elections.

Typically, Americans viewed Korea through the prism of DJ's political yearnings, less than an accurate reflection of all that was going on. DJ had no problem regaining his appointment at Harvard's Center for International Affairs. Edwin O. Reischauer, director of the Harvard-Yenching Institute, former U.S. ambassador to Japan, author of numerous books and co-author of a standard work on the transliteration of Korean Hangul script to Western lettering, had flown to Korea in November 1973 to persuade the government to give DJ a passport so he could take up the appointment offered at Harvard before his kidnapping in August of that year. "Kim still plans to come to Harvard but as long as he remains in Korea, he is in grave physical danger," Reischauer said at the time.[38] In the intervening period, Reischauer remained in close touch with DJ, directly and through Lee Hee Ho. Although Reischauer officially retired nine months before DJ's exile to America at the end of 1982, his influence guaranteed a Harvard appointment. Cambridge would be DJ's base as a fellow at the university's Center for International Affairs in 1983 and 1984.

The position at Harvard gave DJ a platform from which to enlarge on thoughts that he had been formulating in his letters from prison—and in ideas that he could not risk committing to writing that had to pass through prison censors. DJ was busy during this period on other fronts. Most importantly, he established his Asia-Pacific Peace Foundation and the ancillary Korean Institute for Human Rights, not in Cambridge but in the Washington suburb of Springfield, Virginia, as the base from which to gain influence as well as donations with strong support from the large community of well-to-do Koreans in the Washington-Baltimore metropolitan area and elsewhere, many of whom had origins in the Cholla region.

The Peace Foundation's activities during DJ's American "exile" seemed akin to those of the Hanmintong's American branch, the Korean Congress for Democracy and Unification. The latter had laid the groundwork as a strong voice demanding a shift from the ritual support accorded the Chun government during the Reagan presidency. "One of the main activities of Hanmintong's branch office in the United States was to urge the U.S. government to change its policies toward Korea," according to the summary of its activities. "For this purpose, it criticized the U.S. policy that supported the dictatorship regime in Korea through interactions with influential figures in the United States. Such a movement imposed a serious burden on the military dictatorial regime which depended on the U.S." Reischauer and Jerome A. Cohen, a noted Harvard law professor with a special interest in northeast Asia, added important support in the campaign.[39]

The first mission of the Hanmintong's American branch had been to "save Kim Dae Jung after his abduction in 1973 and death sentence in 1980." During DJ's prison terms, the office also proselytized for freedom of other democratization activists, including the poet Kim Chi Ha. Next, "it started a movement that urged changes to American policies toward Korea by contacting important figures—politicians, bureaucrats, scholars and journalists who were interested in democratization of Korea." All the while Hanmintong in America coordinated with Hanmintong in Japan, "building a democratic movement of Koreans living overseas."[40] Among the names with whom the American branch worked in Japan were those whom the KCIA pinpointed as receiving funds from the pro-North Korean organization of Koreans in Japan. DJ in exile aided immeasurably in the mission of Hanmintong's U.S. office to arouse the passions of Korean-Americans while his "peace foundation" became the fulcrum for fund-raising as well as public relations and strategizing in both the United States and Korea, where he was to reestablish his Asia-Pacific Peace Foundation after returning to Seoul in February 1985.

Kim Dae Jung was so busy with his foundation and politicking among Koreans and Americans that he resided in suburban Washington and was not much visible around Harvard Yard. Nonetheless, "For me personally, it was an extremely productive period for both studying and learning," he wrote much later. "To live in the academic environment of such a distinguished university was a cherished experience I shall never forget. Even now, I often reminisce about the campus, with its lush green foliage and stately old buildings." Although as a visiting fellow he did not have to meet formal requirements, "I wanted to conclude my research activity at Harvard with a written paper, as a means of collecting my thoughts."[41] The result was a study of his vision of the economy in a democracy, first written in typewritten form in that pre-computer era, translated as a book in Korean and, finally, published in English.

As in all his oratory and writings on the entrenched government, DJ was totally critical. There was nothing good about anything his predecessors had done, not a passing bow to the problems they faced in dealing with the North Koreans in a time of war and uneasy truce, no credit or thanks to them for building up the economy. "Because I advocated peaceful dialogue and exchange with North Korea, I was immediately accused of dancing to the tune of North Korean leader Kim Il Sung," DJ wrote in the preface to the first edition of the book. "Shortly after the election, however, President Park adopted my proposal for a North-South dialogue and claimed the idea as his own."

This transparently political jab bore no relation to the reality of the desire of the conservatives whom DJ hated, even the incompetent and corrupted Chun Doo Hwan, to establish rapport with North Korea. Nonetheless, DJ claimed to have "fully supported" Park's overture to the North—though "reunification talks went nowhere, because both governments used them to shore up their own positions in domestic politics and were not really interested in reunification."[42] The Red Cross talks had not been about "reunification," but DJ was not concerned with such details when tarring the regime with broad-brushed strokes.

DJ was still more scathing in his assault on the economic policies of Park and Chun. His opposition, he said, was "based on my conviction that I have better alternatives...." His attack resonated among Americans unhappy with U.S. support of dictators elsewhere. "Korea's political and economic problems are in many ways similar to those of other Third World countries," he wrote. "Oppressive and corrupt government backed by military forces, huge gaps between the rich and the poor, crushing foreign-debt burden, and excessive government interference with market functions are commonly found, in varying degrees, in most Third World nations. These countries are America's ideological battleground against the Soviet Union. The United States has done poorly in this battle and is not likely to fare any better in the future unless its Third World policies are based on a better understanding of their problems." DJ was glad to offer "an alternative development strategy" that he believed would "benefit not only the Korean people but also, in the long run, the United States—an idea that resembled that of American analyses of Latin America."[43] In the Korean case, though, the question always was who knew or did more, Park or DJ.

Regardless of the answer, American liberal intellectuals believed in DJ they had found the crusading democrat who could, with a nudge from Washington, turn Korea into a sterling avatar of democracy in action, unlike all those nasty dictatorships whose leaders were an affront to American ideals, an embarrassment to their American benefactor. The longer DJ stayed in the United States, the more fans he recruited from politics, show business, academe, nongovernmental organizations, think tanks, even the U.S. government that persisted in formal support of the military leaders who had persecuted him. In his American exile, DJ won acclaim as the hero who influential Americans came to believe was the one to hold high the banner of American-style democracy in a culture and society steeped in 5,000 years of autocratic traditions.

CHAPTER SEVEN

Birth of Democracy

Kim Dae Jung plotted his return to Korea like a political campaign supported by a well-oiled machine. He broached the plan in one-on-one meetings with journalists, including a lunch in August 1984 with me in a cafeteria a few steps from the offices of *USA Today*, where I was working at the time, near the Iwo Jima memorial in the Rosslyn district of Arlington, across the Key Bridge from Washington.[1] On August 22, he met Elliott Abrams, the assistant secretary of state for human rights and humanitarian affairs, confirming that he was about to get in touch with his nemesis, President Chun Doo Hwan, and tell him he was going home. On September 11, he wrote to Chun announcing his plan, and ten days later the Korean government came back with the menacing promise to "take due process" on his return.

Chun and his aides were alarmed by the prospect of again having to deal with DJ on their own turf. "The South Korean government has reacted negatively, indicating that it would send me back to prison if I returned," DJ wrote in an article published on October 11 in the *Los Angeles Times*, the major paper in the region with the largest Korean-American population, the heart of an influx of immigrants from the Cholla region, and the base for Korean-American financial backers. He left no doubt that he would follow through on his plan. "Officially I have stated that I no longer have any reason to remain in the United States because I have completed the medical treatment and the fellowship at Harvard University on which the South Korean government based its approval for my trip here," he stated. "The real reasons for my return, despite the obvious danger of imprisonment or house arrest, involve more profound moral and political questions."

The article, appealing to American intellectuals, synthesized the rationale for all DJ had been doing in the United States and what he planned for Korea:

> First, during the past two years I have dedicated myself to boosting the popular movement for human rights and democracy in Korea from a distance. Now I feel an obligation to join my people first hand in their struggle.
>
> Also, I sense that a specter of crisis is haunting South Korea. An overwhelming majority of the Korean people loathes the government due to its repression, corruption and military dominance, and because of the rapidly growing gap between rich and poor. Consequently the people have become apolitical and spiritless because they feel overcome by the dictatorial regime and its support from the United States and Japan.
>
> If the situation becomes worse, it would nullify my 30 years of struggle for democracy in South Korea and peaceful reunification of the Korean peninsula.

Kim Dae Jung closed with a painful reminder of U.S. failures to keep alive pro-American regimes in China, Vietnam, Cambodia, Laos, Cuba, and elsewhere. "Today in peacetime, with a per capita income of more than $2,000, Korea does not have a free press, local autonomy, direct presidential elections, an independent legislature or an independent judiciary, all of which existed thirty years ago in wartime," he wrote, full of warm memories, it seemed, for a system that he had excoriated at the time. "The courage of our people during the Korean War was due to their desire to preserve such democratic freedoms."

DJ did not revert to his customary castigation of the Rhee regime, in power before, during and for nearly seven years after the Korean War. Nor did he mention the American role. Rather, he equated his personal crusade with democratization itself: "In a sense, how the Chun regime treats me on my return will be the litmus test of its desire for democracy. Yet I do not seek political revenge against it, and I will handle the problem of my return with prudence." He pledged "my best efforts to restoring democracy in Korea," a vow that could be interpreted in Seoul as a declaration of war. "Even though I feel much apprehension about returning to my country," he concluded, "I am not asking the United States to guarantee my safety but only to respect fully my people's longstanding aspirations for a democratic government."[2]

Kim Dae Jung's departure was preceded by the most massive build-up ever accorded a foreign dissident leader on American soil. On October 16, 22 members of the U.S. House of Representatives sent a letter to Chun asking him to guarantee Kim's safety. "We are writing to encourage your continued progress toward normal function of Korea's democratic political structure," began the letter, couched in the floweriest terms. "In particular we wish to request your assurance of personal safety for Mr. Kim Dae Jung to return to his homeland and the full restoration of his civil and political rights." The letter moved from there to unreserved flattery. "During the past four years of your Government, we have been pleased to note several steps toward normality, such as the restoration of rights of 453 politicians and public figures banned in 1980, the release from prison of several hundred political prisoners and the moderation of your Government's attitude toward student dissent as reflected in the lessening of police surveillance of university campuses this year. We are reassured that your government could undertake these measures without endangering social or political unrest."

Such praise, however, came with an implicit threat that the lawmakers, led by Barbara A. Mikulski, a Democratic member of the House of Representatives, later a senator, from Maryland, believed would catch Chun's attention. "As Korea prepares to host the 1988 Olympics, we are aware there is much to be done," said the letter. "Not only must the physical facilities be built, but the social and political climate must be prepared in such a way as to enhance Korea's standing and reputation in the world community. Further political progress is of great importance, to assure the success of the Olympic Games and a peaceful and democratic transfer of power in 1988."[3]

DJ embellished on the reasons for his trip in an interview with Korean journalists on November 4. "Firstly, I should join my colleagues in fighting under difficult situations in Korea for the democratization movement," he wrote. "Secondly, the absolute majority of Korean people are against the dictatorship now in power." He acknowledged "a few democratic activists are resorting to radicalism"—an approach that he professed not to support: "I understand how they feel, but it would not help democracy. So I decided to go back and discuss with them, encourage them, and exchange opinions with them. By doing so we can be united to recover democracy in Korea."[4]

Jimmy Carter, four years after his loss to Reagan and three weeks after Reagan's landslide election to a second term, added his own encouragement. "To Kim Dae Jung," he wrote on November 28, "On the eve of your departure to return to your homeland, Korea, I send my warm greeting to a fellow champion of human rights throughout the world and wish you Godspeed and a safe return. Your presence back in Korea will be a symbol for people everywhere."[5]

The wish for "a safe return" was not mere rhetoric. Kim Dae Jung's exile to the United States was often compared to that of Benigno "Ninoy" Aquino, the foe of the Philippines' long-entrenched leader, Ferdinand Marcos. Like DJ, Aquino was sent into exile, in his case in May 1980 when he was in the Philippine Heart Center after a second heart attack suffered after seven years in prison under martial law imposed by Marcos. After an operation in Dallas, Aquino settled into a Boston suburb—and a fellowship at Harvard similar to the one that DJ had two years later. Like DJ, Aquino denounced his government in speeches and interviews around the United States and, like DJ, was accused by his government of perpetrating violence. Like DJ, Aquino denied any desire for radical violence but warned that radical acts might happen if Marcos did not change policies. Tired of life as a political émigré, Aquino decided to return to the Philippines despite what he knew was the danger of getting killed when he got there. Accompanied by foreign journalists on a flight from Taipei, he was gunned down on August 21, 1983, as he stepped onto the tarmac at the Manila airport.

Comparisons between Aquino's death at the hands of an American-supported regime in the Philippines and the danger that DJ faced when he got back to Seoul were all too obvious. South Korea and the Philippines were vastly different as nations and societies, but they were both U.S. allies, both had important U.S. bases, both their governments owed their survival to American-led wars, and the leaders of both had resorted to martial law to stay in power.

In an interview with me at his headquarters near Washington more than two weeks before his departure, DJ talked about what to expect. "They say they will put me in prison again," he said. "At least house arrest is possible." He was sure, however, of the support that he needed both at home and abroad. "Even if I am in prison, my return to Korea and my staying with my people must be a most powerful and emotional message," he told me. "If I can inspire my people, then the majority will participate in the force for restoration of democracy." He hinted at another Gwangju-style revolt while disclaiming responsibility. "We can't guarantee there will be no people's uprising," he said, "even though I can't support it."[6]

Whatever DJ chose to do, President Chun faced outrage. A group called the "Campaign to Assure a Safe Return for Kim Dae Jung" wrote to Chun demanding "safety and freedom" for DJ to prove "your government's growing confidence." Signers included Reischauer and Patricia Derian, assistant secretary of state for human rights under Jimmy Carter and wife of Hodding Carter, the former State Department spokesman, along with the former U.S. ambassador to El Salvador, Robert E. White, a critic of Reagan's policy in Central America, and two Democratic Party members of the House of Representatives, Edward Feighan of Ohio and Thomas Foglietta of Pennsylvania. As DJ's departure neared, he was lionized at send-offs beginning with a farewell at the Felt Forum in Madison Square Garden attended by 3,000 people. At a reception crowded with think-tankers and do-gooders in the main dining room at Woo Lae Oak, a Korean restaurant near the Pentagon, Mary Travers of "Peter, Paul and Mary" fame sang their mega-hit, "I'm Leaving on a Jet Plane."[7]

The State Department had already demanded—and received—confidential assurances from South Korea of DJ's safety when he landed, but DJ cast himself in heroic mold. "I am afraid there will be another Aquino case," he said at the farewell. He also warned of the opprobrium that would befall the Reagan administration if it failed to defend him—and change its policy of unwavering support for whoever ruled in Seoul. "We are not asking America to provide help, only to respect the people's will for restoration of democracy," he said. "America is in a position to keep our military from moving."[8]

DJ's send-off from Washington's National Airport on February 6, 1985, was a media happening. Aboard the plane with him and his wife were about 50 journalists and 22 other escorts and well-wishers, including Derian, congressmen Feighan and Foglietta, ex-ambassador White and Mary Travers. His arrival at Seoul's Kimpo Airport on February 8 was even more of an event. No shots were fired, but DJ and some of the others got into a shoving match with security guards who wanted to hustle him off right away. DJ demanded the right to go through immigration formalities like any ordinary passenger. In the melee the guards got him onto an elevator, out of sight of hundreds of his followers outside the terminal, and finally to his familiar home in Seoul's Mapo Gu. Technically, DJ had more than 17 years left to serve of the 20 to which Chun had reduced his term, but instead he was placed under tight house arrest, banned from contact with outsiders, forbidden from attending a church service or receiving a Catholic priest at his home.[9]

DJ's stormy homecoming turned into a cause celebre for Americans fighting U.S. policy. The U.S. delegation filed a complaint with the Korean government charging the government "broke its promise" of a "trouble-free return." The delegation also charged that the U.S. ambassador, Richard L. Walker, known for his conservative views, had not informed the State Department fully of what had happened. Some members of the delegation stayed on in Korea for several days as they focused on Walker's claim that they had gone back on an agreement not to lock arms as they attempted to escort DJ through the airport. DJ's American escorts said the deal was void after Korean police separated them from DJ and dragged him away. "We were attacked by plain-clothed goons," said Derian after getting back to Washington.[10]

The U.S. Embassy in Seoul defended Walker, saying that the State Department had formally protested not only DJ's treatment but also the entire incident in which Feighan and Foglietta said they were beaten. An embarrassed State Department spokesman said that Walker's remarks were "in response to an accusatory statement" in which the group claimed he had failed to display an interest in the airport fracas. Secretary of State George Shultz, interviewed on NBC, acknowledged "things didn't go according to the agreements that we had thought we had worked out." Still, he insisted there had been "some progress" toward democracy though "they are a long way from where we'd like to see them." Backing up their secretary, State Department officials cited National Assembly elections coming up four days later, on February 12, in which 24 million Koreans were eligible to vote.[11]

DJ's return would be an overriding issue in the assembly elections in which he had a clear and quick opportunity to renew in earnest his bid for national power.[12] The newly formed New Korea Democracy Party expected to win a small but significant percentage of the seats. DJ himself was banned from voting—a show of government defiance of official American hopes "that restrictions placed on him will be lifted." To the consternation of the government, however, the New Korea Democratic Party made surprising gains, winning 50 National Assembly seats, more than twice the number forecast. The guards outside DJ's home had no way to stop him from showing his exultation through family members, visitors and calls. The outcome, he said, represented "a great success for democratic forces," the more so since he and Kim Young Sam, his dissident ally of convenience and rival within the opposition, also under house arrest, had only formed the party a month earlier. A sign of popular interest was that 84.2 percent of the eligible voters went to the polls.[13]

The New Korea Democratic Party, to be sure, had no chance of upsetting the government machine. Chun's Democratic Justice Party won 88 seats and would gain still more thanks to the provision that called for divvying up nearly half the seats in the 287-member assembly on a proportional basis depending on how many each party won at the polls. Chun, however, was keenly disappointed. His response was not to reconcile with the opposition but to intensify his power with a cabinet shake-up in which he appointed the chief of the KCIA, Loh Shin Yong, as prime minister. Now he had to pursue a careful policy of repressing his foes, often with the same brutality as that of Park Chung Hee, while convincing the world that he was not that much of a dictator.

The problem was all the more complicated as the government sought to project a pleasing if not altogether democratic image in the run-up to the 1988 Summer Olympics, on which Korea had staked its prestige as a chance to showcase the country's achievements. While DJ and Kim Young Sam were under house arrest, the government masterminded a program to rev up national interest and collect funds for an event that would cost at least $3 billion, far more than the 1984 Summer Olympics in Los Angeles. The country made it an Olympic goal to erase the old-time image of Seoul, then the world's fourth largest city with ten million people, as a crowded Third World capital, but Chun and his military sidekick, Roh Tae Woo, chairman of the Seoul Olympic Organizing Committee, had overlooked how to rid themselves and their government of the image of a bumbling dictatorship. Many Koreans shared in the national pride of hosting the Olympics; some worried that a superficial show of success would do little for "the democratic system."[14]

Looking three years ahead, Chun saw 1988 as a crucial political year. He promised to hold elections and step down at the end of his term on February 24, but his foes were increasingly vociferous in their demand for direct elections as opposed to voting by an electoral college largely handpicked by the government. "The attitudes of students and workers are more militant now than they were last year," said Gene Matthews, a Methodist missionary who had come to Korea in 1956, nearly 30 years before our conversation in his office in central Seoul in April 1985. "I could imagine them attempting all kinds of ways to disrupt the situation."[15] This assessment could not have been more accurate. Demonstrators two years later would swarm the heart of the capital, and DJ would lend his voice to demands for sweeping change.

The mood of rebellion, however, contrasted with the Olympic spirit that motivated the games' organizers to make the Olympics an undoubted national success, a coming-out party for a people and a nation anxious to show their ability to compete on an equal footing with the world's most advanced countries, including the old colonial occupier Japan and the new ally, the United States. The games would open "a new and glorious chapter in the history of Korea," said Roh Tae Woo, counting on donations from the *chaebol*. Korean officials did not rule out the long shot that North Korea might attend. "This is one country," said Kim Zohng Chill, vice president of the Korea National Tourist Corporation. "We have one ancestor, one language, one tradition. We always say, 'Why don't we talk?'"[16]

Before Koreans could flaunt their pride over the Olympics the country would go through a traumatic shift in which Kim Dae Jung would initiate a decade-long march to the presidency. Long-feared spring riots broke out in Seoul in mid-April 1987 with worse trouble to come in May around the seventh anniversary of the Gwangju revolt. "Down with dictatorship," was the cry as 13,000 students challenged riot police at 24 universities on April 16. Opposition leaders said the students fomented the riots in protest against Chun's refusal to consider any plan for direct election of the president until after the Olympics more than a year later.[17]

DJ's hand was evident as students protested his house arrest. "Because of this crackdown the student dissident movement will harden," said Lee Keun Pal, secretary of the Korean Institute for Human Rights, the group that DJ had formed in Washington while living in Virginia. "Their activities will accelerate."[18] Lee, one of DJ's closest confidants in the United States, boldly predicted "more action by the students in April and May" and blamed the latest riots on Chun's crackdown on the opposition—including the house arrest of DJ and most of his entourage. DJ and his cohorts rallied around Chun's refusal to engage in "dialogue" on revising his constitution to provide for direct election of a president.

The Reverend Pharis Harvey, one of DJ's avid advocates, gauged the mood: "We're in for a major period of trouble that could undermine the Olympics."[19] DJ walked a fine line, not wishing to appear unpatriotic about Seoul's hosting the Olympics while criticizing the regime on the timing. "We don't want to damage the Olympics," he told me, but he questioned the wisdom of holding the games while the country suffered from severe economic and labor problems. DJ would never recognize that Korea was more prosperous than ever before, but he was well aware of the political impropriety of upsetting his countrymen as they glowed in pride over their country's chance to show off before a vast international audience. "We wish the athletes success," he said. "Let everyone enjoy the games."[20]

All the while, DJ was escalating his campaign. Simmering unrest exploded anew after Chun had his ruling Democratic Justice Party nominate Roh Tae Woo as the candidate to succeed him after his own departure from office in February 1988. "This government cannot last forever," DJ told me on June 10, 1987, as rioting broke out near his home. "The United States must realize the difficulty and cease to support it." He was careful to avoid appearing soft toward North Korea and claimed to be as strongly opposed to the military threat from the North as were Chun and Roh. He vowed to distance himself from extremists demanding withdrawal of all the 40,000 or so American troops and blamed Chun for inspiring a radical response from leftists who saw no other way to change governments. Privately, U.S. government officials were critical of Chun for refusing to agree to any compromise.[21]

The rioting as of June 10, when I was talking to DJ on the phone, had resumed at fever pitch. Demonstrators on June 16 attended a mass at Myongdong Cathedral, a focal point of unrest, as police braced for outbreaks throughout the country and the government considered martial law. "The government has lost its ability to handle the situation," said Lee Shin Bom, a former student leader, one of those tried along with DJ after the Gwangju revolt. Lee, who had been jailed for six years before going to the United States in 1983, from his refuge at the Center for Development Policy in Washington cited participation of "ordinary citizens" in the protests as a breakthrough.[22]

As the protest gathered intensity, DJ, still under house arrest, repeated his plea for direct election of a president and his own freedom as conditions for peace. He counted on Kim Young Sam, freed from house arrest, to specify those conditions in a meeting with Chun, who had broken off talks with the opposition but agreed to see YS. Chun's decision to meet YS reflected U.S. pressure for compromise to stop the worst antigovernment protests since Gwangju. In the two weeks since the latest round of rioting had begun on June 10, the police reported 8,000 people arrested.

The U.S. assistant secretary of state for the region, Gaston Sigur, was on his way to Seoul when I next contacted DJ by telephone at his home on June 23. "We only ask Americans to give us moral support," DJ said. "We want to resolve our problems for ourselves." He went to great lengths to reassure Americans that he was not anti-American.

He denied the main opposition leaders sought a reduction of the U.S. military presence even though extremist demonstrators, rioting in his name, were shouting "down with U.S. imperialism." No, he said, "We don't oppose the American bases." He warned, however, of the potential for economic disruption if the rioting spread. "The disturbances," he said, "will have a great impact on economic development"—a threat clearly calculated to impress American fans of Korea's "economic miracle."[23]

Kim Young Sam's call on Chun had a certain success. On June 23, the same day that DJ talked to me by telephone, Chun abandoned his above-the-turmoil stand. The next day, after Chun's meeting with YS, the government released DJ from house arrest. Neither YS nor DJ, however, was inclined to let up the pressure. YS pledged "to continue our non-violent struggle" as tens of thousands of activists, as well as middle-class office workers, took to the streets. Five days later, on the morning of June 29, Roh Tae Woo, as chief of the ruling party, told the nation that he would resign if Chun rejected his reform program, including direct presidential elections, release of political prisoners and easing or lifting of press restrictions along with a guarantee of basic rights.

DJ was emphatic about the need for U.S. pressure on Chun and Roh. "I am not sure Chun will guarantee a free election," he said. Instead, he called on Chun to step down at once, yielding to a transition government that would "sponsor the free election." In a sign of the deep differences between the two foremost opposition leaders, YS favored letting Chun retire with honor in February 1988 as originally planned.[24] DJ was certain that Chun and Roh had collaborated on how to head off the rioting, especially after Chun on July 1 went on television with a declaration ushering in a new political era. As several hundred thousand demonstrators filled the city hall plaza and the square in front of Seoul station, Chun agreed before the country and the world, on the TV networks that his government controlled, to a "democracy" constitution that called for election of a new president by direct popular vote every five years.

It was, said Chun, in order to "promote epochal democratic development and national harmony" that he had decided to "fully accept" Roh's proposal for a constitution that guaranteed all the reforms that Roh had demanded. In a masterful effort at face-saving, Chun averred that the whole reform program was "in full accord with my way of thinking." The alliance between Chun and Roh had worked to perpetuate the power of both of them. Although Roh "might have suggested the plan," said Lee Keun Pal, DJ's aide in Washington, "it was a kind of joint project between Chun and Roh." A factor in Chun's decision, he told me, was U.S. pressure not to suppress protests through martial law. The U.S. position "prevented the government from involving the military in politics."[25]

The collaboration of the closest leaders in the ruling camp headed off not only the immediate antigovernment rioting but also any danger of overthrow of the government. Koreans would go to the polls to elect a new president in December 1987, and Chun would step down in February, as planned, yielding to the winner of the first presidential election under the new constitution. Sigur made no secret of official American relief. "If things move along well for the next month," he said, Korea could be in for "full-blown democracy." There was no denying, though, the uncertainty of the response. The *chaebol* might demand the return of the old government, and old ways, if nonstop turmoil posed a threat to business. Student activists and leftists might not buy into the program, and the military might step in if reforms showed signs of failing.[26]

The beleaguered government now faced what might be its toughest test after the riots, organizing an election that top officials, military leaders and their diehard critics would agree was fair. The opposition, exulting in triumph, was so convinced of its popularity that it was sure to claim as fraudulent anything less than victory for whomever it selected as its candidate. DJ put it this way in another telephone conversation with me: "If it is truly a free election, there will be no doubt of the result." An intrinsic part of Roh's strategy was his belief that he could get elected on a surge of popularity generated by his stunning proposal for a direct election. The opposition, however, maintained that Roh and Chun had conspired to hold the election in the certainty that it would strengthen their grip. "The overall atmosphere is negative," said Lee Keun Pal, "but if they try to manipulate the election, it will backfire." Like most Koreans, Lee believed "U.S. pressure is critical" and the United States should compel Chun to conduct the election fairly.[27]

Chun had a tough technical problem in arranging for the polling. He had to get the election machinery in place by December. South Korea had not held such an election since 1971 when DJ had challenged Park Chung Hee and won 45 percent of the votes. DJ spoke for the more extremist elements when he reiterated his demand that Chun yield to a transition government. In the end, he predicted, only a free election— and a new government—would endure Chun's dream of holding the

Olympics in Seoul without mishap. "We now have a much brighter prospect for a successful Olympics," DJ told me. "A new government can be sure of holding the games without any threat of rioting."[28]

DJ said repeatedly that he would never run, but the image of DJ getting elected and presiding over opening ceremonies for the Olympics was alluring. Roh surely would not have presented his "demand" for a direct election had he not realized he had more chance of succeeding Chun that way than by a vote of Chun's "electoral college." Roh would have won a vast majority of the votes in the "college," but such an event would have taken place amid rioting that would have forced Chun either to resign or to declare martial law whether the Americans liked it or not.

The point of DJ's remarks was that such a denouement might come to pass. Roh might gain popularity by appearing to rush to the side of the rioters, but no opposition leader believed that he could win an honest popular election. The question, then, was whether Chun and Roh would ever "accept" victory by an opponent, gracefully turning over the government to a peacefully, popularly elected civilian. The atmosphere of euphoria hanging over Seoul since Chun did his about-face hardly jibed with Korean history. Dissidents had eagerly seized on the ideal of democracy with the same devotion with which millions had turned to Christianity, but the country had no democratic tradition. Both the Communist regime in the North and the military-dominated one in the South carried on a legacy of dynastic rule that had endured until the onset of Japanese colonialism.

No matter whom the opposition nominated, DJ deemed electoral corruption and military manipulation as inevitable, and he made no secret of his low regard for the Olympic Games' significance in comparison with Korea's political and social problems. When Chun boasted of his country's economic achievements, DJ called attention to the fact that wealth was concentrated in the hands of a relatively small clique of enormously rich tycoons closely tied to the military establishment. Income distribution may have been among the world's most equitable, but the average Korean still earned only $2,000 or so a year. The government responded harshly to attempts at organizing labor or farmers' groups capable of bringing about reform. The downside of the economic boom was not so much the repression of campus dissidents as it was the intimidation of workers who often had no channel through which to express their grating discontent.

It was one thing for Korea's problems to explode into headlines in the spring of 1987, but such a catastrophe would be unthinkable in

1988—not if the Olympics were to be held, not while the world was watching Korea at its proudest moment. How, if Roh were elected, could the government pacify its critics? And how, if YS or DJ were in office, could either deal with military officers loyal to military rule? Either way, Korea faced a time of testing that might be more severe than the struggle from which had emerged the "democracy" constitution. The refusal of the Reagan administration to back Chun against the demonstrators, the delicate maneuvering by U.S. officials toward reform, were calculated to keep the United States on the good side of rising Korean opposition.

Opposition leaders themselves, however, guaranteed Roh's victory. No way would Kim Young Sam and Kim Dae Jung, each with strong regional backing and separate political organizations, agree on a single candidate holding aloft the banner of hostility toward the generals in power. YS, though a leading dissident, was a conservative mainstream figure; DJ represented dissidents with an agenda that offended not only those loyal to the generals but also millions who saw him as a firebrand with a leftist message that would play into the hands of North Korea. Breaking his frequent vows not to run, DJ broke off from YS and organized his own campaign.

Kim Dae Jung's appeal was messianic. At one rally near Seoul, I stood behind him on the platform as more than a million people broke out in cheers at his every utterance. DJ attacked the government from a rostrum that he shared with Moon Ik Hwan, his compatriot from the trial for the Gwangju revolt. Jimmy Kim, a veteran journalist with United Press International, was not impressed. "Yes, but it's the same million every time," he reminded me, meaning that DJ's fans were Cholla people who followed him everywhere. Buoyed by the economic boom, the ruling party was confident of thirty percent of the vote and counted on the failure of the opposition to agree on a unity candidate. At a rally in Gwangju, YS had to leave under jeers from the crowd. Had DJ and YS placed top priority on democratization, they would have compromised—and DJ might not have felt such a strong need to form his own party.

The atmosphere was full of dire forecasts. At the vanguard of protests were far-leftist groups that opposed the U.S. bases and sought reconciliation with the North. There seemed no doubt that DJ's shock troops would go on a rampage in the event of a Roh victory, but it was less clear how they would respond if YS were to win. The military establishment was far likelier to accept YS in the interests of harmony—and the Olympics. "I'm thinking that democracy will be returned to Korea," said Jane Harvey, who had attended Scarritt College in Nashville with DJ's wife, "but who knows how that's going to happen?"[29]

Come election day on December 16, Roh coasted to a decisive victory, winning 36.6 percent of the votes on a promise of "stability and reconciliation" as a prelude to the Olympics and his prediction that North Korea would not "dare to risk disrupting" the games. YS finished second with 28 percent of the votes, and DJ came in third, one point behind with 27 percent. Kim Jong Pil, "JP," clinging to his own dreams, was fourth with 8.1 percent. There would be no concession speeches, no congratulatory phone calls to the victor, no appeals by the losers to unite behind the winner. Refusing to accept the results, DJ and YS accused Roh's Democratic Justice Party of stealing three million votes. "Null and void," they said in separate statements. DJ in particular was inconsolable. "We cannot admit the results," he said. He and his followers had no immediate alternatives, but students promised more protests in the face of media criticism.[30]

If many Koreans did not believe that Roh's victory was credible, the Reagan administration endorsed him with alacrity. As Edward Poitras, a Methodist missionary who had spent a quarter of a century in Korea, observed, "The United States was quick to express its pleasure."[31] Roh himself, at a news conference two days later, appealed for "national harmony" and called for "peaceful transfer" of power. "My major task is to heal all wounds which came from the bitter campaign," he said. "When all parties agreed to have a direct election, it does apply that any winner will lead this country."[32]

DJ did not seem to have considered that he was at fault for running a campaign separate from that of Kim Young Sam. Even as Roh spoke, the long-feared violent response to his victory erupted in DJ's Cholla region. Quick to shout down the election count, DJ said nothing to discourage the rioters as they carried on late into the night in Gwangju and in half a dozen towns in South Cholla province. Police also had to break up leftist protests in Seoul, beginning with a dawn attack on several thousand radicals who had held a ward office since election day. By the time the police took back the building, 36 people, two-thirds of them policemen, were injured; a dozen vehicles were wrecked by firebombs and rocks thrown by leftists and about 1,000 people were under arrest. Another 1,000 or so students clashed with police around the Myongdang Cathedral, seat of power of DJ's ally, Cardinal Kim.

As the fateful year neared a close, the losers appeared in no mood to compromise. Kim Young Sam, blasting "continuation of military rule," predicted the government's overthrow "by peaceful and non-violent means" and vowed to spearhead an "election revolution" in National Assembly elections. DJ said there would "not be political stability" under Roh and "the condemnation must be heeded."[33] Differences between YS and DJ, however, were far more pronounced than were evident in the 1987 campaign. YS, ideologically, was closer to Roh than the most cynical observers could have predicted. DJ would go on blasting the government for all it did, economically or diplomatically, counting on support from the Cholla region, supplemented by the sympathy he had among American liberals, to buoy him when all appeared lost.

CHAPTER EIGHT

In Democratic Opposition

From the time of his exile in the United States, Kim Dae Jung had his heart set on the Nobel Peace Prize. His closest American friends and confidants had convinced him that the Nobel would be the reward he deserved even if he never achieved his other goal, that of election as president. Moreover, a Nobel would be a great boost for his presidential ambitions. In 1986, as DJ was establishing the nationwide support needed to drive the Chun regime over the brink, he was also proselytizing for the prize. It was not his first bid for the accolade but was his most intense so far. As a prelude to politicking in Korea, he put together a book, *Philosophy & Dialogues*, a compendium of speeches, interviews, even a press conference, from his years in the United States.

The cover of the book, published in Hangul and in English, touting DJ's "unshakable faith in the Korean people and their ability to build democracy," carried two lines of identification. "In January 1987, Kim Dae Jung was honored by being nominated for the Nobel Peace Prize in recognition of his three-decade struggle for democracy and human rights," it said. "This nomination is a tribute to Kim Dae Jung and an honor for the Korean people he has so proudly served."[1] DJ did receive one consolation prize. The American Federation of Labor-Congress of Industrial Organizations (AFL-CIO) in 1987 bestowed on him its George Meany-Lane Kirkland Human Rights Award—an encomium that would build up the case for the highest honor of all.

DJ's drive for the prize provided a framework for much that he was to do in his parallel drive for power, in relations with the United States, in his anxiety for dialogue with North Korea. His right-hand man from his days in American exile was Park Jie Won, a political and business operative from South Cholla Province who had made a fortune in the United States from the sale of wigs, a line in which Koreans had been remarkably successful thanks to the acumen of Park and others. Kim Kyung Jae, publisher and editor of *Philosophy & Dialogues,* gave due credit to Park: "Publication of this book would not have been possible without the help of a devoted supporter of Kim Dae Jung and my esteemed friend, Park Jie Won."[2]

If Roh Tae Woo's victory in 1987 was a severe disappointment for his foes, Roh's record as president justified much of their harsh criticism. Inaugurated on February 25, 1988, Roh served out his five-year term despite a rising crescendo of accusations. It would not be until the presidency of his successor, Kim Young Sam, that both he and Chun Doo Hwan would be tried and convicted for the Gwangju massacre and for massive corruption in which they were revealed to have diverted hundreds of millions if not billions of dollars into their own coffers and those of relatives. Chun in the later years of his presidency had been less severe than Park Chung Hee, preferring to focus on amassing wealth for himself and his extended family. Roh promised still greater tolerance but had to face a storm of criticism for his own and Chun's wrongdoings from the very foes he had defeated months earlier. Too divided among each other to support a single candidate for president, critics united in their hatred of Roh. The voters believed the charges, as seen in National Assembly elections on April 26, 1988, in which DJ, YS, and JP all were elected on the strength of strong followings in their native regions.

The 1988 Olympics were looming, but that event, recognition of Korea as an economic power, would provide only a brief respite in which conflicting forces and factions had to temper their campaigns in the interests of Korea's image before the world. None of "the three Kims," DJ, YS and JP, wanted to be accused of spoiling the party. Several weeks before the Olympics opened in September, I saw Chun Doo Hwan's younger brother, Chun Kyung Hwan, his hands tied in ropes, wearing a pale blue prison uniform, bundled off in a van for another session of his highly publicized show trial for embezzling funds from the Saemaul movement, a rural development program through which Chun was perceived to have collected much of his fortune. Chun Kyung Hwan was a scapegoat whose arrest would mollify the critics, but his conviction and sentencing did not exactly satisfy those who saw Roh as a compromising figure committed to the same policies and outlook as his friend, ally, and predecessor in the Blue House.

On the day that Roh proclaimed the opening of the games on September 17, 1988, the date eight years earlier on which the court had sentenced DJ to death, I saw students piling up hundreds of Molotov cocktails behind the student union building at Korea University in northern Seoul while policemen waited on nearby streets. On the western side of the city, at Yonsei University, a similar confrontation was about to explode. As the familiar scent of tear gas hung over the streets around the universities during the Olympics, the games went off without a hitch other than scandals associated with a couple of boxing matches and outcries against critical reports by NBC News.[3] Once the games were done, demonstrators resumed full-fledged protests almost daily on campuses and downtown streets. Marches to Chun's residence, not far from the Yonsei campus, accompanied investigations in which 14 more of his relatives were arrested. Chun himself fled to a monastery in the mountains east of Seoul after acknowledging some of his wrongdoings in a television address on November 23.[4]

The atmosphere was charged with defiance of longstanding policies. DJ's compatriot from the 1980 trial and the 1987 presidential campaign, Moon Ik Hwan, flew on March 25, 1989, to Pyongyang where he met Kim Il Sung before leaving for South Korea on April 3. Student Im Su Kyong went there in July for a 45-day youth festival before going back by road through Panmunjom, normally closed to all North-South traffic, where she was seen off by weeping North Koreans. Arrested on their returns to the South, Moon and Im were venerated as heroes by followers of Kim Dae Jung and, to a lesser extent, Kim Young Sam. So deep was the hostility for the misdeeds of Chun and Roh that Roh, unable to get anything done, appealed to the three Kims for a figurative ceasefire. DJ joined YS and JP in a statement on December 15, 1989, in which they agreed "to completely settle" problems relating to Chun's rule if Chun testified before the National Assembly. Chun spoke before the assembly on national television on December 31, and Roh proclaimed an end to all such issues on January 3, 1990.[5]

No sooner had Roh reached a truce with his enemies than the fundamental differences between Kim Dae Jung and Kim Young Sam surfaced dramatically. In a display of unadulterated political opportunism, YS, deeply conservative despite his record of dissidence, and JP, never anything but conservative, merged their parties in a coalition with Roh's Democratic Justice Party to form the Democratic Liberal Party, a name whose English translation bore a disturbing similarity to that of Japan's long-entrenched, conservative, nationalist Liberal Democratic Party. DJ's Party for Peace and Democracy was now the only real opposition, a rambunctious grouping that held 76 of the National Assembly's 299 seats and tried to make up in protests whatever it could not achieve by votes.

"As anticipated the merger intensified political conflicts by radicalizing the remaining opposition, the Cholla-based PPD, led by Kim Dae Jung," observed Kim Choong Nam, serving at the time as deputy secretary for political affairs on Roh's Blue House staff after holding the same position under Chun. "The opposition resorted to sit-ins, walkouts, public denunciations, and even hunger strikes. The opposition spared no effort to block the passage of government bills. On July 17, 1990, after weeks of fruitless negotiations, the ruling DLP unilaterally pushed 26 bills through the National Assembly in only thirty seconds." DJ and his allies did not care if the bills had the support of the great majority of assembly members. Instead they decried the action as "legislative tyranny," wrote Kim Choong Nam, choosing to leave the legislative process "completely paralyzed" for months.[6]

DJ's wrath knew no bounds. "The merger of the three political parties was greatly condemned by the people as unethical and undemocratic," he stormed in early 1991 after returning to the assembly. It was typical of DJ's populist approach that he believed his minority grouping had the support of the vast majority of the people. DJ tore into Roh, limited to a single five-year term by the constitution that Roh had helped to formulate, with all the ferocity with which he had once assailed all Roh's predecessors from Rhee onward. "We cannot deny that the repeated acts of deliberate steamrolling of parliamentary votes," he declaimed, "invited wholly negative popular reaction." He praised "the opposition"—him and his followers—for having "successfully stopped another round of villainous constitutional revision." He did not, of course, give the slightest credit to Kim Young Sam, viewed now as a traitor to the cause.[7]

DJ had to broaden his appeal beyond his party's Cholla support base if he were to realize his ambitions. In September 1991, a year and two months before the 1992 presidential election, resorting to a familiar name, he formed the New Democratic Party through a fusion with allies in the southeastern provinces, the conservative stronghold of YS as well as the generals who had held power since Park Chung Hee's takeover in 1961. Thus "for the first time in Korean politics, all political parties and organizations engaged in the democratic movement are united in one grand opposition party," said a statement issued by the NDP, calling the fusion "an epoch-making event...."[8]

DJ was convinced that he and his allies could demonstrate their popularity if only they had local autonomy, to be achieved "through fair and honest" elections. He could hardly believe it when candidates of his party won only 165 of 633 seats in contests for city and provincial councils in July 1991. He knew that "our people are said to have voted on the basis of their hope for stability," he said, but "stability under the Roh regime" means "a temporary silence imposed by oppressive means by the regime in power." He had lost none of his predilection for rabble-rousing, judging "the most important task" was to achieve overall "solidarity" of the "dissident movement." Thus he proposed a "Grand Democratic Alliance" of "all the forces opposing the reaction rule of the Democratic Liberal Party," which he labeled the "Grand Alliance for Keeping the Old Order."[9]

DJ battled the alliance of the parties of Roh, YS, and JP with all the fury that he had summoned for his defiance of Rhee, Park, and Chun. He would never accept the notion that they might represent the country's conservative majority against his Cholla-dominated minority. "The merger scuttled the political order and dynamics intended by the people," he told a press conference timed for the 46th anniversary of Korea's liberation from Japanese rule on August 15, 1945. "All political reforms being implemented under the majority opposition leadership came to a halt," he went on, rejecting any idea that he himself was the minority, the odd man out, an unwelcome voice among the three Kims who had formed that "opposition" before YS and JP broke with him. "A predictable and stable political future became an impossibility," he ranted, "and invisible reactionary forces loomed over all walks of society—political, economic and social."[10]

In this period, Kim Dae Jung, eyes on the prize, built on a program for peace and reconciliation with North Korea that was to dominate much of what he said and did for the rest of his career. Ever since his first run for the presidency in 1971, DJ had been advocating what he called his "three-stage" plan for reunification of the two Koreas, beginning with a confederation in which North and South would work together for a decade or so before achieving a federated state and, in the final stage, a reunified Korea. The plan was visionary, a fantasy that could never happen, any more than Rhee Syngman would ever achieve his fantasy of conquest of the North, but DJ never tired of presenting it as a counterpoint to the tragedy of war, the endless incidents, recriminations and perpetual division. DJ as he prepared for his next run for the presidency harked back to the Korean War. He had become interested "in the issue of national unity," he said, concluding that "without reunification, there could never be national reconciliation or happiness for our people."[11]

DJ took pains to deny that his proposal was unrealistic. "I entertain no cheap nationalistic sentimentalism, and am not seeking instant reunification through unrealistic means," he told an interviewer from the *Monthly Chosun*, at the forefront of conservative criticism. Realistic or not, his plan was disarmingly simple. "Of the Three Stages, the First Stage is 'one confederation, two independent governments'—the structure of the 'Confederation of the Republics,'" he said. "The Second Stage or phase refers to 'one confederation and two self-governing regional governments,'" and "The Third Stage is the phase of completion—'one nation, one government.'"[12] DJ had to allay doubts among those who feared he was playing into the hands of the North. With that aim in mind he advanced the theory that the "political structure" of the second phase would be "similar to that of the United States of America."

Did DJ have the impression that the American states, with all their constitutionally guaranteed "states' rights," really comprised a confederation? What about foreign and defense policies, federal laws, and federal courts? These were details that DJ left unmentioned. He was more anxious to show that he had come up with his plan years before North Korea's Great Leader Kim Il Sung had presented a somewhat different scheme for establishing the "Koryo Democratic Confederate Republic" at the Sixth Congress of the Workers' Party in October 1980.

The questions posed by the *Monthly Chosun* in a three-hour conversation overflowed with skepticism. DJ's plan and that of Kim Il Sung were too similar for coincidence, in the view of DJ's critics. "Indeed, the prerequisite conditions attached to the 'Koryo Confederation' posit that 'a new democratic government'" should rise in the South "through the liquidation of its military fascist rule and the achievement of democracy," the *Monthly Chosun* writer observed, asking, "Don't these prior conditions" translate into the North's "continuing commitment to stirring up a revolution in the South?"[13]

The debate was intended to discredit DJ, who never had a specific agenda for achieving his grandiose goals. DJ believed, however, that he could convey his position more effectively by talking than by refusing requests to meet with a journalist from a conservative publication. Might conservatives recognize that reunification, if carried out peacefully, had to be through gradual integration? In that spirit, DJ's response was as diplomatic as it was ambivalent. Rather than appear to be siding with the North, he said that he considered "our government's position on this reasonable," a note of approbation that he had not used previously to describe anything Roh Tae Woo had done. Reverting to form, he called the government's plans for rapprochement "insincere, clearly superficial and *pro forma*."

But how, asked the interviewer, did the North's "Koryo Confederal Republic" differ from his proposal for a "Confederation of Republics?" Again DJ fell back on the American precedent. He believed that the interviewer was "well aware that the term 'federation/confederation' was first used by the United States." His own "political problem was caused by a plot," he alleged, "deviously hatched by those who were infantile in their thinking—people who had falsely accused me for mimicking Kim Il Sung's ideas, when in fact I had used the term 'confederation' as early as 1973—before North Korea."[14]

So who was copying whom? The answer made little difference since the plan was so devoid of reality as to make it irrelevant other than as a sign of his thinking. "North Korea's reunification plan calls for a political structure similar to that of the United States of America," he rambled, again confusing the issue with the American analogy, "in which the central government exercises not only the power of diplomacy and national defense, but also important internal political powers of government."

Did DJ really think the North would become a democracy in which the people had a say, that was willing to share these powers with the South? "As North Korea itself is changing according to current circumstances," he went on, "such policy concerns of their plan may also shift." Meanwhile, under his dream of a "Confederation of Republics," both republics "will continue to retain their independent powers; both governments will empower an equal number of representatives who will then establish a confederal government; and proceed to discuss ways to secure peaceful coexistence, exchange and reunification."[15]

DJ was anxious to explain away issues that got at the heart of the contradictions. If he had been ahead of Kim Il Sung in coming up with the confederation scheme, he had more difficulty making any such claim about his opposition to the National Security Law. North Korea had long called for complete repeal of the law, whose language was deliberately vague. A suspect might be subject to prosecution for having acted "with the knowledge that he might endanger the existence or security of the State or the basic order of free democracy, praised, encouraged, propagandized for, or sided with the activities of an anti-state organization."[16] South Korean activists routinely echoed

North Korea's demands for the law's repeal though North Korea's own laws were infinitely harsher.

As the *Monthly Chosun* interviewer pointed out, "there are some people who criticize your position on this." DJ had a ready response to such carping, one that justified his outlook while denying any affinity for Communism, much less North Korea's brand. "It is ridiculous to be misunderstood, simply because my demand happens to correspond with that of North Korea," he said. He went on to an analogy that would fall apart in a cursory look at history. "Simply because East Germany was a dictatorship, founded upon evil laws, and because West Germany was defending itself from the Communist menace, did West Germany resort to dictatorial rule," he asked rhetorically. "When we claim to fight against the evils of Communism, and we imitate their evil methods to do so, can we claim that we are better than they?" And "Didn't West Germany go one step further, by legalizing the Communist Party and by allowing it to function freely?"[17]

The great flaw was that East Germany, in its darkest periods, was never so cruel a dictatorship as North Korea. East German troops never invaded West Germany. There had been no German equivalent of the Korean War that had cost at least four million lives, military and civilian, North and South Koreans, Chinese, Americans, and soldiers from Allied nations. Despite the pervasively notorious Stasi, East Germany's security ministry, East Germany did not confront West Germany with more than a million troops across a long "demilitarized zone." East German guards did fire at would-be defectors as they tried to flee across the Berlin Wall, erected in 1961 as a tall barbed wire fence and later a reinforced-concrete edifice with more than a hundred watchtowers. Unlike North Korea, however, East Germany did not perpetrate innumerable shooting incidents against West German soldiers, and from the mid-1960s did not shut its borders so tightly to visitors from the West as did North Korea to South Koreans and foreigners.

Nor did East German leaders order any crimes so horrific as the explosion of a Korean Air flight on November 29, 1987, over the Andaman Sea, killing all 115 passengers and crew members, or the murder on October 9, 1983, of 17 South Korean officials and 4 Burmese by a bombing in Rangoon intended for the visiting South Korean president, Chun Doo Hwan. And North Korea's gulag system, holding more than 200,000 political prisoners at any given time, in addition to thousands imprisoned elsewhere for other crimes, according to heart-rending tales told by defectors and later information gleaned by spy satellites, was comparable in torture and killings only to the concentration camps of Hitler's Nazi Germany, not to East Germany's own brutal prison system.

DJ embroidered on the German comparison with another analogy that again seemed compelling except when measured against experience. "If we are to win in our fight against Communism, we will have to see the truth in Aesop's famous tale," he said, "in which only the hot sun can take somebody's heavy coat off, not the blustery, wintry northern wind." West Germany had "won by its own balmy sun," he argued. "One cannot rely on the northern wintry wind to win our case."[18] As he spoke, North Korea was entering one of its worst phases of cruelty toward its own people as well as a new era of global terrorism in the form of a nuclear program highlighted by fabrication of warheads with plutonium at their core at a complex whose construction was identified in the 1980s in the town of Yongbyon, 60 miles north of Pyongyang.

Overlooking reports of the North Korean program, DJ downplayed the significance of Roh Tae Woo's declaration of July 7, 1988, declaring that North and South Korea were members of the "same national community" and promising to "promote exchange of visits between the people of South and North Korea," to "open doors of trade" between the two Koreas, to approve North-South contacts at conferences and to "cooperate with North Korea" in improving relations with Japan and the United States—all efforts for which DJ would have loved to take the credit. Patronizingly, DJ acknowledged the Roh government—not Roh—had made "a considerable achievement" but attributed "the success of the Northern Policy" to "changes in the international arena," "the end of the Cold War, the collapse of Eastern Europe" and the Soviet policy of *perestroika* for restructuring the economy under the man who would be the last Soviet leader, Mikhail Gorbachev. Moreover, said DJ, Seoul had paid too high a price in committing three billion dollars to economic cooperation after normalizing relations with Moscow.[19]

Although "military rule" is often described as lasting through the Roh presidency, Roh pursued "Nordpolitik" with Communist and former Communist countries shedding Communist leadership. Even as the Berlin Wall was falling, from late 1989 through 1990 and into 1991, North-South reconciliation appeared to be moving at a pace that no one could have anticipated. North and South Korea joined the United Nations on the same day, September 17, 1991, and on December 13 North and South signed off on an "Agreement on Reconciliation, Non-Aggression, Exchanges and Cooperation" and a "Joint Declaration on the Denuclearization of the Korean Peninsula." These were milestone dates. The joint declaration in particular seemed to point the way to a new era. It called for verification of denuclearization, promising neither side would "test, manufacture, produce, receive, possess, store, deploy or use nuclear weapons" or "possess nuclear reprocessing and uranium enrichment facilities"—promises the North habitually violated until repudiating the agreement on January 29, 2009.

Roh Tae Woo "had a grand vision for South Korea's foreign policy and reunification and consistently and diligently pursued his policy goals," former aide Kim Choong Nam has written. "He broke through decades-old Korean fears and distrust of Communist nations to open unprecedented relations. He established diplomatic relations of immense strategic and economic importance to South Korea with the Soviet Union and China." One immediate dividend: Moscow no longer dispatched fighter planes and other weaponry to North Korea.[20] Equally important, both the Soviet Union and China stopped accepting North Korean currency at a highly artificial exchange rate, dealing a severe blow to the North Korean economy.

While Roh worked on relations with former Communist adversaries, the flagrant abuse of human rights that characterized the Park and Chun regimes diminished. Like Chun, Roh was if anything more interested in accumulating huge funds for his personal use and that of his close family than in going after his foes. The critics, notably DJ but many others also, were far more outspoken than they had ever been under Park and Chun, and opposition mounted openly. The police cracked down on strikes at Hyundai companies in Ulsan, the industrialized hub that was spewing forth Hyundai motor vehicles and ships. Scores of strikers were arrested in violent clashes, but the Korean Confederation of Trade Unions, the umbrella covering large "metal" industries, though still illegal, won de facto recognition as the voice of thousands of workers.

Roh deprived the left of one talking point, granting amnesty in the run-up to the presidential election of December 19, 1992, to Im Su Kyong, the activist who had gone to North Korea in 1989. The loosening of constraints set the stage for the rise of Korea's first civilian leader since Park Chung Hee seized power in 1961. Kim Young Sam carried the banner of the Democratic Liberal Party against Kim Dae Jung and a third-party candidate, Hyundai empire founder Chung Ju Yung.

Kim Dae Jung was an easy target. YS charged him with leaning to the left, favoring North Korea and the Communists, the familiar complaint of the military leaders whom YS had opposed in his dissident days.

Distracted by the need to go on denying pro-Communist tendencies, DJ pressed his scheme for confederation and reunification. That line, repeated in emotional harangues, was less than convincing or credible in view of all that Roh had done for rapprochement with the Eastern Bloc and Communist world, including North Korea. YS just as easily dismissed the challenge posed by Chung Ju Yung. Confident that he could do better than either YS or DJ, Chung, not without justification, denounced YS as "a stonehead idiot" on the economy.[21] YS countered that Chung was a tycoon who believed he could buy the presidency with the ease with which he consummated a business deal.

Grandly, YS promised "to listen to all supporters of other candidates" while repeating pledges of "democratization" and "a new Korea." There was speculation that YS strategists had planted "upset" talk in order to get out the votes of YS fans who might have stayed home. For all DJ's oratory, however, he had no realistic chance of winning. With 24,095,170, 81.9 percent, of 29,422,658 eligible voters casting ballots, YS had 9,977,332 votes, far ahead of the 8,041,284 votes cast for DJ. The margin would have been still higher but for the well-financed campaign of Chung Ju Yung, who tallied 3,880,067 votes.[22]

DJ as always swept Cholla, winning 95 percent of the votes in Gwangju and 88 percent in surrounding South Cholla Province and in North Cholla, but Chung finished first in Kangwon Province, DJ's one-time stamping ground in the mountainous northeast. The fact that Chung was born and bred in a village on the northern side of Kangwon, many years before the province was divided between North and South at the end of World War II, trumped DJ's early campaigns for a National Assembly seat from the same province, that is, the portion below the DMZ. YS was overpowering in his native Busan and the Kyongsang region, where DJ finished third behind Chung. He had hoped his rabble-rousing would resonate in the industrial centers of Busan, Daegu, Ulsan, and Masan, but regional and Hyundai company loyalties mattered more.

Cheating on the vote count was, for a change, a nonissue. Voters pressed their seals on ballots tallied by the abacus, all watched by each party's observers. Nobody trusted computers for fear of tampering. This time DJ would not assail the election of Korea's first civilian president as corrupt. There had been no "typhoon for Chung," "no late surge," as predicted in London's *Financial Times*, whose representative had perceived Chung winning so many votes "at the expense of Kim Young Sam" as to "tip the election" for DJ.[23] The image of DJ giving a press conference flashed on TV screens saying "I accept the result, and

I want to instruct Kim Young Sam to accomplish national development and improve the life of the people." The victor appeared before an exuberant crowd at his party headquarters. "My victory is a victory for the people who wanted change, reform, stability," said YS. "This is the first civilian government in current history. This is the most clean election. It opens a new stage of political culture."[24]

One special topic that struck a sensitive nerve in Kim Young Sam was the persistence of DJ's campaign for the Nobel Peace Prize. DJ after his defeat in 1992 said that he was through with politics and would never again run for president. Through aides and intermediaries, however, he intensified his pursuit of the Nobel, which had eluded him before the presidential election in 1987. Much to the annoyance of YS, he seemed to have a good chance of getting it in recognition of his struggle against conservative regimes as well as his oft-stated formula for peace and reconciliation with the North. YS had had his own sights set on the Nobel but decided he had no chance. As president, he instructed the National Security Planning Agency, formerly the KCIA and, later, the National Intelligence Service, to do all possible to keep DJ from wangling the trophy.[25]

At the same time, YS after his inauguration in February 1993 felt a compulsion to demonstrate that he was as much a man of mercy and goodwill as was DJ. Thus YS granted amnesty to Moon Ik Hwan, who had been jailed for going to North Korea in 1989. YS also amnestied 143 others held on security charges and, shortly afterward, amnestied a student activist who had helped Im Su Kyong, already freed, to go to Pyongyang around the same time as Moon. And for Christmas 1993 YS amnestied a score of union leaders and a radical accused of printing material harmful to the nation.[26] As for DJ, in accordance with his vow to leave politics, he again retreated to an academic setting, this time Cambridge University in England whence he could go on campaigning for the Nobel, advancing ideas for peace and reconciliation—and keeping his presidential ambitions alive while denying that he had any.

Still conservative, joined in a marriage of convenience with the political organization that had elected Roh Tae Woo, Kim Young Sam could be expected to pursue a mild line. Despite his one-time dissidence against Park Chung Hee, he sought to alter few if any of the laws responsible for propping up military-controlled regimes. Hundreds were arrested during his presidency for such violations of the National Security Law as praising North Korea, failing to report suspected pro-Communist activities or waving the North Korean flag. "It is still legal in South Korea for the security forces to carry out arbitrary arrests and detentions," said Human Rights Watch in a report on November 1, 1995, three months beyond the half-way point in his presidency.[27] Although YS initially purged the military and other security institutions, his arbitrary reform efforts and poor governance were making him unpopular.

Kim Young Sam early in his presidency espoused reconciliation even though North Korea soon after his inauguration said it was withdrawing from the nuclear nonproliferation treaty and a year later refused inspection by the International Atomic Energy Agency, the IAEA, of its reprocessing facilities at Yongbyon. Alarmed when a North Korean negotiator warned in talks at Panmunjom on March 19, 1994, that Seoul would become "a sea of fire," YS opposed any move to exacerbate tensions surrounding the nuclear complex.

A conservative of convenience, YS was closer to DJ than the generals who had preceded him in the Blue House in his reluctance to risk war. Critical of whatever the YS government was doing for reconciliation, DJ took advantage of the near-crisis atmosphere to advance his vision for dealing with the North. Besides promising never again to run for president, he presented what seemed like a far-fetched proposal for Jimmy Carter, the former president, to go to North Korea in search of a solution.[28] YS at the time was under fire for the conciliatory views of his unification minister, Han Wan Sang, a well-known former dissident who was tried with DJ in 1980 but sensed opportunity with YS.

YS by his own account persuaded President Bill Clinton in a telephone conversation in June 1994 not to stage a strike on North Korea, saying he would never order his troops to enter a war that could kill between ten million and twenty million Koreans.[29] Next, responding to DJ's appeal, Carter came to Seoul en route to Pyongyang by road through Panmunjom and a meeting with Kim Il Sung. In a leisurely conversation in a boat on the Daedong River on June 17, Carter won from North Korea's "great leader" the promise of a freeze of the North's nuclear program in return for construction of twin light-water nuclear reactors to help fulfill the North's energy needs. Nuclear reciprocity was the critical mass: if we stop building nukes for wartime purposes, was the inference, then let us have nukes for peacetime use. Thus Carter laid the basis for what would have been the first North-South Korean summit. Kim Young Sam was busy preparing to go to Pyongyang when Kim Il Sung died on July 8, 1994.

After the death of Kim Il Sung, YS came to be regarded by critics as a foe of reconciliation. There was never talk of a summit between YS and Kim Il Sung's anointed successor, his son, Kim Jong Il, who had already gained command of the armed forces. North-South tensions quickly worsened as YS refused to express condolences over the death of Kim Il Sung, arguing there was no reason to mourn the passing of the man who had ordered the invasion of the South in June 1950. Nonetheless, U.S. and North Korean negotiators returned to the table in August and, on October 21, 1994, signed the Geneva Framework Agreement under which the North shut down its nuclear program at Yongbyon under supervision of IAEA inspectors. The United States assisted in placing the 8,000 spent fuel rods at Yongbyon into canisters in a cooling pond while the five-megawatt experimental reactor and reprocessing facilities were locked up. IAEA teams rotated in and out of Yongbyon, making sure the North abided by the terms.

Most importantly, the United States persuaded South Korea and Japan to agree to invest heavily in the project for building twin reactors on a site at Kumho on the northeastern North Korean coast. South Korea would pay the most, $4 billion, for the reactors to be constructed largely by KEPCO, the government-owned Korea Electric Power Corporation, while Japan would pay another $1 billion. The United States would spend an average of $50 million annually to ship 500,000 tons of heavy fuel oil to the North each year as a stopgap to help meet the North's energy requirements until the reactors were completed.

South Korea's foreign minister, Han Sung Joo, was almost taken by surprise when Robert Gallucci, the chief U.S. negotiator, and Kang Sok Ju, the vice foreign minister in charge of the North Korean team, came to terms. Although the price tag seemed huge, much of the money would revert to South Korea in payments to KEPCO. As a result of the Geneva framework, a new acronym was introduced, KEDO for Korean Peninsula Energy Development Organization, its U.S.-led headquarters in a glitzy office tower on Third Avenue in New York, a few blocks from the glassy monument that is the UN secretariat.

The agreement, however, did not lead North Korea to tone down its rhetoric against Kim Young Sam. In North Korean parlance, he was the incarnation of evil, a "lackey" of the Americans, a figurehead with whom the North would never negotiate. North-South relations threatened to run aground completely when a 325-ton North Korean Shark-class submarine foundered off South Korea's east coast on September 18, 1996. The Americans hoped to forestall disaster while talking the

North into putting off its withdrawal from the nuclear nonproliferation treaty and agreeing to let U.S. teams search for bodies of American troops missing from the Korean War.

In the aftermath of the submarine incident, U.S. officials 14 months later were trying to get the process on track. The Americans perceived a glimmer of hope that representatives of the two Koreas, the United States and China might sit down for "four-party talks" as suggested by presidents Clinton and Kim Young Sam on Jeju Island off South Korea's southwestern coast in April 1996. The sense was that negotiators would come up with a solution to the puzzle: how to get the North to say something that the South could accept as an apology. Tensions had been rising ever since the incident. Only one of 26 crew members and saboteurs was captured alive. One escaped and the others were killed, a number executed by their own mates, while five South Korean soldiers and several civilians were gunned down in the manhunt. YS made the issue of an apology and a promise of "never again" a point of prestige and power.

Right away, the South banned all travel by South Korean businessmen to North Korea. The cancellation threatened a small but promising flow of goods between North and South—not overland, to be sure, but through the West or Yellow Sea corridor between Nampo, the port southwest of Pyongyang, and Incheon. The North stood to suffer far more than the South from the reduction, largely because it had a favorable trade balance, mostly from cheap clothing produced by small textile factories. Why, South Korean officials asked, should the South send food to North Korea while the North refused to apologize for the submarine? It was to obtain direly needed aid at the height of the famine of the mid-1990s that the North, on December 29, 1996, came through with begrudging "deep regret" for the submarine imbroglio, promising, "Such an incident will not recur."[30]

Kim Dae Jung was out of the loop in this momentous process. On the sidelines, he could advance his views but was unable to mount a convincing attack against moves toward a reconciliation that were not antithetical to his own ideas. Marginalized as he was, he wrote an essay on democracy for the prestigious American journal *Foreign Affairs* in which he criticized an unlikely target, Lee Kuan Yew, Singapore's senior minister and former prime minister, for having suggested in an interview in the same journal that Western-style democracy and Western values did not apply to Asia.

"Such doubts have been raised mainly by Asia's authoritarian leaders, Lee being the most articulate among them," DJ wrote. "They have long maintained that cultural differences make the 'Western concept' of democracy and human rights inapplicable to East Asia." As far as DJ was concerned, "The best proof that democracy can work in Asia is the fact that, despite the stubborn resistance of authoritarian rulers like Lee, Asia has made great strides toward democracy." DJ clearly had South Korea's former leaders in mind, Kim Young Sam too, as he embroidered on the theme. "Policies that try to protect people from the bad elements of economic and social change will never be effective if imposed without consent," he wrote, though he would refrain from seeking popular consent for Sunshine while discouraging criticism of North Korea.[31]

Kim Dae Jung's *Foreign Affairs* article offered a surface impression of DJ's thinking, a portent of what he was doing as he planned his comeback into politics. Building up politically as he had diplomatically, he surged back into the public eye in campaigning in mid-1995 for the posts of governor, mayor, and metropolitan and provincial councils. These were the first local elections since the brief experiment in democracy after the fall of Rhee in 1960. DJ spared no effort in campaigning on behalf of his Democratic Party, as it was now called. To the shock of YS, Democratic candidates not only swept Cholla but captured the post of mayor of Seoul and most of the city council seats in the voting on June 27.

"Retired opposition leader comes back in S. Korea," ran the headline over an article three weeks later in *The Washington Times*, owned by the Reverend Moon Sun Myung's Unification Church. DJ was emphatic about his comeback. "Mr. Kim brushed aside accusations of bad faith and declared the creation of a new opposition group," said the dispatch from Seoul, quoting him as saying, "I have gone through many ordeals to work for democracy and peaceful unification in the past forty years."[32] The reference to "unification" referred to North-South reunification but also had a special meaning for the Unification Church, whose Tongil (unification) group had large business interests in South Korea and was expanding into North Korea.

Kim Dae Jung, on the warpath, looked for any opportunity to go after his foes. Soon enough, YS exposed himself in corruption scandals. The corruption issue was hypersensitive since YS had begun his term by ordering the dismissals of hundreds of officials and military officers implicated in bribery cases. In his righteous wrath, he let go the mayor of Seoul, Kim Sang Chul, a week after he had moved into city hall, and also dismissed several ministers and vice ministers. Those cases would disappear into the long and largely forgotten history of Korean scandals, but YS got into trouble midway through his term as pressure mounted for the arrest of the two biggest fish, Chun Doo Hwan and Roh Tae Woo. YS sensed that arresting, jailing, and trying these two would deflect attention from his incompetence and boost his popularity.

Eager to build up his base and avenge betrayal, DJ seized the opportunity to try to bring YS down as well. The day after Roh's arrest on November 16, 1995, on charges of picking up hundreds of millions of dollars from slush funds, DJ staged a rally at which he said that Roh had given him a campaign contribution and therefore must have given more to YS. Then, two and a half weeks later, on December 3, Chun was also arrested not only for corruption but for his role in Gwangju and for the mini-coup of December 12, 1979, in which he had ordered the arrest of the army chief of staff for complicity in the assassination of Park Chung Hee. DJ tore YS apart in rhetoric matched by tirades from Pyongyang. He called the arrests "shock comedy" while his party demanded to know about Roh's contributions to the 1992 campaign. Next, "Kim Dae Jung dropped a bombshell," as recalled by Kim Choong Nam, who had gravitated as a Blue House staffer to the YS presidency. "If Roh gave money to the opposition leader, it seemed reasonable to assume that he had also funded his own party's candidate, Kim Young Sam."[33]

DJ was in no mood to praise YS for his handling of the cases against Chun and Roh even when they went on trial on December 18 on charges ranging from the 12/12 mini-coup to the Gwangju massacre, to massive corruption. Later, long after they had been convicted in August 1996 and sentenced, Chun to death and Roh to 22 years and 6 months in prison, DJ would write that "justice was done eventually" and "the outcome was a victory for democracy."[34] Many asked how YS could indict those two when his own record was suspect—and he had allied with Roh in his quest for the Blue House. "Kim Young Sam did not have 'moral legitimacy,'" said Kim Choong Nam. "In fact, he was elected by illegally spending huge amounts of money." Moreover, in National Assembly elections in April 1996, YS did "whatever it took to win," insuring that he could cobble together a majority "by any means rather than by the 'fair and clean' elections he advocated."[35]

North Korea contributed to Kim Young Sam's cause by sending anywhere from 120 to 200 troops into the Joint Security Area in Panmunjom for several nights in a row before those elections, revving up enough fears of armed conflict for his party to do better than expected. The party fell short of a majority but pieced together an edge with the help of independents and minority party members. YS, however, barely survived accusations of his own corruption and that of his son, Kim Hyun Chul, who went on trial in June 1997 for accepting funds for himself and his father's 1992 campaign from Hanbo, a secondary *chaebol* on the brink of bankruptcy. DJ, looking ahead to the December 1997 presidential election, again pledged to "go after corruption"—a popular rallying cry as rioting students called for YS to resign.[36]

CHAPTER NINE

Dawn of Sunshine

Kim Dae Jung sensed his greatest opportunity for national power—and for the Nobel Peace Prize—lay in reconciliation with North Korea. Even as Pyongyang took to excoriating Kim Young Sam in the strongest language, DJ got to know one of South Korea's most astute figures in North-South relations, Lim Dong Won. A former major general, born in North Korea, Lim had visited Pyongyang many times as a member of the team that negotiated the 1991 peace and denuclearization agreements. In early 1995 DJ appointed him secretary-general of the foundation that he had started during his American exile, founded again in Seoul after his return in 1985 and reestablished in 1994 under the formal name, Kim Dae Jung Peace Foundation for Asia and the Pacific. DJ, of course, was the foundation chairman.

"By luring Lim, DJ thought he could attract former generals to his side," a former colleague at DJ's foundation told me. "DJ had free time. He and Lim talked every night. They got to know each other very well." Just as DJ could claim to have come up with his "confederal" idea long before Kim Il Sung, so he could also say his foundation predated North Korea's Asia-Pacific Peace Committee, established after Kim Il Sung's death in 1994 by North Korea's intelligence chief, Kim Yong Sun. DJ's foundation stepped up activities around the same time, but DJ had laid the groundwork years before in Virginia. The similarity in names hardly seemed coincidental, however, considering that Kim Yong Sun was responsible for inter-Korean relations and a close aide of Kim Il Sung's son and heir, Kim Jong Il.[1]

While DJ and Lim were discussing how to reconcile with North Korea, the YS government was using its intelligence-gathering machinery in hopes of destroying him. The National Security Planning Agency concocted a Machiavellian plot to portray DJ's camp as collaborating with the North. A letter, purportedly written by a South Korean religious leader who had defected to the North, suggested that DJ had been in touch with the North Korean regime. The NSPA publicized the forgery to make DJ appear as a pawn of the North. The goal of the "northern wind" conspiracy was to sway voters against DJ by portraying him as a Communist sympathizer willing to sell out the South.[2]

South Korea by this time, however, was in the throes of turmoil that touched the lives of the people far more closely than that of little understood concerns about North Korea. Like so many other events in Korean history, the economic crisis of late 1997 caught both Koreans and foreigners by surprise. As Korea appeared to have reached a pinnacle of economic success, the system in mid-1997 began to buckle. Kim Young Sam, inept enough at dealing with North Korea, was out of his depth when confronted in the second half of the year with the plummeting value of the won, the precipitous drop in foreign exchange reserves, severely depleted for buttressing the currency, and the failure of *chaebol* and their subsidiaries.

The timing for DJ and his National Congress for New Politics, as he had renamed his party, could not have been better. DJ's critics might attack him on numerous grounds, but no one could hold him responsible for plunging the country into economic crisis. After having balked for weeks against the inevitable, Lim Chang Yuel, the finance minister whom YS had belatedly appointed on November 19 to replace his incompetent predecessor, came to terms on December 3 on an agreement with the International Monetary Fund that called for extensive reforms in the banking system, in the spending habits of the *chaebol* that fed off the banks, and in accounting procedures to insure against future shocks. In return the IMF promised a package of $58 billion in loans from institutions and countries with big stakes in the Korean economy. "The IMF crisis," as it was dubbed in the media, inspired DJ to rhetorical flights in which a real and present danger gave him ammunition. He picked up on the national shame over the country's falling, as many saw it, "under IMF control." To DJ the need for such public humiliation was a "national disgrace."

The candidate of the Grand National Party, the arch-conservative Lee Hoi Chang, a former supreme court justice who had served as prime minister until YS dropped him for seeming to go around him, made it on DJ's list of "enemies responsible for the economic situation." YS, the foremost "enemy," was the easiest whipping boy, but DJ blamed Lee for failing as chairman of the board of audit and inspection to stem the economic crisis.³ Summoning a meeting of candidates, YS asked for "pan-national cooperation" on economic problems. DJ believed an emergency decree could bring reform. When YS scolded DJ for demanding renegotiation of the IMF agreement, DJ backed off, saying he was requesting "supplementary talks."⁴

Kim Dae Jung had the edge over Lee Hoi Chang even though Lee almost closed the gap after disavowing support from YS, who tried to help Lee by making a show of resigning from his party. The IMF crisis was not the only factor that DJ had going for him when voters cast their ballots on December 18. More important was a rift in conservative ranks in which Rhee In Je, former governor of Kyunggi Province, surrounding Seoul, rejected for the conservative nomination, ran a separate campaign. DJ could thank his former dissident ally, now his enemy, YS, for Rhee's candidacy. Rhee, close to YS, decided to run on the advice of YS, who intensely disliked Lee Hoi Chang. "When Rhee organized a new party, many close associates of YS followed him," said YS aide Kim Choong Nam. "YS's critical mistake helped his rival DJ's victory."⁵

More shocking, DJ showed he was no less likely to make a pact with a political enemy than was YS. He persuaded Kim Jong Pil not to run, promising to make him prime minister, the position that JP had held when Park was president, in a reform government. Nor would the prime ministership be the somewhat ceremonial post that it had always been. DJ would press to amend the constitution, giving JP more to do than preside over cabinet meetings. Did it matter if JP were deeply conservative, with a record of corruption exposed during Chun's presidency, if JP had been KCIA director when DJ was in rebellion against Park and then had infuriated him by joining YS in alliance with Roh Tae Woo during Roh's presidency? Not at all, not if DJ could win votes that JP might have received from the Chungcheong provinces and Daejeon, midway between Seoul and DJ's Cholla stronghold.

The stars were aligned for Kim Dae Jung. Here was a campaign with a real point, not a vague apparition such as North Korea or corruption or dictatorship, all issues on which DJ had based earlier crusades, but an economic upheaval in which livelihoods were at stake. DJ wound up winning 10,326,275 votes, 40.3 percent, against 9,935,718 for Lee, a margin of 1.7 percent. Rhee In Je won an astounding 4,925,591 votes, most of which would have gone for Lee. DJ still needed near-unanimous support from the Cholla region, and he got it—97.3 percent from Gwangju, 94.6 percent from surrounding South Cholla Province and 92.3 percent from North Cholla. In front of the South

Cholla governor's office in Gwangju where troops had shot into the crowd in May 1980, citizens shouted "Deejay, Deejay" as returns rolled in.[6] His victory electrified a world that ranked him with South Africa's Nelson Mandela and Lech Walesa of Poland as a hero victorious over evil.[7]

DJ at once dropped the criticism of the IMF that had made fine campaign cant but would do no good if Korea were to recover from near-collapse. He was realistic in a "conversation with citizens" in January in which he warned of "terrible hardships" if the country were forced to declare a moratorium on debt repayment. In the "conversation," before more than 800 people at the state-owned Korean Broadcasting System, he said bluntly that "in a few days the country can go bankrupt unless we cope with the situation." He appeared in good humor as he reminded the audience, "I have prepared for the presidency for many years," telling the millions watching the live broadcast on a cold Sunday evening, "I know I can do it, just trust me." He did not "want to be admired during my presidency," he said, preferring to be "admired after my term" and "missed by the students after my death."[8]

But could DJ transcend his Cholla origins and govern a nation in which a sizeable majority opposed him? And could he overcome the regional prejudices always paramount in Korean politics? In the month before the inauguration on February 25, DJ's aides drafted laws for recovery, including a bill to legalize layoffs by companies that had to guarantee lifetime employment. The need for loans also helped to bring about not only DJ's victory but also an atmosphere conducive to reform in human rights. A great irony, as DJ embarked on reforms on the economy, human rights and North Korea, with which he would renew the quest for reconciliation after disposing of the economic issue, was that he persuaded YS to grant amnesty to Chun and Roh. Both of them sat somberly on the dais at DJ's inauguration as DJ took the oath of office and YS yielded power to his old foe.

The line-up of foreign guests arrayed behind them, including such diverse figures as George Soros and Michael Jackson, suggested the extraordinary breadth of the contacts DJ had made during his American exile. So moved was the red-hatted Jackson that he hugged the new president, then traveled to Incheon to inspect reclaimed land that he was thinking of developing for a Neverland-type amusement park. Soros was less effusive but more encouraging, investing in a fund after predicting plunging stock prices and devaluation of the won would lure foreigners. (Jackson never invested—but returned the next year to give an elaborately produced performance before wildly cheering fans, proceeds to benefit children's charities.)[9]

On the steps of the domed National Assembly building, DJ blamed his predecessors, a few feet away, for the suffering inflicted on ordinary citizens. Enlarging on his oratory and writing of the past three decades, he charged "the political, economic and financial leaders of this country" were all "tainted by a collusive link between politics and business." Hinting at vengeance, he said "we must calmly and squarely look back to find out how we have arrived at this state of affairs." Reforms, including transparency, downsizing and shareholders' rights, would be "carried out by all means." Battling the nationalism and antiforeign sentiment that pervaded the society, he assured his countrymen, "Inducement of foreign capital is the most effective way to pay back our foreign debts, strengthen the competitiveness of business and raise the transparency of the economy."[10]

If DJ was not about to reconcile with his historic tormentors, he wanted full reconciliation with South Korea's enemy to the north. He was fully aware that consensus-forming would be difficult as long as many viewed the North Koreans as enemies. Proclaiming himself ready for a summit with Kim Jong Il, whom he did not mention by name, he pronounced "three principles" as the basis for talks: "First, we will never tolerate armed provocation of any kind. Second, we do not have any intention to undermine or absorb North Korea. Third, we will actively pursue reconciliation and cooperation between the South and the North beginning with those areas which can be made available to us."[11] DJ called that pursuit his *Sunshine policy*, the term derived from Aesop's Fables about the traveler who took off his coat when warmed by the sunshine.[12]

Before getting around to Sunshine, however, DJ had to deal with more pressing matters at home. Besides investigating the root causes of "the IMF crisis," prosecutors needed to clean out the National Security Planning Agency after the NSPA was determined to have been frantically destroying records in the period between DJ's election in December and his inauguration in February. DJ's aides zeroed in on a Korean-American businessman who had said he had evidence that North Korea was bribing DJ. Prosecutors charged that NSPA officials had paid the businessman to state that DJ was a Communist sympathizer who depended on donations from the North.[13] "Northern wind" blew up into an inquiry into the NSPA's history.

Exposé of "northern wind" gave DJ the pretext to renovate an agency that had long been a bastion of conservatives who shared the view, dating from the Park Chung Hee era, that DJ was a traitor. One of DJ's first moves after his inauguration was to put his team in charge. Two dozen top officials of the National Security Planning Agency lost their jobs, and Kwon Young Hae, the last director before the name was changed to NIS, was arrested. The plot thickened when Kwon, in the hands of prosecutors, was mysteriously stabbed in the stomach by a penknife purportedly hidden in a Bible that his wife had thoughtfully given him as he surrendered for questioning and pretrial detention. Had Kwon committed Japanese-style hara-kiri? Self-inflicted or not, the wounds were not fatal. Rescued when his screams were heard from a toilet, Kwon recovered, stood trial, and was convicted.[14] Thus DJ reversed what he had called the "intelligence politics" of the 1970s and 1980s, repeating the tactics of his predecessors.

Kim Young Sam had already stopped the torture and beatings for which the KCIA had been notorious; DJ during his presidency ordered a halt to the tear-gassing of demonstrators. He was not, however, above resorting to the familiar technique of electronic eavesdropping. Exposure of wiretapping surfaced in bizarre style after he had left office and, before the firestorm of scandal burned out in a pyrotechnic display of headlines, arrests and trials, spread from the Korean embassy in Washington to the Samsung group to the top levels of the National Intelligence Service. The spark was ignited by a disgruntled former agent from NIS, Kong Un Young, who gave tapes of conversations between Hong Seok Hyun, publisher of *JoongAng Ilbo*, a leading conservative newspaper, appointed by DJ's successor, Roh Moo Hyun, as ambassador to Washington, and Samsung Vice Chairman Lee Hak Soo.

Since Hong, as husband of the sister of Lee Kun Hee, Samsung chairman and principal owner of the group, was the brother-in-law of Lee Hak Soo's boss, what could be more natural than for the two to discuss payoffs to candidates? As heard on the more incriminating tapes, they were scheming how to hedge their bets by bribing both leading candidates in the 1997 election, DJ and Lee Hoi Chang. The KCIA had innumerable devices for recording conversations with DJ and thousands of others. Entire floors of Seoul's Westin Chosun Hotel were wired for lines to visitors, including foreign correspondents, many of them in Seoul to interview DJ about dissent. The fact that the NIS persisted in eavesdropping during DJ's administration was all the more significant considering that DJ had pledged during his 1997 campaign to do away with all bugging.

Kim Seung Kyu, NIS director, confessed—he used the word for "confession"—on the nation's television networks on August 5, 2005, begging the public to forgive him after prosecutors seized 274 taped conversations from the home of the NIS person responsible for the actual bugging. Devices had been placed as late as the final months of the presidency of Kim Young Sam beneath desks and dining tables, and they were sophisticated enough to monitor conversations on cell phones as well as landlines. The recordings, however, were all made before 1998. The NIS claimed to have burned the ones covering DJ's presidency. No one believed the NIS assurance that the days of bugging were over. As the leftist gadfly People's Solidarity for Participatory Democracy put it, "We just can't buy it."[15] The scandal was evidence that nothing much had changed, that any leader, however idealistic or initially determined to clean up the mess of his predecessors, would revert to the practices of the bad old days.

Aides said bugging phones had gone on without DJ's knowledge, not a convincing argument though DJ loyalists may have been eavesdropping without letting him know for the sake of deniability. DJ had an acutely tuned sense of what his people were up to, and informants among them would pass on gossip, signs of disloyalty or anything else that might be relevant to his political and personal security. Nonetheless, as long as they and he could say he knew nothing about it, he remained above the fray, beyond reproach. Besides, their own resentment was legendary, not just against his military persecutors but also against conservative figures, including YS, whom he saw as forever against him.

Kim Dae Jung faced a problem of a different sort in countering the agency's transgressions. As a former dissident, he could be expected to order the release of hundreds of "prisoners of conscience"—captured North Korean spies and Communist activists—whom the agency had jailed and, in many cases, subjected to torture. After freeing 74 of them in commemoration of the annual celebration on March 1 of the anniversary of the 1919 revolt against Japanese rule, DJ was reluctant to release any more right away. He could not afford, while dealing with difficult *chaebol* leaders at the height of the economic crisis, to appear pro-Communist. Conservatives would always remind him that he had received only 40 percent of the votes and was "the president of Cholla," not Korea. DJ on August 15, 1998, 53rd anniversary of liberation from Japanese rule, did free another 103 after they had signed a controversial loyalty pledge promising to abide by South Korean laws.[16]

In February 1999, DJ promised amnesty for 17 long-term prisoners who had refused to sign.

DJ was more interested in pursuing corruption among his enemies. His anticorruption campaign bore similarities to that conducted by YS early in his presidency, but the targets this time were YS and his son, Hyun Chul, convicted of accepting bribes from the bankrupt Hanbo group. After YS and Hyun Chul refused summons to testify before a National Assembly committee, Lee Hoi Chang, the defeated presidential candidate, leveled the same charge that DJ had been accustomed to making in his days as a defeated dissident. The government and its allies, Lee said, were guilty of "oppression of the opposition" though DJ shrewdly included Kim Hyun Chul among those granted pardons on the August 15, 1999, Liberation Day. Hyun Chul had already served six months but was free for medical reasons. Short of full amnesty, the gesture relieved him of the need to appeal his two-year sentence—and also got YS to tone down his attacks on DJ.

The corruption issue, though, would return, showing that DJ and his aides were as vulnerable as those who had gone before. As campaigning heated up for National Assembly elections in April 2000, Lee Bu Young, jailed as a dissident by previous regimes but now a conservative, charged that DJ's "reformist government turned out as corrupt as the previous administration."[17]

With politicos trading corruption charges, DJ had to act quickly to bring Korea out of economic crisis. Needing cooperation from *chaebol* leaders and conservative politicians, he refrained from referring to the starry-eyed study on "mass-participatory economy" that he had done at Harvard in the early 1980s. The problem now was different. Calling on the *chaebol* to submit restructuring plans, he berated them for having overextended their empires, overpricing and speculating in real estate. He faced a powerful critic in the form of the Federation of Korean Industries, made up of *chaebol* chieftains who promised reforms to "stabilize the financial markets and the national economy" but demanded that DJ heed "economic realities."[18]

For all his pronouncements on economic issues as a crusading dissident, DJ was hardly an economic expert. In response to suspicions that the *chaebol* were stalling, however, he had the sense to appoint competent people to key positions. Lee Hun Jai, chairman of the Financial Supervisory Commission, the super-agency overseeing reform, led the charge for revising control structures, banning cross-payment guarantees among companies in the same group, and getting rid of bankrupt or severely money-losing entities. *Chaebol* chieftains and their banks should face "criminal punishment," Lee warned, if they violated a law that would "completely ban new cross-payment guarantees of conglomerates."[19] A sign of how clouded was the economic vision of DJ's "mass-participatory economy" was his appointment of Lee Kyu Sung, an economist who had served as finance minister under Roh Tae Woo, as his first finance minister. While Lee Hun Jai battled to get the *chaebol* to shed worthless "zombie" companies, Lee Kyu Sung tried to persuade the World Bank to sink more billions into reducing the debts of troubled *chaebol*.

DJ was more intimately concerned with political than economic subtleties. Having assumed power, he had to rationalize differences between progressives and conservatives. Conflict often revolved around members of the 386 generation—those in their thirties who had gone to universities in the 1980s, having been born in the 1960s. Many "who had fought for democracy and reunification in the 1980s are still confined to the categories, problematics and practices of the 1980s," as scholar Lee Nam Hee has observed. While "neoliberalism became the key economic policy" of the DJ presidency, the government's "mantle of higher moral authority, relative to previous regimes, has helped vindicate their embrace of neoliberalism."[20] If DJ had to deal with criticism from 386'ers imbued in the revolutionary fervor of previous decades, he faced more formidable opposition from conservatives. They, not the liberals, fought assembly approval of Kim Jong Pil as prime minister even though JP's views and deeds had been far more closely attuned to conservative philosophy than to DJ's leftist populism.

Not until candidates of DJ's National Congress for New Politics and JP's United Liberal Democrats won a majority of votes in local elections on June 4, 1998, was JP, already "acting prime minister," approved on August 17 as prime minister. DJ, however, never had any intention of broadening the powers of the prime minister, and JP resigned in January 2000 in favor of Park Tae Joon, the conservative founder of POSCO, Pohang Iron and Steel, a state-invested showcase that was privatized during DJ's presidency. DJ again showed faith in compromise by appointing another conservative, Lee Han Dong, as prime minister in July after Park resigned in a tax evasion scandal. Conservatives complained that DJ and Lee were "devoid of public trust." Would they prefer an avowed leftist to the poaching of one whose views were their own? DJ was undeterred by Lee's record as a Chun loyalist when Chun was on trial for treason. His priority was clear. An aide said DJ had appointed Lee "in the sprit of realizing a coalition."[21]

Nothing showed the contrast between DJ's economic program as president and his populist diatribes against Park and Chun more than his evolving views on labor. The economic crisis resurrected the issue of the right to dismiss workers. On December 22, 1997, four days after his election, DJ reversed his opposition to layoffs after briefings on the economic condition. "I have suffered all my life, but after being briefed I realized our economy is completely at the bottom," said the politician who would never as a candidate have dared to advocate layoffs. "Our economy is in such bad shape, we could go bankrupt even tomorrow." Reluctantly, he conceded, "When businesses cannot save themselves from bankruptcy by reducing salaries, they may inevitably resort to redundancies."[22]

In line with one of the IMF requirements for getting out of crisis, DJ hoped to wrest labor's consent to limited layoffs through a tripartite commission representing government, *chaebol* and the two big national unions. The militant Korean Confederation of Trade Unions refused to go along, demanding that owners and executives suffer equally with rank-and-file. The Federation of Korean Trade Unions, historically allied with the government and sometimes accused of siding with management, did not object formally but expressed similar reservations. The once-leftist DJ, after his inauguration in February 1998, was transformed in the eyes of workers from hero to villain. "Kim Dae Jung is the enemy of labor," was the translation of a headline in a labor newspaper. "The Kim Dae Jung government is deceiving labor," said a KCTU pamphlet distributed on the May Day holiday outside Myongdong Cathedral, rallying point for DJ-inspired demonstrators during the 1980s democracy movement.[23]

During a walkout that had lasted for six weeks at Hyundai Motor's major Ulsan plant, DJ dispatched Roh Moo Hyun, labor lawyer and National Assembly member, to negotiate a settlement. Roh, a determined in-fighter, said there was "no cause to send in the police" after strikers agreed on a compromise. When company executives protested, Roh made clear the government was ready to pressure Hyundai Motor into agreement. "Government-labor negotiations do not exist," he said. "Now there are just government and company negotiations." After the company grimly agreed, union members decamped from the compound they had been occupying. They accepted the loss of 277 jobs, a minimal figure, on the promise of severance pay of seven to nine months' salary. Others would be let go for eight months and then get six months' training for new jobs. Union representatives praised DJ for rebuffing the demands of the owners and managers to send the police into the plant.[24]

The tripartite commission appeared as the solution to strikes that might cripple entire sectors. There was no doubt the rights of workers were improving, but worker unrest was difficult to control. Unemployment one week after the Hyundai Motor strike soared to 7.6 percent, highest in more than 30 years, while exports, the economy's lifeblood, dropped precipitously. Strikes at major companies declined as the country rebounded from crisis, but union leaders often refused to participate in the commission's attempts at intervention. The vaunted commission disintegrated a year after its formation when the KCTU withdrew and the FKTU followed the KCTU example. Strikes against government-owned companies, such as KORAIL, the Korea Railroad, were illegal, beyond the scope of the commission. In the end the commission was not a success.

The labor problem was all the more critical in view of the shrinkage of the motor vehicle industry, one of the most labor-intensive. DJ had to push and prod manufacturers into deals they were slow to make. After the failure of two auctions for Kia Motor, DJ warned that the third auction had to be the last. Hyundai Motor on October 19, 1998, took over Kia, defeating bids by Daewoo Motors and Samsung Motors after Ford was disqualified for failing to bid high enough for Kia's satellite company, Asia Motors. DJ's naiveté was evident in flawed attempts at twisting the arms of *chaebol* chieftains, demanding "voluntary" action, voluntarily or not. He oversaw a "big deal swap" on December 7 for Daewoo Motors to take over Samsung Motors while Samsung Electronics was to get Daewoo Electronics, producer of consumer items like TV sets—an exchange that would never happen. The same day, DJ called on "the tycoons" of the top five *chaebol*, Samsung, Hyundai, LG, SK, and Daewoo, all controlled by founding families, to stop "sabotage and resistance" to restructuring.[25]

The issue of family ownership crystallized tragically around the nation's flagship carrier, Korean Air, the leading company of the Hanjin group, Korea's sixth largest *chaebol*. DJ on April 20, 1999, cited family ownership of the *chaebol* as he blamed the troubles of Korean Air on "mismanagement by the owners of the company and the owners' management style." More than 800 people had died in Korean Air crashes, including 228 when a Boeing 747 slammed into a hill in Guam in August 1997 and 269 when a Soviet MiG fighter shot down a KAL 747 straying into Soviet airspace in September 1983. Korean

Air in 1998 contracted with Delta Air Lines for ten pilots to conduct a safety study, but Delta cancelled the partnership on April 16 after an MD11 cargo jet crashed in Shanghai, killing three crew members and six on the ground. DJ cited Korean Air as "an example" of the problem of ownership by extended families. "Instead of making the best efforts to acquire skilled pilots," he said, owners "concentrate too much on profits."[26] Cho Yang Ho, eldest son of the Hanjin chairman and founder, Cho Choong Hoon, resigned as president, only to become chairman while his father remained group chairman.[27]

The Daewoo empire of founder Kim Woo Choong presented more problems. Daewoo's impending collapse by mid-1999 become all too clear as Kim, responsible for the group's accumulation of $57 billion in debts, resisted reform. While the economy appeared to be recovering, DJ's top aides battled for Daewoo's survival through emergency loans. Like a corporate chairman leaving details to underlings, DJ remained aloof. He indicated his displeasure, however, promising on August 15, 1999, liberation day, to be "the first president" of Korea "to reform *chaebol* and straighten out our economy." His goal, he said, in an echo of his forgotten views on "mass-participatory economy," was for the economy to grow "on the basis of the middle class."[28] The next day, Daewoo agreed to retain 6 of 25 companies, but that plan failed after all of them fell into the hands of creditors, mostly government banks.

On November 1, Kim Woo Choong and a dozen other executives resigned. In hiding in Europe, soon to go on the Interpol list as a wanted man, Kim apologized on November 25, 1999, for "errors of judgment, mistakes and negligence."[29] While the boss remained in exile from which he would not return to face arrest for another five and one-half years, more than 20 Daewoo executives were tried and jailed. General Motors, a partner in his motor vehicle venture until Kim drove GM out in 1982, recovered Daewoo Motors in a complex deal in 2002, two years after Renault, the French manufacturer, had rescued fledgling Samsung Motors in September 2000 by buying most of the equity.

DJ had little to say about the entry of specific foreign companies into Korea's motor vehicle industry. These were maneuvers he viewed from afar, leaving aides to monitor and facilitate. Foreign investment, however, had his blessing as he sought to persuade Koreans to change historically negative attitudes at a time when foreign funds were so needed. He vowed in early 1999 to do away with regulations "hindering foreign investment" and set a goal of $15 billion for the year. In his first 11 months in the Blue House, DJ claimed to have cut by half the "11,000 regulations" that made life difficult for foreign companies.

"This year," he said, "we will make sure the regulations are all abolished." DJ acknowledged the underlying problem. "Koreans in the past have had a very negative attitude toward foreign investment," he said, but "we were able to convince the Korean people" of the need to take a positive view.[30]

Still, foreign investors wondered how much Koreans wanted foreign investment as the economy picked up from the depths of 1998. The *chaebol*, when in need, welcomed transfusions of money, but management control remained in the hands of shadowy family groupings whose inner workings and power relationships, rivalries and trade-offs were largely hidden. DJ's windy promises did not keep Doosan's OB Brewery from rigging the bidding in July 1999 to keep Coors from recovering Jinro Coors. Nor did it stop SK Telecom in August from diluting the holdings of Tiger Management, the U.S. investment fund, in a rights offering.[31]

With DJ showing signs of overconfidence, James Rooney at Templeton Investment Trust warned in January 1999 of "the risk of declaring success prematurely"—and losing competitiveness—"by premature strengthening" of the won. He feared financial institutions were "putting their money in the market rather than the real economy" while eschewing "fundamental changes in the way Korean companies do business."[32] Delegating the task of paring down banks and companies, DJ showed his customary finesse. "DJ had a lot of good people," Rooney said later. "He was a master politician. A total of 2.5 million jobs were lost in the crisis, and those jobs came back. You can give DJ credit for taking good advice. He was clearly astute. He had grown up in a political environment. In his own way he managed to pick his way through that." Later in his presidency, however, DJ's "energy was going elsewhere, on the Sunshine policy," said Rooney. "DJ lost his focus on things that were important, the momentum that drove Korea successfully."[33]

Moody's Investor Service in February 1999 raised Korea's sovereign ratings from junk to investment grade, an international seal of approval. With this endorsement, officials expected the equity and foreign direct investment essential to fulfilling the forecasts of the finance ministry and the IMF of a two percent growth increase in 1999 from 1998 when the economy had registered negative growth between 4 and 5 percent. Moody's cited Korea's "vastly improved external liquidity position" and steps to liberalize foreign investment and "put into place a comprehensive framework for reform and restructuring of the financial and corporate sectors." Thomas J. Byrne, Moody's top analyst of sovereign risk, saw optimism as helpful. "The psychology is changing," he told me. If people feel their jobs and income are more stable, they'll start spending again."[34] A decade after the crisis, however, Byrne remarked that basically "Kim Dae Jung wanted the Nobel prize" while leaving fine-tuning of the economy to subordinates.[35]

In the context of animosity toward those in power since the division of the peninsula in 1945, DJ would be as good as his word in courting North Korea. He talked of "engagement" with the North as a break with the South-style dictatorship under which he had suffered. Thus his rise to the presidency marked a milestone in North-South relations though the policy he enunciated built on the groundwork laid by administrations he had denounced. Under DJ, whatever offences the North would commit, the South would perceive Sunshine. Keeping his promise of reconciliation, he avoided offending the North by any mention of human rights for millions of North Koreans in the throes of famine, disease, and persecution after more than half a century of Communist rule.

"Engagement" began right after DJ's inauguration with word the South was lowering barriers blocking South Korean companies from investing in the North. The government planned "to radically simplify administrative procedures on investment in North Korea," Yonhap reported. The government would more than double the $5 million limit on investment by South Korean companies in North Korea and ease restrictions on travel. The $5 million ceiling, set by YS in 1994, had discouraged all but a handful of investors. Another measure that might encourage investment in North Korea was a proposal for compensating businesses for losses there. While hoping for increased commerce, DJ renewed his call for exchanging envoys and holding reunions between families separated by the Korean War.[36]

South Korea revealed its plans for improving trade with North Korea on the eve of talks in Seoul on March 2, 1998, with a U.S. team led by Charles Kartman, in charge of U.S. diplomacy vis-à-vis the North. Kartman was in Seoul to discuss the next round of four-party talks in Geneva two weeks later among representatives from the Koreas, the United States and China. DJ's aides indicated they would not object if the United States were to recognize the North Korean government in Pyongyang and lift trade sanctions.

As delegates from the four principal Korean War protagonists gathered in Geneva on March 14, there were hopes, said a U.S. diplomat, of moving "beyond sterile debate and into matters of substance." Whether teams from North and South Korea, China, and the United

States could turn rhetoric into action depended on how the North viewed DJ's policies. The talks could be a success if the North budged on one issue that had frustrated a lasting peace—North Korea's refusal to negotiate with South Korea. South Korean and American negotiators delineated goals. Negotiators must discuss the "peace mechanism on the Korean peninsula," including steps for reducing forces, while North-South talks should cover economic cooperation, exchanging envoys and reuniting families separated by the Korean War.[37]

Kim Kye Gwan, North Korea's vice foreign minister, responded with the usual rhetoric. In the first session on March 16, 1998. he reiterated, as he had in the first round of the four-party talks in December 1997, two central points of North Korean policy: the United States had to withdraw its 37,000 troops from the South and negotiate a bilateral peace treaty formally concluding the Korean War. The talks broke down but not before Kim Jong Il on April 18 wrote "an open letter" calling for "a wide-ranging, nationwide dialogue" to bring Koreans together. All Koreans, "North, South, and abroad, must visit one another, hold contacts, promote dialogue and strengthen solidarity," he said.[38] In Seoul, DJ told Japanese editors "in the course of South-North contacts" that he and Kim Jong Il would talk. There was no stopping the Blue House drive to encourage rapprochement through dialogue, if not between governments, then between groups and individuals.[39]

The road to the Pyongyang summit would be treacherous. The patience of Kim Dae Jung was needed to avoid a major rift after North Korea sent a Yugo-class midget submarine into South Korean waters in June 1998, complicating efforts at bringing representatives from North and South together. The submarine, snared in the nets of a South Korean fisherman on June 22, was towed into the east coast port of Sokcho, where a demolition team broke in and found bodies of nine North Korean sailors and agents. The latter, to avoid the capture of any of them, had shot the former and then committed suicide. "This incident will have a serious impact on North-South policy," said the Korean Broadcasting System, but DJ vowed his government would pursue "a flexible North Korea policy."[40]

The Hyundai Group, led by founder Chung Ju Yung, went ahead with plans to open tours to the Mount Kumkang region of North Korea despite the test-firing on August 31, 1998, of a long-range ballistic missile from the village of Musudan-ri, in the district of Taepodong, on North Korea's northeastern coast. Alarmingly to Japan, the missile, dubbed the Taepodong by Americans, not North Koreans, arced over the main Japanese island of Honshu before landing harmlessly in the sea 800 miles from the launch site. By coincidence, KEDO had issued a resolution the same day, August 31, reconfirming the commitment of all the governments to build the twin light-water reactors promised by the 1994 Geneva framework. South Korean officials minimized the missile, calling the firing a politically inspired device to build up Kim Jong Il before a meeting of the Supreme People's Assembly. DJ as always was looking for sunshine in the clouds.

Kim Dae Jung's Sunshine policy and the North's need for money ensured the success of one project that seemed to exist separately from diplomatic or military confrontation. Far from retaliating with sanctions for the missile and submarine incidents, undeterred in the pursuit of Sunshine, South Korea reaffirmed its commitment to 70 percent of the $5 billion cost of building the nuclear power reactors in the North. The South was more anxious than ever to pursue economic ties as the best antidote to North Korean threats. The venture into North-South tourism by the Hyundai Group, with the full backing of the governments of North and South Korea, came to signify the opening of the North to a range of opportunities.

The day after North Korea published a new constitution, on September 6, 1998, naming the late Kim Il Sung as "eternal president," DJ's government authorized Hyundai to ferry boatloads of South Korean tourists on five-day trips to view Mount Kumkang. Hyundai's total investment in the North would come to well above $1 billion. Hyundai planned to pack a maximum of 1,250 tourists for each cruise aboard a chartered vessel from the east coast port of Donghae on a 12-hour journey of 105 miles. The 28,000-ton Hyundai Kumkang left on November 14, 1998, with 441 passengers and 415 crew members. Once cleared through immigration the next morning, the passengers boarded buses for a 10-mile ride and a 2-mile hike, then went on a 14-mile ride and a walk of more than a mile.

U.S. negotiator Kartman arrived in Seoul the next day, November 15, anxious to enlist South Korean support for inspection of a suspected underground nuclear site at Kumchangri, about 25 miles northwest of North Korea's nuclear facilities at Yongbyon. Fighting to avoid damage to Sunshine, DJ noted lack of "conclusive evidence that the intended purpose" was nuclear-related. He agreed, however, on the need for access. William Perry, former U.S. defense secretary, whom Clinton had asked in 1998 to coordinate policy on North Korea, sought to win assurances four months later that China would persuade the North to open Kumchangri for inspection. Stopping off in Seoul on March 8,

Perry viewed DJ's "engagement policy" as "a very important factor" on which to build.[41]

Fears of an imminent crisis were resolved when U.S. and North Korean negotiators, meeting in New York on March 16, agreed on U.S. inspection of Kumchangri in return for 500,000 tons of food aid. The deal called for two inspections, one in May 1999, the next a year later. A 14-person U.S. team arrived in Pyongyang on May 18 for a one-week mission. On May 25, the day after the team was there, having inspected the cave and confirming, to no one's surprise, that the North Koreans had cleared it of anything incriminating, Perry flew to Pyongyang. Lim Dong Won, appointed by DJ as senior secretary for foreign policy and national security soon after his inauguration, saw Perry in Tokyo to fine-tune the message of reconciliation that the South wanted him to deliver, including a plea by DJ for an "inter-Korean summit" with Kim Jong Il.

Sunshine was to endure seemingly insuperable trials before reaching its zenith at the inter-Korean summit of June 2000, the brightest moment of DJ's presidency. One of the most formidable was the confrontation of naval forces in the West Sea that culminated in a 10-minute gun battle on June 15, 1999, in which South Korean ships sank a North Korean gunboat and heavily damaged another North Korean vessel, killing some 40 North Korean sailors. The North Korean vessels retreated from south of the Northern Limit Line, the marker on maps that the North refused to recognize, beneath which boats from the North were not to venture even on fishing expeditions. DJ stuck to his own guns, defending his "policy of warm partnership" with the North as the way to "peace on the Korean peninsula" and ordering a shipment of fertilizer as U.S. warplanes crisscrossed the skies. "Negative factors have not been eliminated completely," he acknowledged, but North and South were "beginning to cooperate on exchanges in many areas including economic and cultural fields."[42]

CHAPTER TEN

Sunshine at Its Zenith

Lim Dong Won, now unification minister, back from talks with William Perry, said on August 29, 1999, that the United States was ready to "relax economic punishment" and expand relations with North Korea if the North abandoned plans to test-fire Taepodong-2 on August 31, first anniversary of the firing of the first long-range Taepodong on August 31, 1998. Lim hoped North Korea and the United States would come to terms in talks between Charles Kartman and Kim Kye Gwan in Berlin. American, Japanese, and South Korean alarm increased as Taepodong-2 was rolled onto the launch pad at Musudan-ri under the watchful eyes of spy satellites. The result was vindication for Sunshine when the North agreed on September 12 not to launch the dreaded missile. Kim Dae Jung, President Clinton, and Japan's Prime Minister Keizo Obuchi got the word in Auckland during the annual session of APEC, the Asia-Pacific Economic Cooperation group. "We agreed to make further efforts to solve apprehensions," said Kim Kye Gwan.[1]

The maneuvering showed the powerful influence of Lim, the architect of Sunshine, in the first phases of the tortuous process of rapprochement. Driven by DJ's urgent desire to keep up the momentum before talk of a summit bogged down amid economic problems at home and lukewarm support from the new U.S. administration, Lim masterminded policy for DJ against a drumbeat of rising criticism from political foes. Elevated in December 1999 from unification minister to the omnipotent post of director of the National Intelligence Service, Lim in his first year as intelligence chief established three main avenues for dealing with a regime that had previously seemed unapproachable.

First, he formed a liaison office at the truce "village" of Panmunjom, in the demilitarized zone that had divided the two Koreas since the Korean War. From there, NIS officials could telephone and fax their North Korean contacts. Although the NIS denied direct links between Seoul and Pyongyang, the agency patched calls through to Pyongyang directly from its barricaded granitic headquarters complex in a wooded greenbelt on the southern fringe of the capital. Then, at Lim's behest, one of his top deputies, Kim Bo Hyun, opened a dialogue with North Korean officials in Beijing in early 2000 while negotiating for the summit. Kim Bo Hyun led the NIS division that specialized in North Korean affairs both in classic intelligence-gathering and, since Lim took over NIS, in negotiations and contacts at all levels.

Lim, who had fled the North at age 17 as Chinese troops were driving out UN forces in January 1951, revisited Pyongyang in secret in May 2000 to negotiate the agenda for the June summit, including the joint statement to be issued by Kim Dae Jung and Kim Jong Il. DJ's foes found Lim an easy target for one basic reason. In pursuit of rapprochement, they charged, the president and the NIS chief compromised the mission of the NIS as a gatherer of intelligence on the North—and on subversion in the South. The marriage between the dreams of DJ and the expertise of Lim Dong Won evolved in the long years before DJ's victory in December 1997 at the height of South Korea's economic crisis.

While DJ turned to people from his native Cholla for aid and advice, he found that Lim suited his interests as a former general who, unlike virtually all other senior military people, had come to adopt a "liberal" outlook toward the North. The son of a Christian pastor in North Korea who was executed during the Korean War, Lim attended the Korea Military Academy after settling in the South and for years shared the strongly anticommunist views of his fellow officers. At the same time, he developed a reputation as "a scholar-soldier," writing a book called *Revolutionary Wars and anti-Communist Strategy*.[2] Ambitious and hardworking, Lim was by no means purged after he was forced to retire in 1980 as Chun consolidated his rule with cronies from around Daegu. Exiled as ambassador to Nigeria and Australia as DJ was going on trial, he returned to Seoul eight years later as head of the foreign ministry's Institute of Foreign Affairs and National Security.

Gravitating to the center of power as deputy chief of the unification board under Roh Tae Woo, Lim was able to advance his softline views on trips to Pyongyang in 1991 during which he argued for the Agreement on Reconciliation, Non-Aggression, Exchanges and Cooperation that took effect in February 1992. Lim's origins in North Korea inspired suspicions, however, when the North Koreans set up a meeting with a long-lost sister in the North. The experience made him receptive to DJ's overtures. In early 1995, he joined DJ's camp as secretary-general of his Asia-Pacific Peace Foundation, a base for DJ's power ambitions—and a receptacle for "donations."

In promoting an inter-Korean summit, formally proposed in DJ's inaugural address, Lim realized that one of the main challenges was to convince the Americans. His meetings with Perry had a significant influence on "the Perry Review" in which Perry recommended a moderate approach toward the North. Lim's talks with Perry were in turn part of a strategy that paralleled the ongoing secret talks that Kim Bo Hyun had been conducting in Beijing since December 1998 after the North had indicated its interest in dialogue.

The signal for an inter-Korean summit was passed through top executives of the Hyundai group, Hyundai group founder Chung Ju Yung and one of his sons, Chung Mong Hun, Chung's fifth son and chairman of Hyundai Asan, the Hyundai firm responsible for dealings with the North, including trade and investment. They bore the word on getting back from a trip to Pyongyang in December 1998, after which Lim ordered Kim Bo Hyun to meet with North Korean representatives in Beijing.

A year and three months later, on March 9, 2000, near the end of the talks in Beijing, Kim Dae Jung enunciated his "Berlin Declaration" at the Free University of Berlin, announcing, "We are willing to provide the infrastructure" needed to jumpstart the North's collapsed economy.[3] The Berlin Declaration caught American diplomats by surprise. The Blue House had not told them about it. With the Perry review out, however, they had to endorse it. The U.S. administration was now on the side of whatever DJ wanted.

Park Jie Won, formerly DJ's spokesman, now his culture minister, entered the dialogue, going to Beijing on March 17, 2000, to work out the announcement in April that the two Kims would meet at the summit in June. Lim Dong Won twice flew to Pyongyang to meet Kim Jong Il. Although Park was credited with negotiating details, the process when he came upon the scene was almost finished. One mystery was why he, together with Kim Bo Hyun, had to make a secret trip to Singapore in March for another meeting with deputies on North Korea's Asia-Pacific Peace Committee. The purpose of the Singapore trip was evidently to negotiate conditions for the summit, including an initial secret payoff of $450 million plus $50 million in unspecified goods for the regime.

Such a payoff was necessary in a society where bribery, often in the guise of gift-giving, is a longstanding tradition. A banking center, Singapore was one place outside North Korea and China where contacts were convenient among highly placed figures from both Koreas.[4] The payments were done in dollars, not Euros, even though North Korea decided to make the Euro its preferred foreign exchange currency while banning the dollar. Considering North Korea's financial desperation, Kim Jong Il would probably have been glad to have met any South Korean leader in return for a huge cash infusion. There was no reason to have cloaked the payoffs in secrecy other than the need, for the campaign for the Nobel, to make it appear as if Kim Jong Il seriously wanted reconciliation rather than money.

While Kim Dae Jung's historic journey was in the critical planning stage, a court placed the Reverend Moon Kyu Hyun on probation for having gone to North Korea in 1998 without authorization.[5] It was significant that the court suspended a two-year jail term since the same Catholic priest had been jailed in 1989 for going to North Korea during student activist Im Su Kyong's visit nearly a decade earlier. The time was ripe for a legion of clergy, business people, academicians, politicians, athletes and assorted others to make the trek—all important steps on the way to the Nobel. A trusted aide, Kim Han Jung, coordinating the quest for the Nobel, was also believed to have met Kim Jong Il's oldest son, Kim Jong Nam, in Japan in December 1999 to talk about terms for the summit, clearly critical for the Nobel, and iron out financial details.

DJ by early 2000 was obsessed by National Assembly elections coming up on April 14 in which corruption had become a major issue. North Korea lived up to the bargain in terms of DJ's timing. Several days before the elections, North Korea agreed to host the summit in June. The sensational announcement provided a last-minute burst for candidates of DJ's Millennium Democratic Party, its latest brand name. In a campaign dominated by the usual name-calling and scandal-mongering, however, the conservative Grand National Party won a plurality, 133 seats to 115 for DJ's Millennium Democrats. DJ was steadily losing support amid apathy and hostility created by economic difficulties but hoped to catch up with the help of independents and his reluctant coalition partner, Kim Jong Pil's depleted United Liberal Democrats, plus a few members from the anti-American Democratic Labor Party.

There were still vital issues to settle before the summit in June. DJ did not want to discover, on arriving in Pyongyang, that his interlocutor would not be Kim Jong Il but the titular head of state, Kim Yong Nam, chairman of the standing committee of the Supreme People's Assembly. That concern was eased early in May when the NIS received a message interpreted as meaning the summit was a done deal. The message was a simple question, "Will we have the chance to taste traditional food?" Since Kim Jong Il was known for gourmet tastes, the sense among NIS and Blue House officials was that all was in order. Taking no chances, however, Lim then journeyed to Pyongyang via Beijing. On June 13, as Kim Jong Il prepared to meet Kim Dae Jung, a large refrigerator van passed through Panmunjom carrying the makings of the farewell dinner that DJ would host for Kim Jong Il—to be cooked in Pyongyang by some of Seoul's best chefs.

Could there have been a more unusual backdrop to a summit? Kim Dae Jung hedged bets whenever he talked about the unprecedented mission on which he would embark on June 12. He did not want South Koreans to get their hopes up. As he and his aides persisted in saying, the summit might not produce substantive results. Its value, they said, was for the two Kims to be meeting, getting to know one another—and laying the groundwork for future summits. If the talks got nowhere, there might be an adverse reaction in the South and fast-diminishing support for Sunshine. DJ would regard the trip as a triumph if Kim Jong Il would agree on a return visit to South Korea, possibly on August 15, the holiday celebrated in both Koreas in honor of liberation from Japanese rule.

For all the high-level disclaimers, however, Koreans saw the summit as about the biggest, most promising thing to happen in the cause of permanent peace on the Korean peninsula since the signing of the ceasefire that had ended the Korean War. Just for starters, DJ went to Pyongyang on Monday, June 13, by plane—the first direct flight from Seoul to Pyongyang since the fall of 1950 when U.S. troops rolled up the peninsula before the Chinese came into the war in November and pushed them back again. DJ returned by road—a symbol of the possibilities of opening the border at Panmunjom to regular traffic. In between, Koreans in both North and South witnessed scenes live on TV that until recently had been unimaginable—the two Kims shaking hands, mouthing pleasantries, concluding with a joint declaration calling for reconciliation, cooperation, maybe, some day, reunification.

No one expected North and South Korea to sign a peace treaty formally ending the Korean War. Still, there was an irrepressible feeling in Seoul that this time South and North Koreans had gone beyond generalities and talked sensibly about the incredible range of issues that still impeded North-South rapprochement. Department stores in Seoul were selling North Korean products, such as herbs and liquor. Vendors were peddling T-shirts with pictures of Kim Dae Jung and Kim Jong Il. Books about North Korea were on display. The South Korean government authorized the showing of a North Korean movie and the airing of a few North Korean songs. It was as though North Korea had become trendy even as people expressed doubts that anything much would come of the talks.

The summit, however, was also disillusioning. There was no agenda—something the South Koreans had wanted but the North Koreans opposed. The two leaders theoretically were free to discuss anything, according to Park Jie Won, who had held secret talks in early April with North Korean officials in Beijing and Shanghai. Such freedom meant that they could enlarge on the generalities of the South-North joint communiqué of July 4, 1972, resulting from the North-South Red Cross talks. That document called for adherence to such noble principles as "unification" free of "foreign interference" and cooperation on reuniting millions of families divided by the Korean War. In the years since the signing, however, North-South relations had deteriorated precipitously; only a handful of families were briefly reunited in a single exchange in 1985.

Without an agenda, Kim Dae Jung could not begin to confront Kim Jong Il on the manufacture and export of long-range missiles capable of delivering anything from conventional high-explosives to nuclear warheads to chemical and biological ordnance thousands of miles. DJ sidestepped that issue, listing discussion of a "peace regime" as one of the topics in which he was interested. By adhering to that phraseology, he avoided North Korean demands for withdrawal of U.S. troops from the South. The all-embracing phrase "peace regime" suggested a program for decreasing military establishments on both sides of the demilitarized zone without fixing a schedule.

Surely, however, Kim Jong Il had specific aims in mind in receiving the leader from the South. One had to assume there would have been no summit if the North were not driven by desperation. There were recurring reports of widespread famine in which approximately two million people in the North had starved in the preceding five years. Factories were shut down. The infrastructure was decrepit. If the summit accomplished nothing else, as far as the North was concerned, it would vastly increase prospects for more economic aid. Toward that end, Kim Jong Il hoped to enlist the support of South Korea in persuading the United States to lift the "terrorist" label applied to the North and do away with economic sanctions. He also wanted the United States to speed up shipment of "heavy oil" needed to fuel the economy during construction of the twin nuclear reactors agreed on in Geneva in 1994. Kim Jong Il had even considered suggestions made by Chinese leaders during a trip to Beijing at the end of May that the North consider a market economy to revive dead industries and provide incentives for farmers.

If the summit itself were to be more than an exercise in symbolism, some of the business leaders and officials accompanying DJ would, in separate talks with the North Koreans, have to get down to details. The tradeoff was obvious—DJ might be more amenable to assisting the North economically if the North would agree to his top priority, the reunion of families. And North Korea might go along with an elaborate program for bringing families together if the price were right.

There was solid precedent. The North had compelled the Hyundai group, the South's largest conglomerate, to agree to spend $1 billion on a new hotel and other forms of infrastructure for the privilege of transporting South Korean tourists to the Mount Kumkang region. Once the North had abolished some of the rules and regulations that made investing difficult at best, impossible at worst, the South might be in a mood to authorize another $1 billion to set up a center for family reunions, just one of the deals that people in Seoul were speculating might emerge. The real question, though, was how long the process would last—how many more summits and "working-level" meetings would be needed for a real breakthrough. The answer would be a measure of the urgency the North attached to relief from suffering that might otherwise endanger its ruling establishment, possibly "Dear Leader" Kim Jong Il.

The summit invited comparisons to another case of divided countries—the division between the People's Republic of China, "mainland China" in the Western media and mindset, and the Republic of China, Taiwan. Both cases had one element in common. The divisions of nations were characterized by terrible wars between Communist and capitalist or, as they said in Taiwan, "nationalist" forces, the remnants of the Kuomintang that Generalissimo Chiang Kai-shek had led to defeat before fleeing to his new island home as Mao Zedong's Red Army approached final victory on October 1, 1949.

The division of the "two Chinas" also shared another salient characteristic with that of the Korean peninsula—both divisions were shaped by the same outside forces, Russia, the United States and Japan as well as the Chinese. The comparison quickly broke down, however, when one considered that China was a giant, Taiwan a small island state, whereas North and South Korea divided the peninsula geographically, as decreed in the conferences of allied powers in the latter phases of World War II.

One could go on citing differences between the two cases, that is China/Taiwan and North/South Korea, in population, wealth, and attitudes, but the prospect of talks between North and South Korea held out hope for Korea and the region, including China and Taiwan. The fact that the leaders of the two "halves" of the Korean nation could meet one another after the peninsula was divided not in deals between Koreans but in far-off negotiations by two huge foreign powers, the United States and Soviet Union, demonstrated that not all heavily armed confrontations had to result in debilitating war. This initial North-South summit, if all went well, could result in traffic, trade, mail, communications, and visits directly across the DMZ. The summit would engender high hopes if the North were persuaded to accept such contacts as a matter of common sense, not just humanitarian or propagandistic gestures.

As the visit of the North Korean leader, Kim Jong Il, to Beijing had already made clear, China exercised a qualified influence over the North even though the DPRK rejected Chinese advice to reform and open its economy. China's leaders had been instrumental in persuading Kim Jong Il to agree to talks. They had also been advising the North Koreans of the need to introduce capitalist touches to their economy. If the Chinese could expect to prosper economically in a system that mingled communism with capitalism, so could the North Koreans. There appeared to be no other way to pull the North Korean economy from the depths of poverty.

The stubbornness of the North Koreans in promoting their system, in seeming to believe they would eventually control all the Korean peninsula, was matched only by the Chinese insistence on a one-China policy in which Taiwan had to kowtow to Beijing as a province of China. Politically, China repeatedly shut the door to compromise. Negotiations between the newly installed president of the Republic of China, or Taiwan, and his counterpart in Beijing were not going to happen. On a different level, however, China had for years engaged in compromise. Taiwan business leaders engaged in trade and investment with China to a degree hardly imagined by the hereditary leaders of South Korea's *chaebol* with North Korea. Taiwan businessmen routinely went to China via Hong Kong, and commerce moved between China and Taiwan by sea—perhaps not publicly acknowledged but still carried on. Thus China set an example for North Korea—one that North Korea now might follow.

It was still possible to be pessimistic about the outlook for long-term peace. The North Korean military establishment was so large, and the North so successful in building missiles and weapons of mass destruction, that there was every likelihood of using these threats whenever in need of food, fertilizer, and assistance. There was no certainty that some day North Korea might not be tempted again to take on South Korea militarily, particularly if the South were to drop its defenses while the U.S. withdrew guarantees of ground, air and naval support and failed to provide the latest weaponry. The threat of U.S. retaliation remained a powerful deterrent to such aggressive aims. Just as it was hard to imagine shells falling on Taiwan, so it was difficult to conjure the nightmare of a "second Korean War" engulfing the Korean peninsula.

The best outcome for the Korean confrontation remained a policy of live-and-let-live in which South and North came to terms on relations that were normal between states in peacetime. Since the people of both Koreas shared the same language, were from the same cultural and ethnic backgrounds, it seemed logical the two Koreas would some day close ranks in common cause against surrounding great powers, China, Japan, and Russia as well as the United States. These countries had always seen an advantage, not admitted or acknowledged, in divide-and-rule in which they exercised influence both north and south of the demilitarized zone. The inter-Korean summit would be a success if it contributed to decreasing tensions on all sides. Ideally, North and South Korea, like China and Taiwan, should recognize the advantages of getting along with each other, economically, culturally, and politically, while foreswearing bellicose policies that risked another war.

Kim Dae Jung's arrival at Pyongyang's Sunan Airport at 10:25 a.m., June 13, after a flight of one hour and seven minutes from Seoul Airport, the military terminal at the K-16 base southeast of the capital, provided one of the happiest photo opportunities of modern Korean history. In contrast to all the shots of war and killing, of mass protests and demonstrations, the image of Kim Jong Il embracing DJ on the red carpet before a military honor guard offered hope after half a century of armed conflict and venomous rhetoric. Footage of the two leaders cruising in a motorcade into Pyongyang, cheered by 600,000 citizens decked out in their finest traditional clothing, was almost as compelling. In a gesture well choreographed in advance, Kim Jong Il ordered the motorcade to stop long enough for both to get out and shake hands like politicians on the campaign trail. For the benefit of TV cameras, the motorcade wended its way by the Supreme People's Assembly, the War Memorial and the huge bronze statue of the Dear Leader's father, Great Leader Kim Il Sung, on the six-mile route to the Paekhwawon guesthouse.

DJ was accompanied by 130 top bureaucrats, politcos, and business leaders, including Chung Mong Hun, whose financial finagling would be exposed as vital in making it all happen. With 50 South Korean journalists also in tow, DJ was treated as the most important visitor ever to set foot in the North Korean capital. Overwhelming success was prescripted. "The unification delegation from the South must live up to our expectations," an anonymous North Korean was quoted as telling Yonhap.[6] The two sat down for hard talk on June 14 before coming up with a joint declaration the next day. As General Hwang Won Duk, one of DJ's advisers, described the conversation, DJ wanted more than pro forma verbiage. "If we were to repeat our past practice of restating general principles, this summit will be meaningless," said DJ as quoted by Hwang, who sat through the conversation. "Instead, we must discuss practical matters, those items that can be achieved realistically, and present them to our people as tangible gifts."[7]

Hwang reported after getting back to Seoul on intriguing interplay. "The Korean problems must be resolved by the Koreans themselves," he quoted Kim Jong Il as saying. "Don't you agree?" To which DJ responded: "Yes, indeed. That is what we have been asking for and we agree with you completely." In response to Kim Jong Il's question, "Then why do you promote your alliance with the United States and Japan to stifle us," DJ replied: "That is a misunderstanding on your part. The three-nation alliance is not for the three nations to conspire to destroy you. On the contrary, it is to help you. Why should we help you? The alliance was formed in 1998 to coordinate the three nations' dealings with North Korea." His own "North policy," DJ assured Kim Jong Il, "is 'Sunshine' for peace, reconciliation and cooperation," and it was "because of my Sunshine policy that we are here today." Indeed, "Our policy of reconciliation is to help you—not to destroy you," and "the three-nation alliance is to support my Sunshine policy."[8]

DJ also wanted it understood, while the United States was "our ally," that South Korea received assistance from China and Russia in the form of deals on trade and investment and that Japan and the United

States "have been trying to normalize relations with you." DJ's logic: "We have also advised you to make peace with these nations. If we were after your neck, why would we be seeking normalization with you?" But did Kim Jong Il really say, as DJ later alleged, that he wanted American troops to stay on bases in South Korea, providing geopolitical "balance" against conniving powers? Hwang failed to mention any such remark, raising a serious question as to whether DJ made the claim to mollify U.S. officials and conservative South Koreans dubious about his overture to a sworn enemy whose propaganda machine frequently called for withdrawal of all American forces.

The joint declaration as proclaimed the next day, June 15, did not repeat the empty rhetoric of the agreements of 1972 and 1992. Rather, said Hwang, this one emphasized "practical steps toward unification." The two Koreas would achieve unification without outside interference, merging the North's proposal for "federation" with the concept of "confederation" long espoused by DJ. They would "settle humanitarian issues," reuniting families divided by the Korean War, and they would cooperate economically, opening up social and cultural exchanges. And, one final point: Kim Jong Il would pay a return visit to Seoul.[9] If those promises appeared to go further than previous declarations, however, they were so vague as to leave plenty of scope for Kim Jong Il to back away from them. Just as Kim would never consider a trip to Seoul, so talk of "federation" and "confederation," viewed as a sellout by South Korean conservatives, was not likely to advance beyond the level of abstraction without upheaval in both Koreas.

Lim Dong Won, who also sat through the conversation between DJ and Kim Jong Il, offered no evidence of Kim Jong Il's enthusiasm for keeping U.S. troops in South Korea. Rather, as Lim later recounted, the Dear Leader said he would hardly mind if American troops stayed on provided they abandoned their anti-DPRK position—in other words, became a ceremonial force with no strength at all. Lim elaborated on Kim's feelings about the United States and his eagerness to soothe any fears DJ might have about reconciliation. "Kim distrusts the United States," Lim wrote in his memoir. "He is afraid of the United States. But he desperately hopes to normalize relations with the United States." As director of the South's National Intelligence Service at the time, Lim played up the relations that he had formed with Kim Jong Il. "If you have problems in putting our agreements into practice," Lim quoted the Dear Leader as remarking to DJ after the signing of the joint declaration, "please send Mr. Lim to Pyongyang frequently." A bonus, said Lim, was installation of a North-South hotline in response to DJ's proposing it. "That is a good idea," Kim replied. "Let's put it up"—a feat that Lim called "one of the summit's greatest achievements" as a conduit for resolving differences and arranging high-level inter-Korean visits.[10]

No sooner had DJ come home to a triumphant welcome after three days of greeting and meeting Kim Jong Il, however, than the hoopla faded into questions about how much he had accomplished. "The agreement was short on concrete detail," said Han Sung Joo, foreign minister in 1994 when the United States and North Korea negotiated the Geneva framework. "There is too much emphasis on matters of principle. We should think of it as a start rather than a finished product."[11]

Accustomed to deep disappointment in dealings with the North, analysts believed the agreement at least offered more hope than two other "landmark" pieces of paper that yielded disappointing results in the long run. "The possibilities of implementation are higher than in 1972 and 1992," said Choi Won Ki, specialist on North Korean affairs for the conservative newspaper *JoongAng Ilbo*, even though the North-South agreements of those years covered much the same points as those discussed at the summit. Choi was "disappointed," however, that the two leaders had not agreed on details for reuniting families and, on a broader scale, that their declaration did not specifically allude to "peace" or "reduction of tensions."[12]

Such comments typified the mixed opinions of commentators and editorialists as they evaluated what the summit had really meant, who, if anyone, was likely to benefit—and whether the initial rush of enthusiasm would endure. Among the most skeptical was South Korea's biggest-selling newspaper, *Chosun Ilbo*, a long-time conservative critic. *Chosun Ilbo*'s biggest concern was that the euphoria of the summit might undermine South Korean security, buttressed by the presence of those 37,000 U.S. troops. "North Korea has long made unreasonable demands of us, demands we could never accept as part of negotiations, such as the withdrawal of U.S. troops," the newspaper editorialized. "We still have to wonder whether there has been actual change in this area." There was no way to be sure "that the North is not just putting on a show for the sake of practical advantage."[13]

JoongAng Ilbo, while more enthusiastic, reflected much the same concern. "The two leaders agreed to 'achieve reunification independently,'" said the newspaper, noting that the North had previously "insisted that 'independence' means the denunciation and rejection of foreign powers" and "ejection of U.S. troops." If the North had transformed its attitude "from its former hostility," it said, the summit "could indeed be heralded as a tremendous victory." Otherwise, the paper warned, the summit could become "a major stumbling block to progress."[14]

Debate over the meaning, significance, and value of the summit was sure to boil over into national politics, where DJ faced severe opposition. The Grand National Party, which held a majority in the assembly, charged that a pledge to work for "national unification in an independent manner" was an invitation for North Korea to demand withdrawal of U.S. troops. The party also worried that the joint declaration of the summit said nothing about "curbing mass destructive weapons such as nuclear warheads and missiles." The government team responsible for planning the summit sought to put a positive spin on it all by distributing "an analysis of the outcome" of the talks. The document said the two Kims had "confirmed that they have no intention of invading the other side" and would "refrain from any acts threatening the other side." Thus, it said, the summit had contributed "to the elimination of international apprehensions about instability on the Korean peninsula."[15]

As negotiators from North and South Korea edged toward inter-Korean reconciliation on July 30, 2000, specific agreements marked the first significant steps beyond the general principles of goodwill enunciated at the summit. The two negotiating teams issued a joint statement committing their governments to regular talks between ministers, reopening liaison offices and designating a week of reconciliation surrounding the August 15 holiday. The agreement signaled the desire of both Koreas to keep up the momentum of the summit.

The negotiators appeared, however, to have avoided one major topic—that of a return visit to Seoul by Kim Jong Il. The understanding at the inter-Korean summit was that the North Korean leader would visit the South Korean capital in the near future, but the date was never set. Negotiators also avoided any mention of the military impasse that had left the Korean peninsula divided since the Korean War. The U.S. secretary of state, Madeleine Albright, raised the topic of the threat posed by North Korean missiles when she met Paek Nam Sun, the North Korean foreign minister, at the regional forum of the Association of Southeast Asian Nations (ASEAN) in Bangkok on July 28, 2000, six weeks after the summit, but admitted failing to "glean" much from the brief conversation.

American diplomats were playing a careful game. Albright after the forum warned against feeling overly confident about prospects for peace. The United States had to get along with DJ as the leader of one of America's closest allies. The U.S. ambassador to Korea, Stephen Bosworth, in just about every speech he made, aligned U.S. policy with Sunshine. Nobody spoke more optimistically than American policy makers about rapprochement bursting forth. They did not want to appear dubious about DJ. A misstep, a misstatement could upset South Korean leaders as they built up the summit before the high-sounding expressions of the joint declaration were forgotten in another round of North-South acrimony.

Similarly, the Americans prayed that no untoward incident would provide more ammunition for anti-American demonstrators. It was because of such sensitivity that the American military command made an abject apology in July for dumping into the Han River about 20 gallons of formaldehyde from the American mortuary in the U.S. headquarters complex at Yongsan after a worker at the base exposed the deed. The question, however, was whether U.S. forces in Korea could endure for long in a time of heightened concerns. American commanders were impatient with demands that they give up training at the bombing and strafing range in Maehyang-ri, about fifty miles southwest of Seoul, which the U.S. command finally had to abandon. They were annoyed by South Korean reluctance to engage in joint exercises that might offend the North and were miffed by demonstrations outside American bases. Were not U.S. troops there to defend the South, to guarantee the freedom to protest, the Americans asked. Not really, South Koreans would respond, they were there to defend American interests.[16]

Not unexpectedly, support for reconciliation was strongest in the first few days after the summit. A survey conducted by the unification ministry on June 17 and June 18, 2000, showed that 96.7 percent of respondents believed it had been very effective while a mere 2.3 percent said it had not. The primary reason cited for admiring the summit was that it had happened—43 percent of those polled cited the holding of the summit as the most important aspect of the meeting while 29.1 percent were most impressed by the prospect of inter-Korean family reunions and 11.3 percent by the possibilities for finding common interests that would lead to reunification. A mere 7.8 percent cited deals on economic cooperation, 5.1 percent Kim Jong Il's promise to come to Seoul and three percent the agreement on North-South communications.[17]

In the newly engendered atmosphere of goodwill and friendship, 78.7 percent of respondents said that Kim Jong Il would be most welcome in Seoul as opposed to 14.9 percent who would not welcome him, five percent who would welcome him even though they did not think he should come and only one percent who neither agreed he should come nor were prepared to welcome him. Views on whether the North would keep promises made at the summit were less favorable. A majority 55.6 percent had confidence in the North while 32 percent did not. Nearly the same majority—55.3 percent—favored providing rice for North Korea while 42.6 percent disapproved. Reasons for sending aid ranged from the fact that all Koreans were of the same nation, as noted by 58.3 percent of respondents, to the desire to promote a peaceful relationship, cited by 15.1 percent, to needs to form a national economic community, 13.4 percent, and to establish peace on the Korean peninsula, 8.6 percent.[18]

The lure of reconciliation would remain a powerful force a year after the summit when DJ hoped that Kim Jong Il would express firmly his determination to come to the South. As a prerequisite for Kim Jong Il to make this commitment, the North had not only to see the results of the review of policy under the fledgling American president, George W. Bush, elected just five months after the summit, but to conclude that the Bush people stood for continuity in the policy of the Clinton administration, which had expressed total approbation of Sunshine.

North-South negotiations after the June 2000 summit focused on issues that might clear the way to reconciliation—and possibly to reunifying the peninsula in the distant future. The agreement to "normalize liaison offices" reflected "the spirit" of the declaration as did an understanding on reconstructing the North-South rail link that was bombed out in the first months of the Korean War. Reconstruction of the railway could lead to normal inter-Korean commerce—something not seen since Japanese colonial days. Although the two countries were doing several hundred million dollars worth of trade a year, all goods moved by sea—several times more expensive than by land.

North and South Korea escalated their pursuit of reconciliation into the fall of 2000 amid mounting criticism in Seoul—and speculation that DJ would win the Nobel. In the onrush of contacts with the North since the summit, NIS Director Lim Dong Won insured continuity by broadening the structure for dealing with the North inside the NIS and installing the expertise and equipment to support it. He starred in a one-man show in implementing Kim Dae Jung's wishes, stage-managing policy from his aerie in the NIS headquarters, rarely appearing in public. Under his instructions, the NIS after the summit coordinated with the North on visits of members of divided families and talks on reopening rail links and on supplying the North with electric power, food, and fertilizer.

If colleagues described Lim as "quiet and scholarly," he broke his rule against public appearances when he was seen in September 2000 accompanying Kim Yong Sun, founder of the North's Asia-Pacific Peace Committee, to Jeju Island, the Pohang Iron and Steel plant at Pohang and other centers. "People are wondering how the director of our National Intelligence Service could be Secretary Kim Yong Sun's personal escort for almost the entire duration of his visit," editorialized the critical *Chosun Ilbo*. "The work of the director of the NIS is to protect the country from espionage, terror, and threats both foreign and domestic," the paper lectured. "This is supposed to be done in as much secrecy as possible."[19]

The critics were not mollified when Kim Yong Sun's sortie to Jeju turned out to have been a prelude to an unprecedented meeting there between the defense ministers of the two Koreas—and, it was rumored, to Kim Jong Il's promised visit to Seoul. "Lim Dong Won is a defender of our system, but he seems to serve Kim Jong Il, head of our main enemy, with utmost reverence," said a spokesman for the Grand National Party. "Lim should resign." Lim got upset by shrill attacks on his tactics and strategy. "He has requested reporters not to write about him," said Cho Gab Je, author of a book on the intelligence service and editor-in-chief of the *Monthly Chosun*. "He wants to be left alone from internal politics. He provided extraordinary service for the president. For most, however, it has been a risky position. Historically, many people have been jailed or killed after serving as director of the KCIA."[20]

Despite his legacy of success in the secret history of Sunshine, Lim was acutely aware of the danger he faced while wary of antagonizing the North. On October 7, 20 representatives of both government and nongovernmental organizations flew to Pyongyang aboard a North Korean plane for observances the next day marking the 55th anniversary of the founding of the North Korean Workers' Party. At the same time, North Korea's second most powerful leader, Jo Myong Rok, left Pyongyang for meetings with the three Americans with the greatest influence on U.S. policy on Korea—President Clinton, Secretary of State Albright and Defense Secretary William Cohen.

This sequence appeared to bring efforts at rapprochement to a new level even as DJ's foes stepped up their campaign against its pace and form. The South Korean government, after ruling that no one could accept invitations to attend the Workers' Party celebration, imposed one condition. Nobody from the South, said the unification ministry, could comment on the observances while in Pyongyang. Critics charged DJ with falling for North Korean propaganda in the run-up to announcement of the winner of the Nobel Peace Prize at the end of the week. Aides of the president, nominated annually for the Nobel from the mid-1980s until he got it, believed the prize, besides giving him the recognition he deserved, would counter domestic critics.

The Grand National Party accused the government of compromising with the North from the moment the summit was over. Denouncing the government's "unprincipled policies," *Chosun Ilbo* said the Workers' Party observance was an occasion for the party to "reconfirm its legitimacy and its basic tenet regarding communization of the peninsula." Hwang Ha Soo, a senior unification ministry official, defending the decision, argued that South Koreans were too "mature" to fall for North Korean propaganda.[21]

The Workers' Party staged its celebration even as Jo Myong Rok met Albright as the highest level North Korean visitor ever to go to Washington. Jo, who served as vice chairman of North Korea's National Defense Commission, chaired by Kim Jong Il, was viewed as more powerful than Kim Yong Nam, chairman of the presidium of the Supreme People's Assembly and titular head of state. At the top of Jo's agenda during his visit from October 9 to October 12 was North Korea's drive for final removal from the State Department list of countries supporting terrorism—a prerequisite, in the North's view, for opening diplomatic missions in each other's capitals. Washington insisted on proof the North was taking definite steps to prove it was no longer a terrorist state. U.S. leaders, raising such issues as the export of ballistic missiles to middle east countries, wanted to know if the North were really abiding by the 1994 Geneva agreement.

DJ had high hopes of U.S. support for reconciliation when Madeleine Albright journeyed to Pyongyang on October 22, 2000, to reason with Kim Jong Il. It was apparent, though, that Kim's purpose was to turn her visit into an occasion for his own propaganda coup when he inveigled her into committing one of the great blunders of U.S. diplomatic history, having her and her subordinate and friend, Wendy Sherman, stand beside him at a gigantic display of rhetoric and propaganda in May First Stadium. Albright and Sherman had to watch as posterholders in the packed stands flashed cards to portray the test-launch more than two years earlier, on August 31, 1998, of the long-range Taepodong missile.

"In our meetings, Kim and I mixed tough talk about human rights and military intentions with more reflective discussions about the reasons for our lack of mutual trust," Albright wrote. "It became evident to me the longer we talked," she concluded, "that Kim was prepared to trade military concessions for a combination of economic help and security guarantees."[22]

Albright seemed to believe the man whom she addressed as "chairman," in deference to his post as chairman of the all-powerful National Defense Commission, when he assured her there would be no more Taepodong missile launches. This promise was made only to be broken, as happened when Taepodong-2 was launched on an abortive flight on July 5, 2006, flying briefly from the coastal site at Kumho before plunging into the sea in a trajectory that resembled that of a giant Roman candle in a fireworks display, and again on April 5, 2009, when a second Taepodong-2 was fired on a mission whose sole purpose, North Korea insisted, was to put a satellite into orbit.[23] Kim did not appear to have offered Albright any such reassurance about testing nuclear warheads, which she may not have thought was likely until North Korea conducted its first underground nuclear test, a small half-kiloton blast that may have been a failure, on October 9, 2006, and another, more powerful one, estimated at four kilotons, on May 25, 2009.

Albright's gullibility in judging Kim Jong Il became clear more than seven years after her visit when North Korea, having agreed a year after its first underground nuclear test, to a timetable for disabling its nuclear complex and itemizing its inventory, delayed turning over the list. "Frankly, I was surprised," she told me. Asked whether she really believed Kim Jong Il would reveal his nuclear program, she said, "Yes, I did."[24] Convinced that the "hard-line" policy of President George W. Bush had led to the failure of the 1994 Geneva framework, she overlooked the enriched uranium program whose revelation in October 2002 was to precipitate the breakdown of the agreement.

Albright, moreover, did not see human rights as an urgent issue. "Your administration should push for progress on human rights," she advised the next American president in a new book, but "if we refuse on moral grounds to negotiate with the North Koreans on security matters, we may end up with no improvement on either security or human rights—hardly the outcome you will desire."[25] Basically, that remark was the rationale used by Kim Dae Jung and Roh Moo Hyun for never mentioning the unpleasant topic of human rights in hopes of bringing the North to terms.

CHAPTER ELEVEN

Sunshine under Fire

At the North-South summit in June 2000, the topic of human rights was left unmentioned other than in Kim Jong Il's request for the return of North Koreans held for many years in the South as North Korean spies or guerrilla fighters. Kim Dae Jung was eager to respond with a show of his concern for human rights in dealing with them. In a gesture appropriate for his campaign for the Nobel, DJ ordered the release of 63 elderly men, all originally from North Korea, and then agreed to let them go "home." An official report from Pyongyang made much of their return on September 2, 2000, after "all sorts of persecution and sufferings" in the South: "The DPRK Red Cross Society, on the basis of a comprehensive and intensive medical examination of the unconverted long-term prisoners, has taken concrete measures for their medical treatment and... steps for their reunion with their families and stable life...."[1]

Among them was Shin Kwang Soo, who had confessed to inviting a Japanese cook, Hara Tadaaki, in 1980 to a beach and hustling him aboard a North Korean espionage vessel. Shin, arrested after entering South Korea on Tadaaki's passport, was convicted and sentenced to life for espionage; DJ's government rejected Japan's request to question him before freeing him to return to North Korea.[2]

In a nationwide address two days later DJ said North Korea still held 800 South Koreans as prisoners, including soldiers captured in the Korean War and fishermen whose boats had strayed within territorial limits as defined by North Korea or were seized by North Koreans in international or South Korean waters. Criticized for failing to demand an exchange in return for the North Koreans, DJ hoped to head off domestic criticism and possibly move the North to free some of them.

He was mistaken on both counts.³ At the apogee of his career as dissident and national leader, in Oslo on December 10, 2000, to receive the Nobel Peace Prize, DJ faced such opposition at home as to frustrate his efforts for his remaining two years and two and one half months in office. "There is no question his popularity is decreasing," said Choi Jang Jip, a Korea University professor who had accompanied him to Pyongyang. "The declining economy is affecting the middle and lower class. The gap between rich and middle class is increasing."⁴

Certainly the opposition Grand National Party, whose candidates had won the first two presidential elections under the 1987 "democracy" constitution, had been exploiting the trend, combining muted congratulations for the Nobel with not very subtle criticism. Kwon Chul Hyun, GNP spokesman, said DJ's mission to Oslo was "indeed an auspicious occasion" but chided the president for extending the trip to a full week overseas rather than returning "in consideration of the urgent domestic situation."⁵

Kim Dae Jung may have believed that the Nobel Peace Prize, the apotheosis of a lifetime dedicated to personal struggle against dictatorship, placed him above petty carping. "Human rights and peace have a sacred ground in Norway," he declaimed as he received the prize on December 10. "I think of the countless people and colleagues in Korea, who have given themselves willingly to democracy and human rights and the dream of unification." Having paid obeisance to human rights, DJ moved quickly to "the breakthrough in South-North Korean relations that the Nobel Committee has judged worthy of its commendation"—his meeting in Pyongyang with the North Korean leader, Kim Jong Il.

Unctuously, DJ referred to Kim Jong Il as "chairman," though the title reflected the Dear Leader's chairmanship of neither his government nor his Workers' Party but of the real center of power in North Korea, the National Defense Commission. "I went with a heavy heart not knowing what to expect," said DJ, in a histrionic touch that contrasted with the ecstasy with which the Blue House had announced the summit. "There was no guarantee that the summit meeting would go well." It was "to replace the dangerous stand-off with peace and cooperation," he explained, that he had "proclaimed my Sunshine policy" at the time of his inauguration in February 1998.⁶

The discontent of millions of Koreans, fearful of a relapse of the economic crisis that almost bankrupted the country in 1997, extended to why Kim was receiving the prize—his success in beginning the process of reconciliation with Kim Jong Il the previous June. "Citizens have an exaggerated impression and ask how we can do all this for the North in the midst of our own suffering," complained Wi Pyoung Ryang, vice director of policy research at the Coalition for Economic Justice, a citizens' group. "Some people criticize his North Korean policy for not having a consensus." Hardest to believe for Wi and others who saw DJ as steering the country through economic turmoil was that many conservatives, clearly a majority, did not think he should have left Korea. "People say the economic situation has gotten very difficult," he said. They want to know, "Why is he going outside the country?"[7]

The question was so compelling that the employee-owned *Kyunghyang Shinmun*, a mid-level newspaper in circulation, sold in metropolitan Seoul, conducted an internet poll asking people whether they supported the trip. "There is a huge debate about President Kim's participating in the Nobel prize ceremony," said a note on the *Kyunghyang Shinmun* website, announcing that 54 percent of the 17,346 respondents were opposed and 45 percent in favor.[8] To many observers, such adverse sentiment was unfathomable. "It's a bit churlish," said David Coe, representative in Seoul of the International Monetary Fund, which had just completed the three-year arrangement for staving off bankruptcy in the 1997 economic crisis. "He's the man who pulled the country out of crisis, but they cut him no slack. It's a real paradox. This is a man who has the moral authority of Nelson Mandela outside Korea, yet he's a prophet without honor in his own country."[9]

Nor was the economy the only reason for such seeming ingratitude. Many distrusted DJ for promoting Sunshine on the way to the prize. The government's efforts at turning DJ's visit to Oslo into a public relations mission had a rebound effect. Kim Dae Joong, editor of *Chosun Ilbo*, summarized the difficulties in an editorial that ran on December 7, 2000, three days before the ceremony. DJ "became so obsessed with being the first Southern President to set foot on North Korean territory that he came to ignore public opinion about the speed of his approach to North Korea, and the serious conflict within the South," he wrote. "The Nobel Peace Prize and resulting international diplomacy may have done a lot for our international image, but it got him overexcited at a time when the people are struggling to make a living. He doesn't seem to realize that the congratulatory signs everywhere have been put up with little true feeling behind them."[10]

On the same day, Euh Kyong Taek, chief editorial writer of *Dong A Ilbo*, also highly critical of Kim Dae Jung despite its liberal heritage, deemed it "a shame that the nation is not in a particularly festive mood." He too cited the enthusiasm with which Koreans "carried out the gold collection drive to overcome the foreign currency crisis three years ago." At that time, "people still had dreams and hopes amid the difficulty," he wrote. Now, "not only his old-time friends, but many of the voiceless supporters have turned their backs." As evidence, Euh Kyong Taek cited a survey of public opinion in the early days of DJ's presidency that showed he had the support of more than 80 percent of the people. "Today, the public support stands at 30 percent," he wrote. "Many who had supported the president are now withdrawing their support," he went on, bemoaning the void created by "loss concerning political leadership."[11]

Such judgments ran the risk of a certain confusion or ambiguity. It was one thing to castigate the president politically, on the basis of factors that might have to do with regional and class differences or with economic problems that he could never eliminate regardless of policies. It was another, however, to suggest that Koreans did not favor reconciliation with the North, did not want Kim Jong Il to come to Seoul, did not want a peaceful ending to the armed confrontation that had existed ever since the end of the fighting in 1953. Polls still had most Koreans favoring moves toward lasting peace. The *Korea Herald* had one survey conducted by the Korea Research Center showing 89.7 percent of respondents approved of Kim Jong Il's coming to Seoul while 79.6 percent favored engagement with the North.[12]

If a majority liked the idea of reconciliation, however, many disapproved of the decision-making process. Suspicion of DJ's motives as self-interested and insincere led to widespread disapproval of Sunshine. Critics cited a litany of incidents giving rise to the feeling that DJ should spend as little time away as possible. Among them were bribery scandals, some involving bureaucrats at the Financial Supervisory Commission responsible for economic reform. There was also debate in the National Assembly in which conservatives sought to impeach the government's top prosecutor on the grounds that he was pursuing cases that suited the government's interests.

Add rising unemployment, a declining stock market and the bankruptcy of more companies, said Han Sung Joo, former foreign minister, and "people have a sense of crisis." On top of all else, "There's not much real communication with the top, people don't get much explanation what's going on.... People see the president as going out of the country again for this grandstanding, and there's a little cynicism." Han doubted if "dialogue with the people," as promised by DJ after Oslo, would work "if it means a meeting where people give staged questions."[13]

Foreign observers, caught up in near-universal adulation for DJ overseas, found antipathy toward him quite mystifying. Ronald Meinardus of Freidrich-Naumann-Stiftung, a German foundation that had formed a cordial relationship with the president's Asia-Pacific Peace Foundation, reflected the puzzlement. "South Korea has one of the most tremendous men in international history, and the way he is treated shows the immaturity of these people," he said. "Some of them say he is not doing anything in the field of restructuring, but if he does something they start crying that it will cause unemployment. I am most disappointed to see intellectuals and journalists do not appreciate the difficult position he is in." DJ was the victim of "micro-partisan bickering," in Meinardus' view. "One of the tragedies is that South Koreans do not love him like South Africa loves Mandela."[14]

Michael Breen, a British commentator in Seoul, saw envy behind the criticism. "Koreans can be startlingly mean when it comes to applauding individual success," said Breen, musing over the contrast between DJ's image at home and abroad. "While he is known internationally as a democrat, domestically he is widely viewed as just another leader of a political faction that is no different from any other."[15] There was a real disparity between views internationally and inside Korea. Rhee and Park were if anything more kindly remembered than DJ as seen in National Assembly elections in which conservatives consistently won a majority. DJ did not gain confidence when he remarked, in an address on August 15, 2000, 55th anniversary of Korean liberation, that North Korea opened the Korean War as an attempt at reunification. That remark, intrinsic in the quest for the Nobel, implied a degree of support for the dictator Kim Il Sung whose invasion had cost millions of lives.

The contrast in views about Kim Dae Jung was most evident in comparisons between the commentaries in Korea and the praise from Oslo, which might have been on another planet, so disconnected did it all seem from Seoul. "Through his 'sunshine' policy, Kim Dae Jung has attempted to overcome more than 50 years of war and hostility between North and South Korea," said the Norwegian Nobel Committee, announcing its decision on October 13, 2000, two months before the ceremony.[16] If pictures of DJ and Kim Jong Il embracing, saluting one another and exchanging toasts made for enduring photographs, the image in the minds of many Koreans was that of a wounded hero or a lame duck whose power was falling in the countdown to the next presidential election in December 2002. Although he could not, under the constitution, run for a second term, he dearly wanted a successor to carry on his policies.

While DJ was basking in glory, conservatives in Seoul and Washington feared that moderates would be taken in by the negotiating skills of Kim Jong Il and his underlings. As an example, they had only to cite Albright's mission to Pyongyang. Clinton talked about going there to meet Kim Jong Il in the waning weeks of his administration, but the mission failed to materialize while Americans were mesmerized in early January 2001 by the infamous Florida recount of votes that tipped the balance in the electoral college in favor of George W. Bush as Clinton's successor over Vice President Al Gore. It is doubtful, however, that Clinton would have gone when it became clear that Kim Jong Il did not have concessions in mind. In any case, the sympathetic Democratic administration had run out of time.

Already there were signs that engagement might grind down as happened soon after Bush's inauguration. Overly anxious to convince Bush to follow Clinton's example with whole-hearted support for his policies, DJ went to Washington in early March 2001 to plead his case. He was confident that a séance in the White House with the new incumbent would produce, if not endorsement of Sunshine, at least understanding. The trip, begun in high hopes of fostering warm relations between the two presidents, turned into disaster when Bush, far from emitting sweet talk in the style of Clinton and Albright, shocked the South Korean entourage by expressing "some skepticism" about Kim Jong Il. What would be the point of a deal with him, Bush asked, if there were still a problem with "verification" on any agreement for the North to stop producing, testing and exporting missiles, mostly for middle eastern countries at odds with Israel? With that, Bush suspended dialogue initiated in the Clinton administration until his people had completed a "review" of policy vis-à-vis the North.

Unless the United States wanted to jeopardize U.S.-South Korean relations and risk a second Korean War in a game of dare-and-doubledare, however, there were not many alternatives to Sunshine. All DJ had done was to say he would like to settle outstanding issues with the North peacefully and amicably, without the rhetoric that characterized the pronouncements of his predecessors. By the end of spring, approaching the first anniversary of the inter-Korean summit, Washington seemed in line with Seoul. Secretary of State Colin Powell endorsed Sunshine in terms that were far more convincing than those used by Bush, and the White House said it was open for dialogue. There were two issues it wanted on the agenda beside missiles—first, nuclear weapons and nuclear power, second, conventional forces. The North could talk about anything it wished. There would be no "preconditions."

As far as Pyongyang was concerned, however, Washington had crossed the divide from reconciliation to hostility. The suggestion that negotiations cover "conventional arms" was seen as a precondition since the Clinton administration had never broached the issue of the presence of most of North Korea's 1.1 million troops within 50 miles of the DMZ. Kim Jong Il's formal call for withdrawal of the Americans from the South did not leave any wiggle room. The only explanation from Seoul for his seeming duplicity was that he had said what he believed in his summit with DJ but had to grandstand for his critics and would-be destroyers at home. That explanation appeared more an exercise in wishful thinking than a sober appraisal. The rhetoric of editorials had been too vituperative to believe that Kim Jong Il did not mean it when he gave his name to a statement saying the Americans had to leave.

Kim Jong Il's posture put DJ in an embarrassing position. The conservative opposition had a field day raising the possibility that the president had lied in his account of his conversation with Kim Jong Il. There were no minutes, no transcript of the meeting; we have to take Kim Dae Jung's word for what was said. Lending credence to the president's account, Jimmy Carter, visiting Seoul in August 2001 on behalf of Habitat for Humanity while Kim Jong Il was calling on Russia's President Vladimir Putin in Moscow, said that Kim Il Sung had given him a similar reassurance in 1994. The elder Kim had seemed to talk reasonably about the need for an American presence when Carter saw him shortly before he died.[17]

The beginning of construction of rail links between North and South Korea—on the west side across the DMZ, into the industrial complex beside the ancient Koryo capital of Kaesong, on the east coast 16 miles north to the Mount Kumkang tourist complex—seemed to presage the resumption of routine commerce. The process stopped dead in its tracks, however, after Bush spoke out in Washington in March. One had to ask whether it was going anywhere anyway. The most often heard criticism in Seoul was the South was making all the concessions while the North was conceding nothing.

Family visits, for starters, turned into a debacle. The North Koreans who came South were party hacks who had gone there during the Korean War, some under duress, some of their own volition. There was no attempt by the North to send ordinary people who happened to have been caught on their side. All the North Koreans whom South Koreans visited in Pyongyang were tutored to tell their long-lost relatives how wonderful was life under Kim Jong Il, how much they loved the Dear Leader. The North had no intention of opening up the country to normal visits. There would be no resumption of mail privileges, except for one mailing of stilted, formal letters, no telephone calls, no emails, none of the normal communication that goes on even between people of countries not on good terms.

From the outset, the family visits exposed the insincerity of Kim Jong Il's overtures. Initial brief meetings of 200 families in mid-August 2000, half in Seoul, half in Pyongyang, would fail to lead to reunions of millions of other divided families. Another 200 families met in the North and South Korean capitals in December 2000, but North Korea demanded that subsequent meetings, 14 more by 2008, be held inside the North at the Kumkang resort where North Korea could control them and keep North Koreans from returning with tales of the wonders of modern Seoul.

Rightists complained that the North was dictating the course of rapprochement while South Koreans were concerned about their own economic problems. The Grand National Party cited the case of Chang Chung Sik, head of the Korean Red Cross, declared persona non grata by Pyongyang for his disparaging observations about the North Korean visitors who had come to Seoul for the first reunions. One mocking if accurate remark was that these dedicated party people, who had done years of faithful service since leaving the South, all wore the same suits for the whole visit.[18]

As punishment, Chang had to remain in Japan while the second round of reunions was held in Seoul in December 2000—proof, said the opposition, of the North's "muzzling our press and people." Declining support for Sunshine had consequences in the way the administration was behaving. The opposition was only scantily informed of what was going on—usually after the fact. "There has been too little effort," said an opposition official, "to sell the policy to the people, many of whom do not necessarily share DJ's outlook on unification." A member of the Grand National Party created a furor in the National Assembly, saying DJ's Millennium Democratic Party had become a "subsidiary" of the Workers' Party of North Korea.[19]

As the nature of the family visits became clear, South Koreans were increasingly critical of DJ's persistent efforts at courting Kim Jong Il. DJ was under fire not just for failing to negotiate the release of South Koreans held in the North but for not pressing for a commitment on pulling troops away from the DMZ, for selling out the country when economic problems were far from resolved. As talk of a lame-duck presidency gained currency, there was a sense that he would finish his days in failure as had all his predecessors after having risen to power amid great proclamations.

DJ would have to improve his standing among his countrymen even though the Nobel would enhance his global image and confirm his enduring legacy as a campaigner for democracy. "Asia's Nelson Mandela" though he was in editorials and encomiums from world leaders, he risked going down in history as the one who brought about reconciliation only to succumb to factional splits in the South. Never, in all his years in prisons or hospitals had DJ faced such hostility from politicians and the media. Who, outside Korea, would have believed that his poll rating had plummeted quite so disastrously since his election as he fought for economic reforms that threatened to deprive several hundred thousand people of their jobs? Even members of his own party said from time to time that he should dedicate more of his energies to dealing with problems at home.

The bloom was fast wearing off the rose. While the state-owned Korean Broadcasting System provided live coverage of the Nobel awards ceremony and newspaper advertisements and supplements hailed DJ's "glorious achievement," the polls had his popularity descending to perilously low levels. Hangil Research, an independent polling organization, in a poll near the end of 2000 had only 18.9 percent of 500 people surveyed in Seoul still supporting DJ compared with 81.3 percent in March 1998, two weeks after his inauguration. That poll, published in *Naeil Shinmun*, founded three months earlier as a left-of-center paper that consistently supported Kim's policies, said that 34.8 percent were "against" him while 27.9 percent were "neutral," 12.4 percent supported no one, and 5.8 percent had "no opinion."[20]

The conservative *Munhwa Ilbo*, Seoul's only afternoon newspaper, revealed some of the concerns. "Economic expertise" was the quality that 72 percent of the 1,000 respondents said they would most like to see in Korea's next president, said the paper, once part of the Hyundai empire, now independent but reliant upon Hyundai interests for advertising and circulation. Only 3.2 percent of the respondents cited "North-South Korean relations and foreign policy" as important—"evidence," said an opposition official, "that the people are getting tired of DJ's obsession with North Korea and blaming him for economic failures."[21] A spokesman for DJ, one of at least three public relations people in his 54-person entourage to Oslo, said "the polls are different." DJ himself promised a shakeup, probably another cabinet reshuffle, when he returned and faced "the second stage" of restructuring. Yong Sun Mok, a senior Millennium Democratic Party official, acknowledged "in a sense" DJ's popularity was declining but said the impression was "stimulated by some political propaganda."[22]

DJ remained a victim of rivalry between people from the Kyongsang provinces in the southeast, embracing the independent cities of Busan and Daegu, and the southwestern Cholla provinces, encompassing Gwangju. As president, he often discussed this topic as he traveled around the country, attempting to unify a disparate people as he strove to reunite a divided peninsula. On one trip to the Kyongsang region, he remarked, "The biggest obstacles are politicians" for they "abuse regional antagonisms at elections and incite people with lies." Moreover, he added, undeniably, "Some media report their actions provocatively for commercial purposes and build animosity between the people."[23] But who abused regional rivalries? In his appeals to Cholla, DJ demanded absolute fealty from a region where Park had had strong support in the 1963 elections before DJ's emergence as a regional figure.

As a result of his waning popularity, DJ faced an uphill battle in efforts at reforming the banking system and curbing the power of the *chaebol*. A sign of recognition of the difficulties was that aides said he would no longer attempt to revise the National Security Law for fear of antagonizing conservatives. In frustration, DJ's government succumbed to the temptation of a traditional form of abuse. Reviving memories of Chun's crackdown on the press beginning in 1980, prosecutors in early 2001 opened an investigation into the income and taxes of a wide range of media enterprises. On August 16, the publishers of *Chosun Ilbo* and *Dong A Ilbo,* both hereditary bosses, anticommunist and supportive of the *chaebol,* were indicted and jailed without bail. Prosecutors spared Hong Seok Hyun, publisher of *JoongAng Ilbo,* brother-in-law of Lee Kun Hee, chairman of the Samsung group, which had founded *JoongAng* in 1965 and only nominally made a show of giving up ownership while supporting it with advertising. *JoongAng Ilbo* had already toned down its editorials after Hong in 1998 was arrested on tax charges, detained and then given a suspended sentence and hefty fine.

The opposition media would maintain its high level of criticism of both economic policy and North-South relations even after 23 organizations were ordered to pay $388 million in back taxes and penalties, most of them owed by the "Big Three" newspapers, *Chosun Ilbo, JoongAng Ilbo* and *Dong A Ilbo.* The accused publishers doubtless owed taxes, but the impression remained that the purpose of the investigation was to intimidate them into muting their criticism. The publishers of *Chosun Ilbo* and *Dong A Ilbo*—along with the publisher of the much smaller *Kookmin Ilbo*, owned by the evangelical Full Gospel Church—were eventually let off with fines and suspended sentences. In another inversion of the past, *Hankyoreh Shinmun*, founded in 1988 through the sale of shares to more than 7,000 crusading contributors as a voice of the oppressed left, emerged after DJ's election as a proponent of government policy and a staunch critic of its much larger "Big Three" rivals. *Hankyoreh*, now pro-government, was not the target of criminal prosecution.

The punishment meted the publishers of *Chosun* and *Dong A* did not inhibit their editorialists from a steady stream of criticism, especially of moves toward reconciliation with North Korea. The government then sought to curb them with a media reform law, enacted in 2004, that said the media must observe certain tenets of "social responsibility"—a catchall phrase that carried the threat of censorship—with internal readers' committees in place at each media organization to weigh complaints charging articles were not "objective." More practically, the law limited the Big Three to 60 percent of the market with no single newspaper exceeding 30 percent of total circulation while advertising was limited to half the space in any edition.

Since the Big Three among them claimed 70 percent of the market, since *Chosun Ilbo* had more than one-third, and since advertising typically filled two-thirds of each edition, the law was welcomed as a way to keep them from suppressing smaller papers in economic distress but decried as a device to muzzle a free and critical press.[24] The government, meanwhile, exercised unchallenged control over the national television networks—the biggest, KBS, the Korean Broadcasting System, was government-owned; the other two major networks, plus the 24-hour-news YTN cable network and two smaller networks, were government-invested and government-dominated. Government agencies also owned two other networks, one of which, Arirang, carried English-language programming in Korea and abroad. Critics charged all of them went along with government policy, sublimating if not suppressing real criticism.

For DJ, there was one answer. Kim Jong Il would be his savior. All that was needed was for his host in the North to pay a reciprocal visit to Seoul, as he had promised at the Pyongyang summit. Long before DJ made his pilgrimage to Washington, however, there was speculation that Kim Jong Il would think of excuses not to come to Seoul. Word was he wanted a guarantee of crowds similar to those that had greeted DJ in Pyongyang. Cheering throngs would have to line the streets from the airport, and God forbid there should be any demonstrators shouting epithets denouncing him over mega-loud speakers. DJ wanted Kim Jong Il to come so much that his pleas became embarrassing. He missed no opportunity, including a "tea party" for correspondents on one of the expansive Blue House lawns, at which he suggested that the anniversary of the first summit, on June 15, 2001, might be the perfect occasion for "Chairman Kim" to accept the invitation.

While DJ remained hopeful, the North responded both by suspending North-South dialogue, including a fourth round of family visits after the third round in February 2001, and by blasting the United States with daily propaganda barrages. Kim Jong Il, receiving a delegation from the European Union led by the Swedish prime minister, Goran Persson, in May, said that he could not consider the long-awaited return visit to Seoul as promised in the communiqué that emerged from the June summit until Washington had completed a "review" of North Korean policy.

DJ placed all his prestige on the line as he battled for the Bush administration to resume the dialogue that the Clinton administration had been conducting. There could be no meaningful North-South Korean dialogue, he said in May 2001, without a Washington-Pyongyang dialogue "in parallel." As long as those two were not talking, DJ knew that Kim Jong Il would never make the gesture that would ensure his place once again as the father of peace on the Korean peninsula. Washington by this time was glad to cooperate by calling on Kim Jong Il to come to the South since the Bush administration had completed its review and could claim to be ready for dialogue that still seemed unlikely.[25]

For Pyongyang, the game was to raise the stakes, getting Washington to back down on a position interpreted as "hard line" before considering fresh overtures to the South. By this logic, if Pyongyang waited long enough, DJ would get Washington to soften its policy. Thus the North could dangle the promise of an inter-Korean summit before DJ's hungry eyes as a bargaining tool in the power game. Clever though that policy might have seemed, it too was flawed. Kim Jong Il had no solution to the North's economic problems even as North Korea responded with increasingly rude rhetoric to Bush's pejorative remarks about him and the plight of his country in a complete reversal of Clinton policy.

The tough talk climaxed famously when Bush in his first state-of-the-union address, on January 30, 2002, described North Korea, accurately, as "a regime arming with missiles and weapons of mass destruction, while starving its citizens." Next, he charged that Iran "aggressively pursues these weapons and exports terror" and that "Iraq continues to flaunt its hostility toward America and to support terror" and had "plotted to develop anthrax, and nerve gas, and nuclear weapons for over a decade"—the accusation that provided the rationale for the United States to overthrow Saddam Hussein. Bush went on to define the sharp shift in U.S. policy on North Korea when he said that "states like these, and their terrorist allies, constitute an axis of evil, arming to threaten the peace of the world" and "by seeking weapons of mass destruction, these regimes pose a grave and growing danger"—indeed "could attack our allies or attempt to blackmail the United States." The United States, he promised, "will not permit the world's most dangerous regimes to threaten us with the world's most destructive weapons."[26]

The speech came to be known as Bush's "axis-of-evil" address, and the term "axis of evil" entered the lexicon of U.S.-Korean relations. Almost at once U.S. and South Korean diplomats scrambled to reverse the negative impact not just on any hope for dialogue with North Korea but also on U.S. relations with Kim Dae Jung as he pursued reconciliation. Three weeks later, visiting Seoul for the first time, Bush met with DJ at the Blue House.

In a sense Bush was going along with the inevitable. His remarks in Korea were attuned to make up for slights. "I made it very clear to the President that I support his Sunshine policy," he said, standing beside DJ at a Blue House press conference, professing to be "disappointed that the other side, the North Koreans, will not accept the spirit of the Sunshine policy." Bush had to wonder "why the North Korean President won't accept the gesture of goodwill that the South Korean President has so rightfully offered," assuring DJ "that we, too, would be happy to have a dialogue with the North Koreans" but "there has been no response." As for "my very strong comments about the nature of the regime," he said, it was all because "I love freedom, I understand the importance of freedom in people's lives, I'm troubled by a regime that tolerates starvation, I worry about a regime that is closed and not transparent, I'm deeply concerned about the people of North Korea."[27]

Rushing 40 miles north to Dora Station, an imposing edifice in aluminum, glass, and concrete on the new line through the DMZ into North Korea, the presidents again stood side-by-side. They uttered separate statements, to be permanently inscribed in the station's spacious lobby, and Bush, in a meticulously planned touch of drama, scrawled on a railroad tie, "May this railroad unite Korean families."[28]

But how much were attitudes changing? The sight of a gaggle of North Korean women rooting in unison at the Asian Games in Busan in October 2002 illustrated both the hope and the failure of Sunshine. The North's carefully guarded athletes, band members, cheerleaders and officials bunked on a boat in the harbor when not preening at the Games—emblematic of the Dear Leader's desire not to reform but to survive.[29] The North Koreans might have convinced some South Koreans, and much of the rest of the world, that change was afoot, that Kim Jong Il had awakened to global realities, that he was transforming North Korea's economy and wanted peace and dialogue. From participation in the Asian Games to announcement of an economic reform program to diplomatic moves, his greatest success had been a monolithic disinformation campaign.

The worst blow to Sunshine was about to fall. Shortly before the opening of the Asian Games, U.S. envoy James Kelly, assistant secretary of state for East Asia and the Pacific, visiting Pyongyang on October 4, 2002, told North Korea's first vice foreign minister, Kang Sok Ju, that U.S. satellite technology, electronic eavesdropping and documentary evidence proved the existence of a uranium program separate from the one at Yongbyon, suspended under the 1994 Geneva agreement, for producing plutonium warheads. The relationship between the summit and the purchase of components for uranium bombs, including centrifuges from the network of the rogue Pakistani physicist Abdul Qadeer Khan, "father" of the Pakistan A-bomb, was clear.[30] Kelly and others with him heard what they took as Kang's acknowledgement of what was going on.

After Kelly got back to Washington and announced what veteran interpreter Tong Kim understood Kang to have said, the debate entered a new crisis stage.[31] Acknowledgment of the uranium program, denied by North Koreans, set in motion a chain reaction that detonated the elaborate Geneva framework. The United States refused in November 2002 to go on shipping heavy fuel oil, as it had been doing under terms of the agreement, and North Korea expelled IAEA inspectors from Yongbyon at the end of December. On January 10, 2003, North Korea withdrew, formally and fully, from the nuclear non-proliferation treaty, and technicians restarted the five-megawatt reactor at Yongbyon in the final weeks of DJ's presidency. Finally, North Korea boasted in June 2003 of having extracted plutonium from the 8,000 spent fuel rods, enough for between 25 and 30 kilograms of plutonium.[32]

Prospects for meaningful reconciliation appeared bleak. Attempting spin control, South Korean officials said the revelation might be good news. With the truth out, some believed, the North might advance to the next level of dialogue. So far the North's ruses appeared to have been largely taken at face value at the highest levels in Seoul. There had been acceptance of the North's claims to be reforming when there was no evidence of anything beyond what foreigners might see on shepherded excursions. There was a firm belief the North was planning to open up for normal traffic from the South as workers hacked away on the northern side of the DMZ within range of tourists' binoculars at the Dorasan observation post on the southern side overlooking the rail route to Kaesong.

Signs of real change were cosmetic. For eight years, Kim Jong Il had seemed convinced that he could get twin light-water nuclear power reactors for nothing, under the 1994 Geneva agreement, by persuading fearful world leaders that the $5 billion giveaway was a fair price to avoid a holocaust. While more North Koreans clamored to escape, refugees reported starvation, famine, executions and persecution as they had for years.

For Sunshine to survive, a transformation was needed in attitudes, terms and conditions. The North had to put down the nuclear club, talk sense about jumpstarting its economy and cease human rights abuses. No figure was more important in this controversy than Kim Dae Jung, now on the threshold of international greatness. It was DJ, once the persecuted dissident, now the leader of a country of more than 48 million people, who had first opposed and then transformed old-style confrontation. DJ now had to bridge gaps that still seemed too wide for compromise. He was not about to endorse U.S. accusations of the existence of the North's uranium program. There were other standoffs, other confrontations that DJ had to moderate, to rationalize, if he were to bring about reconciliation. They assumed much greater significance when viewed against the backdrop of the inter-Korean summit.

Contrasting tensions were evident in the response to two bloody episodes in June 2002 that would test DJ's will, policies and outlook toward both the United States and North Korea. The first was the killing of two 13-year-old schoolgirls, run down by a 45-ton U.S. armored vehicle during an exercise 12 miles north of the northern fringe of Seoul on June 13. The protest built up slowly since the girls were killed in the midst of the World Cup 2002 soccer tournament, co-hosted by Korea and Japan, while Koreans focused on the performance of their beloved Red Devils, who would finish a surprising fourth.

The protest reached a crescendo five months later after the acquittal by a U.S. military court of the two sergeants in the vehicle. The court-martial ruled the girls had been walking with their backs to traffic on a narrow two-lane road, had been listening to music plugged into their ears; the soldiers said they failed to see them until it was too late. When the soldiers were let off by the court-martial at Camp Casey, the major U.S. base on the old Korean War invasion route to Seoul and home of the Second Infantry Division, the last full-scale U.S. army combat unit in the country, tens of thousands of Koreans took to the avenue through the heart of the capital. Nightly for weeks, protesters carried candles in paper cups, shouting slogans and making speeches while rows of police buses blocked them from getting to the American embassy—and the Blue House beyond. A flashing neon-lit caricature of the girls' bodies—spilled guts in lurid red—was displayed atop a car as anti-American NGO's claimed the accident was premeditated murder.[33]

The second incident was the shootout on June 29, two days before the end of the World Cup tournament, after two North Korean patrol boats crossed the "northern limit line" in the West Sea below which North Korean vessels were banned. North Korea, refusing to recognize the line, set by the UN Command three years after the war, sparked the incident as a challenge to several South Korean patrol boats. It was the height of the crabbing season, and North Korea wanted to demonstrate its rights as it had in the naval battle of June 1999. The defense ministry, hoping to keep a low profile in keeping with DJ's policy, had failed to apprise front-line commanders of intelligence on North Korea's plan to challenge South Korean vessels.

This time the North Koreans, three miles into South Korean waters, opened fire with a heavy machine gun, killing six South Korean sailors and damaging one boat so severely that it sank under tow. Fire from a South Korean corvette severely damaged one of the North Korean boats, after which they fled, presumably with casualties.[34] The South Koreans suffered far more in the 2002 battle than in 1999, and military people blamed DJ for telling the defense ministry to order commanders not to fire warning shots, to fire only in self-defense, forcing the South Koreans to rely on loudspeakers and visual signals to tell the North Korean to turn back.

Defense Minister Kim Dong Shin, scouring the area in a patrol boat afterwards, put on a show of toughness to compensate for the failure to stop the intrusion before the North Koreans opened fire. North Korea accused him of "a premeditated provocation to ignite a new armed clash," to which a South Korean spokesman responded, "If another North Korean ship comes down south of the line, we'll show them."[35] South Korean defense officials hoped the attack was an isolated incident ordered by a local commander, but such an attack had to have had the full support of Kim Jong Il as he asserted his supremacy before his own top commanders, the mysterious power behind the throne.

Around the same time, the North Korean media published demands for tearing down a large bronze statue of General Douglas MacArthur that stood at the crest of a hill in nearby Incheon. About a mile from the foot of the hill were the beaches that U.S. marines had stormed in September 1950—the invasion, planned and ordered by MacArthur, that turned the tide against the North Koreans in the South two months before the Chinese entered the war in the North. The memorial "clearly proves that the U.S. imperialists are the real ruler of South Korea," said one Pyongyang newspaper, calling it "an intolerable national disgrace that the statue of MacArthur, the sworn enemy of the Korean nation, remains standing in South Korea until now."[36]

How DJ would respond to the outpouring over the deaths of the two girls and the attack on South Korean boats would say a great deal about his basic outlook. DJ made no statements, no appeals for calm. He did not acknowledge profuse American apologies, possibly seen as hypocritical and self-serving if not culturally inept, extended first by top U.S. commanders and, as demonstrations reached fever-pitch after the acquittal of the sergeants, by Bush in a message read by the U.S. ambassador on November 27. Nor did he mention the U.S. right, under the Status of Forces Agreement with Korea, not to surrender the soldiers to Korean civil authorities for their conduct during a military operation.

As protesters carried signs blaring "Murderous G.I.'s" and "American Soldiers Go Home," DJ, sensing the mood, joined those demanding retribution. "Our people don't understand why nobody has been held responsible," he told two visiting American senators, Ted Stevens of Alaska, and Daniel Inouye of Hawaii. Failure to provide a credible answer, he warned, "is causing difficulty" for both South Korea and the United States as activists gathered signatures for a petition demanding the surrender of the two sergeants to Korean authorities.[37]

As for the West Sea shootout, DJ accused the North of "a flagrant violation of the ceasefire agreement" but said and did nothing to offend the North Koreans after they offered a pro forma apology. If the battle never caught on as an issue, anti-Americanism raised the overriding question of whether U.S. troops were wanted or needed. Korean officials still saw the Americans as a balancing force, warning foes to the east, west and north that another power was there to block any ideas of domination. DJ had to temper reconciliation with reminders that U.S. withdrawal would be premature, but he never wavered from his belief in gradualism as an alternative to war. From small beginnings, he believed, the two Koreas might reconcile.

Lee Hoi Chang, whom DJ had narrowly defeated in 1997, was again running for president. Although the 1987 "democracy" constitution barred DJ from a second five-year term, Roh Moo Hyun, the labor lawyer nominated by the ruling party, was dedicated to Sunshine, which he formally renamed "engagement." Too unpopular to campaign for Roh, DJ modulated his comments for leftist sympathy. As the protest over the deaths of the schoolgirls slipped into the mainstream, Lee tried to show his empathy by attending a rally several days before the election on December 19. Unable to reverse the tide, he lost to Roh by 2.3 percent of the votes, a wider margin than his defeat by DJ in 1997. The deaths of the two girls had far more to do with Lee's defeat than did the breakdown of the Geneva agreement. DJ had contrived to fire up the fury. There was no such response to the deaths of the six sailors.

For Kim Dae Jung, Sunshine eclipsed hostility toward the North, seen by his followers at the close of his presidency as less a threat than the Americans with whom they lived in uneasy alliance. Whatever they might think of DJ, Koreans preferred peaceful solutions to rhetoric and propaganda. Debate over "verification" and a halt to construction of those light-water reactors at Kumho, as agreed in Geneva in 1994, cast shadows over Sunshine.

Stunning events at the dawn of the twenty-first century produced new tensions. The dream of a strong united Korea, "neutral" among much larger surrounding nations, seemed as impossible as in the sad final years of the Yi dynasty and the far worse tragedy of the Korean War. The struggle for influence and domination would go on even as DJ lost popular support on regional and economic issues—and North-South relations.

CHAPTER TWELVE

Time of Corruption

The death of Chung Mong Hun, inheritor and caretaker of Hyundai Asan, spearheading South Korea's economic drive into the North, provided tragic evidence of the greed and suffering behind the headlines of bribery inextricably linked to the quest for Sunshine. In the ensuing burst of publicity, a complicated web of sub rosa payoffs, contractual arrangements, and understandings that defied categorization was revealed. Behind them lay Kim Dae Jung's maneuvering to perpetuate the glory of the summit and the Nobel.

Chung at 54 should have been at the peak of the career bequeathed him by his late father, Chung Ju Yung. Instead, he jumped—or was pushed—to his death early one Monday morning, August 4, 2003, from his twelfth-story office at the headquarters of the Hyundai group beside the sprawling Secret Garden, historic playground of dynastic royalty in central Seoul. His body landed in bushes behind the building where a night watchman found it. (The flattened bushes offered mute evidence of the tragedy when I arrived several hours later.)

Next day, North Korea's Asia-Pacific Peace Committee suspended tours from South Korea to Mount Kumkang "for a certain time to honor the memory" of Chung, who had dedicated all he did to carrying out his father's wishes for inter-Korean commerce.[1] The elder Chung had initiated the tours in November 1998, a shining moment in his long-term effort to open up the Kumkang region, an hour's drive south of his native village of Asan up the east coast on the way to the port city of Wonsan. The North Korean statement ran counter to Mong Hun's final wishes as expressed in a handwritten note found in his office urging Hyundai Asan, the company that he served as chairman, to carry on the tours in his father's memory. Doubts arose as to whether the program would go on.

Hyundai Asan the week before had resumed tours by road to Mount Kumkang, a cluster of several thousand jagged granitic peaks, after beginning and then halting them earlier in the year. The company had also pressed North Korea to open the border on the east coast to tour buses after a sister company, Hyundai Merchant Marine, had lost major money by operating cruise boats to the small port built by Hyundai at the base of Kumkang. Mong Hun's brothers had torn their own companies away from the core Hyundai group, making separate *chaebol* of their inheritances. Mong Hun was losing everything while elder brother Chung Mong Koo's Hyundai Automotive group, South Korea's second largest *chaebol* and by far the country's largest motor vehicle manufacturer, and next younger brother Chung Mong Joon's Hyundai Heavy Industries, the world's largest ship builder, were rolling in record profits.

Ominously for the future of the tours, Mong Koo, who had briefly co-chaired the Hyundai group with Chung Mong Hun in the late 1990's, opposed "any project that would not make money," as a Hyundai Automotive official put it, and was "adamantly against engaging in business projects in North Korea." Mong Koo, the official assured me, "reconfirmed his opposition after hearing about his brother's death."[2]

Immediately, questions arose as to whether Mong Hun had committed suicide or was the victim of a complicated plot that had to do with Sunshine, carried on in the name of engagement by the left-leaning President Roh Moo Hyun. A former labor lawyer who had battled for the rights of workers arrested in "illegal" strikes at Chung Ju Yung's motor vehicle and shipbuilding companies, Roh at his inaugural nearly six months before Mong Hun's plunge had promised to build on DJ's policies. Two months before his death, Mong Hun was indicted for channeling several hundred million dollars through Hyundai Asan— not a bribe, DJ insisted, but payment for the right of Hyundai Asan to do business in North Korea despite attempts of Sunshine's enemies to sabotage the program.

One thing was certain: Chung Mong Koo had expressed interest in taking over Hyundai Asan and redirecting the company's energies. Hyundai Asan had spent $1 billion so far on a project that had severely depleted the resources of Hyundai Merchant Marine as well as Hyundai Engineering and Construction, once the Hyundai group flagship, now in the hands of bankers. Mong Koo, whose leadership of the immensely profitable Hyundai Automotive Group made him the most powerful of Chung Ju Yung's five surviving sons, opposed plans for Hyundai Asan to develop a huge industrial park at Kaesong in North Korea beside Panmunjom. Hyundai Asan was already far along in calling for South Korean companies to invest a total of $20 billion, and strong opposition to further investment in the North would be an embarrassment to Roh. A spokesman for Roh said the government would "help Hyundai in its effort to continue the North Korean projects," meaning that the government would be willing to extend subsidies and loans to Hyundai Asan as it had for at least the two previous years.[3]

North Korean rhetoric evinced no doubt as to the motive behind Chung Mong Hun's death: he had died as a result of investigation by the special prosecutor into payoffs to the North. The same Asia-Pacific Peace Committee that announced the suspension of tours said that Mong Hun, the North's closest business contact in South Korea, had been the victim of "murder committed by the sword called 'special inspection,'" a reference to the investigation. Mong Hun, at his death, faced trial for approving alteration of documents disguising transfer of approximately $100 million to North Korea before the summit. That sum was part of $450 million that Hyundai Asan claimed to have paid the North strictly for business. The North's Asia-Pacific Peace Committee made clear the impact of the tragedy. "The murder of the man who started the tour of Mount Kumkang," it said, "put cooperation projects between the North and South, including the tour of Mount Kumkang, at an unpredictable peril." The statement called the program "a symbol of inter-Korean cooperation."[4]

The indictment and death of Chung Mong Hun reached into DJ's inner circle. Nearly six weeks before he died, two of DJ's one-time top aides, Park Jie Won and Lim Dong Won, were indicted on charges of transferring the $100 million to North Korea. Eight people—seven after Mong Hun's demise—faced trial for participation in the payoffs in a case that raised grave doubts about Sunshine. The prosecutor, Song Doo Hwan, recognized that the payoffs were needed to carry out the policy, but there was no denying they were "linked to the summit." The payoffs, he noted, went to North Korea before the summit with no attempt at "seeking the understanding" of the South Korean people.[5]

The news was not all bad. Song more or less cleared DJ of direct complicity in the payoffs, citing lack of evidence for why DJ was never summoned for questioning, and he narrowed the extent of the alleged bribery, focusing on $100 million of the $450 million transferred to

North Korea. The government "in pre-summit talks," he told the nation at a news conference carried on South Korea's television networks, "promised to provide $100 million to North Korea, and the Hyundai group was asked to transmit the money...." The government, he went on relentlessly, "was involved in secret cash remittances...through improper channels." Song hoped "there will be no more political wrangling," but that pious view did not let off Park, Kim Dae Jung's closest aide, and Lim, the mastermind responsible for engineering Sunshine. Park was in jail awaiting trial; Lim and Chung Mong Hun were not jailed, just humiliated, in a corruption case unique in modern Korean history.[6]

DJ would never veer from the disingenuous claim that all the payments for the summit were fees for doing business in the North. Apologizing for misunderstandings, he admitted having sent $450 million to North Korea but insisted that Hyundai Asan and North Korea were on a definite "payment schedule" in which the National Intelligence Service had expedited the movement of the money. That said, he claimed "sovereign immunity," meaning that he was immune from questioning for acting in the national interest.[7] Lim Dong Won offered a variation on the theme, describing the payments as "not a reward for the summit but economic assistance our government decided to provide to the North in consideration of North Korea's difficult situation at the time the agreement was reached to hold the inter-Korean summit."[8]

No one seemed to have considered freely and openly acknowledging the payoffs as the price to pay for peace and reconciliation. While DJ and his aides hoped to persuade Roh Moo Hyun not to appoint a special prosecutor, public pressure was too intense for Roh to avoid this responsibility. Roh was committed, however, to building on DJ's legacy. Prosecutors might have delved still more deeply had it not been for the intervention of Roh, who refused Song's request for a 30-day extension of the investigation. Instead Roh on June 23, 2003, called for an end to "political wrangling" over a scandal that had severely embarrassed the government and elicited protests from North Korea. Still, he shrewdly pretended to leave open the possibility of further inquiry. "Whatever questions remain must also be investigated so the Korean people will not have suspicions," he told his cabinet.[9]

Two days later, on June 25, 53rd anniversary of the outbreak of the Korean War, one week after his arrest for abusing power by having the state-owned Korea Development Bank give funds to Hyundai companies for transfer to North Korea, Park was indicted. Lee Keun Young, then KDB governor, and Lee Ki Ho, DJ's economic secretary, were also awaiting trial. The Supreme Court threw out a lower court verdict that Park was guilty of accepting a 15-billion-won ($12.5 million) bribe from Chung Mong Hun allegedly relayed through the former chief of Hyundai Securities, one of the few profitable entities left in the Hyundai core group.

The investigation was the topic of heated debate over DJ's policies. The Grand National Party, the conservative opposition that had a majority of National Assembly seats, called for passage of a new special prosecutor's bill. The party, promising "a full-scale struggle after mustering every power," threatened to blockade other bills and to press investigations into other scandals unless Roh renewed the probe."[10] The vacuity of Roh's pledge to extend the investigation if needed was obvious when, on July 22, he vetoed the bill for a second special counsel.

As it was, the arrest of Park Jie Won posed a serious threat to the legacy of DJ and Sunshine. Park, who had traveled secretly to China to arrange the summit, told reporters as he was handcuffed for the ride to a detention center near Seoul that he was proud of what he had done. Reciting a line from a Korean poem, he compared himself to a petal falling from a flower and defended his boss's eagerness to meet Kim Jong Il. The summit, he said, echoing DJ, had "saved the Korean peninsula from threats posed by North Korea" and created "a safe environment" for South Korea to co-host with Japan the 2002 World Cup soccer finals and then to host North Korean athletes at the Asian Games in Busan.[11] Park's suggestion that he was acting in the interests of reconciliation, however, was blemished by the charge that Chung Mong Hun had given him the 15 billion won two months before the summit as part of the larger bribery scheme.

DJ's critics were clearly miffed by Roh's refusal to broaden the investigation. The government faced demands from conservatives opposed to moves toward reconciliation. "In the worst case, Kim may be indicted and convicted," said Jang Song Hyon, longtime business consultant. "There's strong public pressure to prosecute. There are such doubts. By granting an extension, Roh will get more support."[12] Moon Jae In, Roh's chief of staff, offered the rationale for stopping short, saying the government opposed any investigation unless there was "clear suspicion of criminal activities."[13] The fiercest opposition to the investigation, not surprisingly, came from DJ's fans in the Cholla region.

By the time of these indictments, however, DJ was accustomed to legal assaults on those closest him. All three of his sons faced criminal charges for corruption. Influence-peddling lay at the heart of the investigation into the activities of Kim Dae Jung's third son, and wife Lee Hee Ho's only son, 39-year-old Hong Gul, indicted on June 5, 2002, more than a year before Chung Mong Hun's death, on charges of accepting $2.7 million in bribes and using his influence for companies in search of government contracts. Hong Gul got the news in his cell in the detention center where he had been held since May 19 while under investigation in a scandal that had undermined his father's power and the continuity of his policies in a critical presidential election year. DJ had already resigned as leader of the Millennium Democratic Party in a scandal involving relatives of wife Lee Hee Ho and then had to go through the formality of resigning from the party altogether before the arrest of Hong Gul.

At his father's bidding, Hong Gul had flown to Seoul from Los Angeles three days before his arrest as pressure intensified for him to submit to interrogation. He apologized profusely for embarrassing his father while the media reported on his expensive lifestyle as a student and "researcher" at the University of Southern California; a South Korean network filmed the luxurious home in Palos Verde in which he lived with his wife and two children. The most serious charge against Hong Gul was that he had accepted funds that prosecutors said were transferred by a prominent lobbyist, Choi Kyu Sun, as well as the president of Tiger Pools International, a sports lottery firm, both of whom were also under arrest. The court said that Hong Gul had received the payoffs through the lobbyist in the form of 66,000 shares worth $1,050,000 in Tiger Pools, whose boss believed Hong Gul's influence would win a contract to conduct a national sports lottery, plus $870,000 in separate bribes.

The scandal came close to ensnaring DJ when it became known that lobbyist Choi had worked for DJ in his 1997 presidential campaign. The opposition demanded that DJ submit to questioning, but he stayed away as he would also do during the North Korean payoff investigation. The Blue House feared the scandal might blacken Korea's image during the 2002 World Cup soccer tournament, and the press dubbed it the "prosecutor's World Cup" after the arrest of DJ's second son, 52-year-old Kim Hong Up, on June 21. Advisers in DJ's former party urged older brother Hong Up to agree to interrogation rather than postpone questioning until after World Cup. On July 8, 10 days after the West Sea attack, Hong Up was indicted for tax evasion and bribery for receiving $3.7 million from nine companies, including $2 million in return for his promise to use his influence in steering contracts.

Might DJ secretly intervene for his sons? "There is no place for the president to engage in the process of investigating," said political commentator Jeong Woo Il.[14] The Blue House wanted to tamp down suspicions that the sons of this president, lofted to power on promises of sweeping reforms, were above the law. DJ's press secretary quoted him as expressing "boundless regret toward the nation." Sanctimoniously, DJ promised that "all matters" pertaining to his sons "will be handled strictly according to law." In a televised address on June 21, after Hong Up's arrest, DJ covered himself in humility. "Over the past few months, I have felt thoroughly responsible for not taking proper care of my sons," he said. "I have lived in shame and apologize for hurting the hearts of people who supported me. Again, I express my apology." His sons would be "sternly punished under the law."[15]

The Grand National Party, happy to exploit DJ's troubles, called for a broader investigation into the Asia-Pacific Peace Foundation, as the Kim Dae Jung Peace Foundation once led by Lim Dong Won was now called. DJ may not have craved hundreds of millions of dollars in payoffs as had Chun Doo Hwan and Roh Tae Woo, and prosecutors never cited the handout-hungry foundation while investigating Hong Up, its deputy chairman. Although DJ had not held an ordinary job since his days as a businessman and newspaper publisher in Mokpo, he perfected the aura of one motivated by a desire for reform.

The sources of support for the Asia-Pacific Peace Foundation, its name so similar to North Korea's Asia-Pacific Peace Committee, were never clear. The foundation was assumed to have been pulling in the donations while the family was close to Choi Kyu Sun, the businessman responsible for selling electronic equipment for fighter planes made on license in Korea. The same businessman, from DJ's political base in Mokpo, had agreed to buy a house where DJ had lived in the high-rise suburb of Ilsan northwest of Seoul. Sensitive to the corruption charges, DJ vowed to turn the foundation, a magnet for gifts, into a nonprofit corporation. As reports spread of corruption in his government, DJ shook off suspicions by donating the foundation to nearby Yonsei University as the Kim Dae Jung Presidential Library and Museum while living in a spacious residence next door where his old home had stood in Seoul's Mapo district.

DJ's critics reveled in the scandals, issuing frequent statements on the need for reform. The sons' trials dragged the popularity of DJ's government to a new low and endangered reconciliation. The brothers would not see much of each other in jail, the public was assured. "They will have separate cells," said an official at the Blue House, though they might meet during exercise periods.[16]

DJ's political foes, however, did not necessarily intend to wreak vengeance on him. The Grand National Party did not expect prosecutors to question the president even after he stepped down in February 2003. "Nobody wants chaos," said a party spokesman, wary of a rebound effect if DJ were made a victim. "The arrest of the two sons is enough." Prosecutors questioned more than 100 people about reports of bribery and influence-peddling on the part of both sons and hinted at expanding the investigation to include other relatives and in-laws as had happened when the law closed in on DJ's arch-enemy, Chun Doo Hwan. Among high-fliers who got the summons were Yoo Sang Boo, chairman of Pohang Iron and Steel, and two of his executives, interrogated about the purchase of shares by subsidiaries at inflated prices in the sports lottery firm. Hong Gul was charged with having steered the contracts.[17]

Confidently, an official in DJ's party said "people respect DJ for what he has accomplished" and "the mood can change"—always possible in the hothouse of Korean politics. One factor that DJ and his followers believed might influence voters was a thriving economy, revived and roaring ahead five years after the 1997–98 economic crisis. DJ, the liberal, underlined his support for the *chaebol* that remained the pillars of the economy, inviting executives to luncheons and meetings, while the finance ministry predicted a growth rate of as much as seven percent for 2002.

DJ would have more difficulty diverting attention from corruption and North Korea. Criticized for his perceived weakness against the North, most recently in the West Sea, unwavering in his commitment to Sunshine but in need of a scapegoat, DJ dropped Kim Dong Shin as defense minister on July 11, 2002, while his sons were on trial.

Scandal of one sort or another, however, would never go away. On the day that DJ fired Kim Dong Shin, he named Chang Sang, president of Ewha Woman's University, as Korea's first female prime minister. One week later, on July 18, a cartoon in *Chosun Ilbo* showed her pointing to scribblings on a pad of paper. She's "having to explain a problem a day to reporters," said the caption as DJ tried to persuade the National Assembly to approve her appointment. There was, said DJ, no reason to doubt Chang's integrity. The Grand National Party complained that her son, born in the United States, had retained U.S. citizenship to avoid conscription, that her degree was from Princeton Theological Seminary, not Princeton University, as she claimed, and that she and her husband had enriched themselves off real estate during her presidency of Ewha. In vain did DJ declare "no one knows her character and ability better than I" and she "was not chosen because she was a woman."[18] After weeks of tendentious debate, the assembly on July 31 rejected her by a vote of 142 to 100.

In the month before the December 2002 presidential election, Kim Hong Up and Kim Hong Gul were sentenced to prison as well as heavy fines. Hong Up, whose offences were judged greater than those of his younger brother, was given three and one half years on November 1 but pleaded health problems and remained free. Again sentenced to two years in December 2003, he was not paroled until June 30, 2005. On November 12, 2002, Hong Gul was sentenced to two years but freed on probation. Their cases faded as another couple of scandals of the rich and famous. If both had taken advantage of their influence as sons of a president, their conduct was not unusual in a culture of corruption where nepotism was a birthright. (In that spirit, Roh Moo Hyun granted Kim Hong Up full amnesty on August 15, 2005, Liberation Day, enabling him to turn to electoral politics.)

It might be difficult to feel sorry for the president's two younger sons, but his oldest, Kim Hong Il, 55, was truly a pitiful sight. A member of the National Assembly, he was disabled by a debilitating disease, rarely mentioned in the media. DJ's aides spread the word that Hong Il had been beaten by KCIA operatives as he shielded his father while Park Chung Hee was president, but his illness bore the characteristics of Parkinson's. He grew progressively disabled, unable to walk without assistance, his speech slow and slurred, his legislative effectiveness minimal. On July 26, 2003, a year after his brothers had gone on trial, he too was arrested on a charge of accepting 150 million won, about $150,000, from the president of a merchant bank who believed he could stop the bank from shutting down. Unlike his brothers, Hong Il was not jailed during the investigation or after his indictment. Like them, he got off with a suspended sentence but endured the humiliation, as a convicted criminal, of losing his assembly seat.

The offences of DJ's sons were highly visible because of who they were. Names of other bribe-givers and bribe-takers were constantly slipping in and out of the headlines, so much so that most people paid little attention. The sense was that politicians, and those surrounding them, were forever buying one another off, and the men who owned controlling stakes in the *chaebol* were no different. The culture was steeped in payoffs on all levels, beginning in school where parents felt obligated to present gifts to teachers in hopes of special treatment for their children. All that differed about the involvement of DJ's sons and aides was that DJ had seemed like such a towering figure of reform and purity as to have risen above tawdry doings, however deeply embedded they were in a society in which many foreigners had seen him as an exception to all that was mundanely evil.

The shock of revelations of the payoffs to North Korea would reverberate far longer than the scandals of DJ's sons. DJ would go on justifying the payoff for the summit as a business deal that "facilitated peace on the Korean peninsula," but this rationale was never credible. Hyundai Asan's public agreement with North Korea called for payment of $940 million over six years, of which $600 million was paid between 1999 and 2003 when Chung Mong Hun pleaded the company had no more money. Companies in the Hyundai core group, all under Chung Mong Hun's overall control, including Hyundai Merchant Marine, Hyundai Engineering and Construction, Hyundai Electronics (renamed Hynix) and Hyundai Asan, were the conduits for the secret payments of $450 million. The North's notorious Bureau 39, under the aegis of the central committee of the Workers' Party, manipulated the flow of funds through Macao and Vienna as well as Singapore.

Chung Mong Hun, after some hesitation, had authorized the deal—for half the $1 billion the North Koreans had hoped to extract—with the blessing if not the connivance of his father, Chung Ju Yung, who had dreamed of garnering a Nobel trophy for himself. More than half the $450 million was transferred from the Korea Development Bank.[19] Hyundai Merchant Marine wired $200 million to three different accounts, including that of the Workers' Party in the Macao Branch of the Bank of China.[20] Some funds also passed through Macao's Banco Delta Asia, clearing house for North Korea's international trade in drugs and arms, through which the North was channelling one-hundred-dollar "supernotes" run off on a highly sophisticated Swiss-made press in Pyongyang. The other $250 million went through Hyundai Engineering and Construction, Hyundai Electronics and Hyundai Asan with the NIS facilitating the transfers into accounts of Kim Jong Il in Hong Kong and Singapore. The final $50 million, bringing the total to $500 million, was to be in the form of construction equipment, unspecified and unrevealed.[21]

All the Hyundai core group companies, with the exception of Hyundai Securities, were in extreme financial difficulty after huge losses in the

North Korean venture. Both Hyundai Construction, "mother company" of the empire, the first company founded by Chung Mong Hun's father in 1947, and Hynix went into court receivership, in the custody of creditors. Hyundai Construction was losing huge sums on building up the tourist complex at Mount Kumkang. Hyundai Merchant Marine lost heavily leasing cruise ships to ferry tourists from the South Korean port of Donghae to the port built by Hyundai Construction near the base of Kumkang before the road route was opened in 2003. The ships were running half full. The company had to sell off most of its own fleet to stay afloat.

Thus Chung Mong Hun was so beholden to the government that he was unable to resist pressure to cooperate; refusal would result in the loss of the remnants of his empire. Under these circumstances, suspicions regarding his death were rife. Some of Mong Hun's executives panicked with the realization that he might implicate them if he told prosecutors all he knew. There were rumors that he had drafted more than one copy of the suicide "note" found on his desk minutes after his body was discovered. Mong Hun's widow, Hyun Jung Eun, fought for the remains of the core group with a steely will that some said was engendered by her desire for vengeance against those she suspected as her late husband's killers—and the desire to stave off his greedy brothers and an uncle, Chung Ju Yung's youngest brother, who wanted to wrest her companies from her by purchasing large blocks of shares.

The scandal was transfixing since the bribes were paid by an elected government in pursuit of a controversial policy to a dictatorship that South Korea's ministry of national defense had described in annual white papers as its "main enemy" until DJ banned the term after the June 2000 summit. Activists had been indicted for violating the National Security Law by going to North Korea, spreading North Korean influence, maybe informing or spying, but none had ever been accused of passing bribes to the North. In the end, no member of the central cast in the North Korean bribery scandal went to jail with the notable exception of Park Jie Won, widely seen as having engineered the payoffs and sentenced on December 3, 2003, to 12 years in prison.

Lim Dong Won, more important than Park as the architect of Sunshine, was found guilty of the secondary offence of violating the foreign exchange transactions act, for which he received an 18-month suspended sentence. Lee Ki Ho, former Blue House economics secretary, was found guilty of the somewhat more serious offence of abusing his authority and pressuring Hyundai Asan to wire the money into North Korean accounts, for which he was sentenced to three years, also suspended.

Lee Keun Young, former chairman of the Financial Supervisory Service, responsible for reforming financial practices after the 1997 economic crisis, also got a three-year suspended sentence for authorizing the Korea Development Bank to loan money to Hyundai. Park Sang Bae, former deputy governor of the bank, got 30 months, suspended, also for authorizing the transfer, and Kim Yoon Kyu, chief executive of Hyundai Asan, got one year, suspended, for actually making the transfer. Choi Gyu Baek, the National Intelligence Service bureaucrat who had formally approved the transfer at the behest of Lim Dong Won, got off with a fine of 10 million won, $8,600.[22]

It was to guarantee Hyundai Asan a monopoly in tours to Kumkang and development of the Kumkang region for tourism that Chung Mong Hun felt compelled to extend largesse to numerous politicians. Naïve and weak, Mong Hun was blindly fulfilling the wishes of his father, Chung Ju Yung, who devoted his energies, in the years before he died in March 2001, to opening North Korea to tourism and commerce. Kwon Roh Kap, once one of DJ's close advisers, whose name came up with intriguing regularity, was sentenced in December 2004 to five years and a fine of twenty billion won, about $17 million, for helping himself to the same sum from Hyundai Asan. Another DJ confidant, arms dealer Kim Yeong Wan, avoided trial for laundering the payoffs to Park and Kwon by taking off for the United States.

What had Park Jie Won done that made him more a target of judicial ire than any of the others? As a businessman in New York, Park had ingratiated himself to DJ as a major donor during DJ's years of exile in America. DJ's spokesman during the 1997 presidential campaign, he became culture minister after DJ's election and assumed greater responsibility as chief of staff in the Blue House, DJ's right-hand man. In his lust for influence, Park came across as more than just a schemer who figured out how to bribe Kim Jong Il to host DJ at the summit.

None in DJ's inner circle suffered more than did Park Jie Won. There was no doubt of his importance in bringing about the summit, for which North Korea gave him full credit. A spokesman for the North's Asia-Pacific Peace Committee made a heavy-handed plea on his behalf, denouncing the sentence as "harsh persecution and suppression and an inhuman action against the man who performed a great feat on behalf of the nation by contributing to the historic Pyongyang meeting." The statement urged "South Korean authorities to take his poor health into consideration and unconditionally set him free so that he may receive medical treatment in peace, not detained in prison or hospital."[23]

The Supreme Court in November 2004 ordered a new trial for Park, saying the testimony of Lee Ik Chi, chief executive of Hyundai Securities, said to have transferred cash to Park, was not credible. Immensely relieved, DJ issued a statement saying that Park had been "a scapegoat of politics" and "his honor is redeemed," but Park was still in trouble.[24] Although cleared in May 2006 of accepting the bribe from Chung Mong Hun, he was sentenced to three years for arranging the payoffs to North Korea and also for taking much smaller bribes, about $100,000, from two other *chaebol*, the SK and Kumho groups. Park, nearly blind from glaucoma, physically weakened, was a shadow of the feisty bureaucrat who had been most often at DJ's side during the 1997 campaign and for much of his tenure as president.

Park remained unrepentant after his name appeared along with 433 others on a list of those to whom President Roh granted amnesty on February 25, 2007, fourth anniversary of his inauguration. "I have fought for the past four years to prove my innocence," he said before his release, asking for full restoration of his rights as a citizen. Amnesty was also extended to another in the scandal, Kwon Roh Kap, who had remained in prison, in his late 70s, suffering from diabetes and depression. As a gesture of mercy, Roh also amnestied DJ's oldest son, Kim Hong Il, who was not in prison but glad to be freed of the embarrassment of probation. The amnesties extended to Kim Hyun Chul, second son of DJ's old-time rival, his Blue House predecessor, Kim Young Sam. Already on probation, thanks to the pardon that DJ had granted him in 1999, Hyun Chul now was exonerated completely from the bribery scandal that had disgraced him a decade earlier.[25]

Always the spirit of give-and-take was at play even as the desire for revenge ran deep. Kwon Young Hae, the former NIS director responsible for the "northern wind" scandal in the 1997 presidential campaign, was ordered in 2006 to begin serving his five-year sentence after having stayed out of jail on medical grounds. Outgoing President Roh did not include Kwon's name on his final list of New Year's pardons before stepping down in February 2008—though Roh wiped out the convictions of two other former agency directors, notably Lim Dong Won, who had received slap-on-the wrist suspended sentences and probation for approving eavesdropping on DJ's behalf.[26]

Beside the money channelled by the government through Hyundai Asan, still more may have gone from Chung Ju Yung and Chung Mong Hun on top of payments openly contracted by Hyundai. Kim Jong Il needed whatever he could get in the aftermath of the drought, famine and disease of the mid and late 1990s that had killed about 2 million people. All these funds bolstered North Korea's Bureau 39, whose multiple roles ran from exporting arms, drugs and counterfeit money to importing food, liquor, gifts and other entertainment for Kim Jong Il, his family and closest aides and confidants. The bureau also had a far more sinister job—that of acquiring nuclear components.[27]

DJ's motive for investing so much in the summit at the risk of public exposure—and a reaction that could downgrade him from elder statesman to another in a line of corrupt Korean leaders—was clear. He could rationalize funding Kim Jong Il as a sacrifice on the altar of North-South commerce, amity and eventual reunification of the peninsula. Korea had after all been a single country under dynastic rule until its takeover by Japan before the signing of the Taft-Katsura memorandum in 1905 that gave the United States the go-ahead to rule the Philippines unchallenged by Japan while Japan turned Korea into a colony.

The summit was the ultimate expression of DJ's quest for the Nobel, the honor that would climax a career of protest. "Short term," announcement of the summit was timed "for the general elections [for National Assembly] in April 2000," said Kim Ki Sam, a former NIS operative who quit in disillusionement and then wrote a scathing report on a Korean website. "In the midterm, it targeted the Nobel Peace Prize." And, in the long term, it schemed for political reshuffling using the development of North-South relations as leverage." Although "the short-term and long-term goals failed," Kim surmised, "the mid-term scheme was fully accomplished."

A law graduate of prestigious Seoul National University, a member of "that special team to hunt for the Nobel Peace Prize," Kim concluded in 2003 that the quest for the Nobel was "not right," was "a scam." The reason DJ pursued "such an unreasonable North Korean policy, for such a long period of time, and so consistently and wrongfully," according to Kim, "is that he was blinded by his extreme greedy desire for the Nobel Peace Prize."[28] DJ promised Kim Jong Il two trillion won, "equivalent to $1.5 billion," to host the summit, he said, after Kim Jong Il asked for $3 billion, as it happened the identical sum that Seoul had loaned Russia years earlier. Including payments for the privilege of running Mount Kumkang tours, "the total is $3 billion," as

Kim explained in a Korean magazine. Chung Mong Hun "knew the amount sent up there, but he died mysteriously." [29]

The payoffs from all sources were probably higher still. A conservative member of the National Assembly, Choi Kyung Hwan, believed all told $8 billion was transferred—many times the $450 million cited by the independent prosecutor. Whatever the grand total, "The money saved Kim Jong Il," said Kim Ki Sam. "It was spent on the military. The purpose was to win the Nobel prize." Granted asylum in the United States after having been told that his life was in danger in Korea, warned not to return, Kim was free to speak out while settling with his family near Harrisburg, Pennsylvania, and attending classes at a local college.[30]

In a culture of corruption, bribing North Korea was to be expected. In DJ's case, however, the process was vastly complicated by the quest for the Nobel. The National Inteligence Service, the agency that had hounded DJ for much of his career when it was called the KCIA, made use of experience looking into Nobel prospects for Kim Young Sam. A special team was set up to do the foreign lobbying, to search out avenues of influence. Once South Korea had overcome "the IMF crisis," said Kim Ki Sam, DJ focused on the Nobel, "creating a favorable atmosphere by positively advertising his achievements and experiences."[31]

NIS director Lee Jong Chan recruited Kim Han Jung, a former press secretary, to coordinate the Nobel operation. The campaign was directed from the newly formed Office of External Cooperation, set up in August 1998 as a Blue House super-agency. Beholden only to DJ, it was responsible for organizing the manpower, money and direction of the Nobel campaign down to the minutest details.[32] There was no doubt of the intense pressure exerted on those who might help—or hinder—the selection process. One Korean-American professor said that he was asked to write recommendations for DJ's Nobel 14 times.

At the center of the Nobel campaign, Kim Han Jung worked with a Philadelphia politician, Thomas Foglietta, who as a congressman in 1985 had been a leader of the entourage that accompanied DJ back to Seoul, to persuade the National Constitution Center in Philadelphia to award its Liberty Medal to DJ on July 4, 1999. The Liberty Medal, which came with a $100,000 award, was viewed as a precursor to the Nobel. Half a dozen previous recipients, including Nelson Mandela, Lech Walesa, and Shimon Peres, had later become Nobelists. (Jimmy Carter, who won the Liberty Medal in 1990, got his Nobel in 2002.) And for Foglietta there was also a reward. By now ambassador to Italy, he was flown to Seoul and honored with a human rights medal.

At around the same time, Kim Han Jung met East Timor independence leader Jose Ramos-Horta, winner of the Nobel in 1996, at a conference in Bangkok in support of Myanmar crusader Aung San Suu Kyi, who had won the Nobel in 1991, and visited East Timor. Eager for commendations, DJ spoke out for East Timor independence and Myanmar democracy.[33] Kim Han Jung also was the go-between for Michael Jackson's concert in Seoul on June 25, 1999, a four-hour performance at the Olympic Stadium. Jackson said he would return for a concert dedicated to "world peace" after reunification—a message inculcated in meetings with DJ arranged through third son Hong Gul in California. (After Jackson's death on June 25, 2009, ten years to the day after his Seoul concert, DJ said, "We have lost a hero to the world.")

Success was in sight when the Rafto foundation in Bergen, named for economist Thoroff Rafto, who died in 1976 seven years after being beaten by Communist police in Prague, named DJ in September 2000 as the winner of its human rights medal. The foundation had wanted to honor someone for work on behalf of human rights in North Korea but settled on DJ on the basis of human rights activities in the South—admittedly a "controversial" choice, said the foundation director.[34] Like the Philadelphia Liberty Medal, the Rafto prize was seen as a precursor to the Nobel; Aung San Suu Kyi won a Rafto in 1990 and Jose Ramos-Horta accepted the award "on behalf of the people of East Timor" in 1993.

Kim Han Jung visited Sweden and Norway at least eight times from August 1998 through December 2000, accompanied by Lee Jong Chan, while South Korea's ambassadors placed top priority on finding and entertaining contacts. Among other projects arranged by the NIS was a deal to have DJ's books translated into Swedish and Norwegian for publication in the two countries involved in the selection. The NIS paid for publication of a Swedish translation of DJ's prison writing called *From Prison to President*.[35]

Aware that bribes "would create a backlash," Kim Ki Sam has written, the Koreans "avoided direct cash payments and instead invited influential people from the awards committee." That approach seemed preferable to offering "money alone to buy the prize."[36] NIS officials, visiting Norway and Sweden in the guise of diplomats, spread the word in dinners, conferences and individual meetings of the humanitarian achievements that DJ had accomplished long before the North-South summit. The strategy called for inviting top officials from those countries on junkets to Seoul underwritten by the NIS. DJ wined, dined, and chatted with them; aides and academicians provided briefings and entertainment.

The most influential Nobel insider, Gunnar Stålsett, bishop of Oslo of the Church of Norway and vice chairman of the Nobel Peace Prize Committee, saw DJ at the Blue House in February 2000, four months before the summit, according to Kim Ki Sam's record. Lee Jong Chan dined with Michael Sohlman, executive director of the Nobel Foundation, on March 3, 2008, when he visited Seoul on a diplomatic mission. The Swedish deputy prime minister, Jan Eliasson, led a delegation to Pyongyang in March 2000 bearing a message from DJ to Kim Yong Nam, chairman of the presidium of the Supreme People's Assembly. The former prime minister of Norway, Kjell Magne Bondevik, president of the Oslo Center for Peace and Human Rights and an influential figure on the Nobel committee, was invited to meet DJ and witness "the sad emotional scene" of family members embracing at the first North-South family reunion in Seoul on August 15, 2000. [37]

How or whether such blandishments influenced the Nobel decision is not clear. Keepers of the Nobel faith in Oslo and Stockholm have staunchly avoided comment. Bishop Stålsett, in retirement, said in an email that "as a matter of principle I do not respond to inquiries re the Nobel Peace Prize." Michael Sohlman, in Stockholm, said he was unaware of of the selection, made in Oslo, until it was announced. Nobel officials in Oslo and Stockholm said they never comment on choosing Nobel laureates.[38]

If flattery was seen as the way to sway the Norwegians, however, money was what mattered for North Korea. An exercise in ego-boosting, the campaign for the Nobel might have been harmless had North Korea not sensed opportunity. Three teams of North Korean officials visited Sweden in 1999 to look into the purchase of heavy excavating equipment, which they paid for in cash. But where and how had North Korea found cash in such an unlikely corner of the world?

When NIS operatives reported what was happening, according to a *Monthly Chosun* investigation, they were asked by NIS headquarters to rewrite the report. The article suggested that North Korea handed over several million dollars for equipment from funds earmarked to promote DJ's cause in Norway—and also from funds given North Korea before the summit. "North Korea bought these excavators for the ostensible purpose of establishing underground crop storehouses," the magazine revealed, but "they have purchased them to build nuclear-weapon-related facilities." The excavators, capable of burrowing 300 meters, approximately 1,000 feet, would be critical to developing and testing nuclear warheads in deep-underground explosions.[39]

Money would lay the groundwork for DJ to realize his Nobel dream, an inter-Korean summit to project him as a man of peace on a global scale, missing only the Nobel to crown a lifetime of struggle. "The structure of the National Intelligence Service and money were used in the process of former President Kim Dae Jung receiving the Nobel Peace Prize," said *Monthly Chosun*. "Intelligence is coming in about part of Hyundai's Mount Kumkang tour profits and the illicit transfer of $500 million for the purpose of holding the summit used by North Korea to purchase weapons." The conclusion struck at the heart of Sunshine: "The national interest was impeded in order to exalt an individual's honor."[40]

Kim Jong Il "purchased key components needed to develop nuclear weapons, such as a high-explosive device, etc. from Pakistan, Kazakhstan and France, with the money," wrote Kim Ki Sam. "Kim Jong Il also purchased state-of-the-art weapons, such as forty new MiG fighters, submarines and tanks etc. from Kazakhstan and Russia." Hyundai Asan relayed the funds from government loans. "Hyundai got an enormous amount of public money from the government and provided a portion of it to North Korea for the consideration of exclusive rights for the Kaesong City Industrial Complex and the Mount Kumkang project," as Kim traced the money trail. "Kim Jong Il helped Kim Dae Jung to win the Nobel Peace Prize by extending a disguised gesture of peace, which was bargained for the bribe."[41]

EPILOGUE

Nobel Oblige

Two years and four months after the North-South summit, North Korea was exposed in October 2002 during the mission of James Kelly to Pyongyang to be developing enriched uranium in violation of the 1994 Geneva framework. When Kim Dae Jung stepped down in February 2003, the five-megawatt reactor and reprocessing facilities at Yongbyon were again producing plutonium for warheads. Funding from the South was essential for renewal of the program. The price paid for the Nobel and the summit helped to finance North Korea's first explosion of a small nuclear device on October 9, 2006, and the second, larger underground test on May 25, 2009.

For receiving the Nobel, DJ owed a tremendous debt of gratitude to those who had made it possible. He campaigned quietly, low-key, for Park Jie Won and second son Kim Hong Up, candidates in National Assembly elections in April 2008. Park, running from Mokpo, and Hong Up, from neighboring Muan County, including DJ's birthplace on Haui-do, were beside him as he returned to the scenes of his childhood. Although DJ described the visit as "a personal trip," not everyone saw it that way. Kim Hong Up "was involved in a bribery case and given a prison sentence when his father was president," said *JoongAng Ilbo*. "Park took a bribe from a conglomerate and was sentenced to prison due to allegations that he abused his authority by transferring money to North Korea."[1]

DJ, who had spent much of his career proselytizing for the rights of the people in his native Cholla region and, by extension, all South Korea, summarized his accomplishments in a speech at the University of San Francisco on April 26, 2005.[2] "I abolished the evil laws remaining from past dictatorship and focused on democratic reform. I guaranteed freedom of labor movements and greatly improved the rights of women." He also claimed the credit for having established a National Human Rights Commission in 2001 to help insure that workers' rights in Korea "reached the global standard." (The Korean Confederation of Trade Unions, with 600,000 members in "heavy metal" industries such as ship-building and motor vehicles, was indeed formally legalized but became a tool for leftist activists, many of whom had never worked in a factory.)

DJ prided himself on probes into "suspicious deaths that had occurred during the rule of the military regime." Investigations into the dark days of the past began to proliferate. Commissions were formed for a wide range of events and incidents, including the 1948 Jeju massacre and the 1980 Gwangju revolt. The Truth and Reconciliation Commission, set up in 2005 during Roh's presidency, exposed the slaughter of thousands of civilians, many of them political prisoners or suspects, during the Korean War.

The government, however, did not do away with the National Security Law, under which radicals suspected of working on behalf of North Korea were arrested despite DJ's reconciliation policy. When the National Assembly began to debate a move to revise or repeal the law in 2005, two years after DJ had stepped down, demonstrators set up tents beside the avenue leading to the assembly displaying exhibits of the torture techniques employed during Park's presidency.[3] Under conservative pressure, the law remained on the books for use against North Korean subversion—or activist enemies.

Although former student demonstrators held positions on the Blue House staff, the government was ambivalent. Leftists in the hierarchy of the Korean Confederation of Trade Unions joined radicals on campuses in anti-American demonstrations whose rhetoric echoed that of North Korea; prosecutors and police went after extremists. If corruption was pervasive under DJ, as it had been under those who had competed with and persecuted him, so was surveillance, including electronic eavesdropping, on enemies real and imagined. The DJ administration, committed to human rights and tolerance, did not order the torture of suspects, but some old habits died hard.

For DJ, the turmoil of his rise, the glory of the North-South summit and the Nobel, the scandals of his sons behind him, the challenge now was to preserve and promote his legacy. Suffering from kidney disease, in need of dialysis three times a week, he dedicated his remaining time and energy to burnishing his international image, rationalizing his policies and fending off criticism. Past 80, an elder statesman attended by his wife, Lee Hee Ho, and young, politely smiling assistants, he treated an interview with a visiting American TV correspondent as another chance to perpetuate his legacy. Garbed in dark suit and white shirt, DJ spoke quietly, amiably as he offered tea to the visitor and his crew in his Peace Foundation on the fifth floor of his library.

Where KCIA goons had once eyed his comings and goings, security guards made sure no would-be intruder invaded his privacy in the gleaming new building on the site of his long-time residence. With halting steps, slowed by the kidney ailment as well as the 1971 traffic accident and the suffering of imprisonment, he led the visitors and assistants into a room set up with camera and lighting for a full-scale interview. It was the perfect time in October 2006, five days after North Korea had tested a nuclear device, to press for dialogue between the United States and North Korea—essential for fulfillment of his dream of inter-Korean reconciliation.[4]

DJ viewed the policies of President George W. Bush with if anything more disdain than did Bush's critics at home. "People risk their lives and fight for democracy," he began, projecting the mystique of his personal and political struggle. "It is almost impossible for dictatorship to return." That said, he had high praise for Bill Clinton, a man of "good heart" and "good virtues," whom he had come to "respect very much" when both were presidents. So much did he admire Clinton that he believed he too was worthy of a Nobel, and he planned to recommend him.

Had DJ become an apologist for North Korea? DJ did not have to name names to convey the contrast that he perceived between Clinton and Clinton's successor in the White House. He said that he had "publicly declared the North Korean test is wrong" but seemed happy to forgive the perpetrators. The test, he said, was "out of their frustration with the U.S. attitude"—"their means to pressure the United States into dialogue." The North Koreans, DJ reminded his American audience, had said they would abandon the project "if the United States guaranteed security and got rid of sanctions," a reference to the U.S. ban on most business with North Korea, including dealings with Banco Delta Asia in Macao, the channel for sales of arms and narcotics and for counterfeit $100 bills. Sanctions, said DJ, solved nothing. "North Korea will try to sell nuclear technology to Iran because they are rich and have vast amounts of oil," he said. "North Korea is threatened"—the reason for "this extreme action."

DJ saw negotiations with North Korea as a panacea. "The United States objects to talking directly to North Korea," he said. "I cannot agree." Richard Nixon as president had visited China "although China was designated as a war criminal," and Ronald Reagan had "launched a dialogue with the Soviet Union" while Mikhail Gorbachev was in power though Reagan had scorned the Soviet Union as "the evil empire." Moreover, "The United States went to war with Vietnam, but through dialogue it was normalized." The lesson: "The only way to resolve these conflicts is through dialogue."

Always, Bush was to blame. "President Bush objected to dialogue. What is the result? Pressure has resulted in North Korea withdrawing from the non-proliferation treaty, kicking out the International Atomic Energy Agency and developing nuclear weapons." Conveniently, DJ forgot that the army of the entity once known as "North Vietnam" had finished its conquest of "South Vietnam" after Henry Kissinger and North Vietnam's Le Duc Tho had signed the Paris peace. (They both were to have received the Nobel Peace Prize, but Le Duc Tho rejected his.) DJ as president apologized to Vietnam's head of state, Tran Duc Luong, when Tran visited Seoul in August 2001, for South Korean troops having fought in Vietnam. Did DJ mean to suggest that "North Korea" take over "South Korea" in a climactic struggle in which millions died or were forced to flee?

Kim Dae Jung neglected these and other considerations too as he waxed nostalgic on his negotiations with Kim Jong Il. "I could sense he is the type of person who respects older people," said DJ, recounting impressions from the inter-Korean summit in Pyongyang in June 2000. "He is not cruel as they say." With that off-hand remark DJ swept away the horrors of a gulag to which analysts believed 200,000 prisoners were regularly consigned, new arrivals replacing those starved or diseased or tortured to death or executed by hanging or firing squad as described by those few who had escaped the system and the country.[5] Again, DJ believed "the only way to resolve the problem is to try to talk to Kim Jong Il." He was confident "we will be reunited because we have been a single country, a homogeneous country for 1,300 years.... It will take time, but we will be reunited."

As disillusionment grew, DJ was ever more eager to throw out numbers showing the benefits of reconciliation while glossing over the downside. About 1.8 million people had visited Mount Kumkang and 16,000 family members divided by the war had seen their relatives at reunions since his June 2000 summit with Kim Jong Il, he said in speeches in April 2008 at Harvard's Kennedy School and the Fletcher School of Tufts University. "The North Korean people were stunned to find that the food and fertilizer were sent by South Korea to help address their hunger," DJ reported. "The hostility North Koreans had against its (sic) Southern counterpart turned to friendly sentiment. And now they envy their brethren in the South and wish to enjoy the affluent life of South Koreans." DJ credited "change of sentiment" as having "led to cultural change as well." Now, he said "people in North Korea enjoy South Korean songs, TV dramas and even movies"—"secretly, of course."[6]

Nowhere did DJ betray doubts about North Korea's policies or the tight controls imposed on visitors to the Kumkang zone or investors in Kaesong. Nor did he hint at the brevity of the family visits, at the North's insistence on holding all of them in the Kumkang zone rather than expose North Koreans to the sights of Seoul, as they had done in the first few visits. Nowhere was North Korea held responsible for stalling on giving up its nuclear weapons.

The villain was Bush for "wasting five or six years" before "trying to pursue peaceful negotiations of this issue." After Bush in January 2002 "described North Korea as an 'axis of evil'... definitely the situation deteriorated dramatically." DJ failed to mention that Bush, eager to be the president who got the North to give up its nukes, under pressure from DJ's government as well as his own divided cast of aides and advisers, had begun to shift course on his first visit to Seoul less than one month later. "The situation is now changing," he preferred to observe, predicting that six-party talks hosted by China, including delegates from the United States, Japan, Russia, and the two Koreas "will have smooth progress."[7]

While DJ was holding forth, Kim Ki Sam, the former NIS operative, publicized his revelations surrounding the Nobel Peace Prize. Park Jie Won, vindicated by election to the National Assembly, seated with DJ and wife Lee Hee Ho at the Fletcher School luncheon, described Kim as "a low-level operative" whose comments did not merit response. "Hyundai transferred half a billion dollars to the north on a commercial basis," said Park, "and as for $1.5 billion dollars going north, there is no evidence." The prize, he said, was "not decided by lobbying" and "the accuser is too low-level in the organization to level such a charge." Kim Ki Sam responded that he would cooperate in any investigation. "The KCIA hurt national security," he said. "It must regret its activities over the past ten years and beg the people's forgiveness and change or suffer another failure."[8]

Kim Dae Jung had little to say about human rights in North Korea, about mismanagement of the North's economy, about the 1.1 million North Koreans under arms. His legacy had been to hold up an illusion of harmony and unity—and to bring American diplomats into line behind Sunshine, "the only way to achieve win-win on the Korean peninsula." As he spoke, U.S. envoy Christopher Hill was pressing hard to get the North to come up with a declaration of its nuclear inventory as promised in the six-party agreement of February 13, 2007, fortified by a second agreement on October 3, 2007, offering the quid pro quo of removal from the State Department list of state sponsors of terrorism.

North Korea made a show of disabling its nuclear complex at Yongbyon, blowing up the cooling tower on June 27, 2008, before a global TV audience, but would never acknowledge all it was doing to develop nuclear warheads with enriched uranium at redoubts far from Yongbyon even after Secretary of State Condoleezza Rice, on October 11, 2008, removed the DPRK from the State Department's list of nations sponsoring terrorism. Nor would North Korea acknowledge its role in designing and equipping the nuclear complex in Syria that Israeli warplanes demolished in September 2007. DJ was oblivious to these omissions in the nuclear inventory that North Korea submitted in June 2008 to the five other nations in six-party talks. Sensing the new American president, Barack Obama, as the true successor to President Clinton, DJ had a typically simplistic solution:

> The United States should assure North Korea of its security and its integration into the world economy and also promise normalized diplomatic ties with North Korea. In return the United States should secure North Korea's agreement on the denuclearization of the Korean peninsula including the complete abandonment of its nuclear program, abandonment of long-range missiles and establishment of a durable peace structure on the Korean peninsula, which will take shape through a declaration of the end of the Korean War, arms control and a peace treaty. Let's give North Korea what they need and take what we need.[9]

No sooner was Obama inaugurated on January 20, 2009, than North Korea stated it would never relinquish its nuclear warheads even if the United States formed diplomatic relations. The North was outraged by the conservative policies of President Lee Myung Bak, former Seoul mayor and Hyundai Construction executive, elected in December

2007 on a tidal wave of revulsion over Sunshine and the economy. Nine days after Obama took office, North Korea renounced the reconciliation agreement reached with the South in 1991 while the disgraced Roh Tae Woo was president. In a disinformation campaign to show that Kim Jong Il was in fine health after suffering a stroke in August 2008, North Korea daily released still photographs of Kim visiting military units, factories, and farms.

Kim Jong Il was shown in motion on North Korean television for the first time since his stroke after the launch of another long-range Taepodong-2 missile on April 5, 2009, Taking his seat before the Supreme People's Assembly on April 9, he clearly was not his usual pudgy self. He had lost weight, his hair was thinning, and he did not move his left hand as he waved his right hand weakly to calm a standing ovation from hundreds of dutiful followers. When he next appeared on North Korean TV, at a ceremony on July 7 marking the 15th anniversary of the death of his father, Great Leader Kim IL Sung, he limped slightly and was visibly more haggard than three months earlier. His greatest concern was arranging for one of his three sons, most likely the youngest, Kim Jong Un, still in his 20s, to succeed him under the cover of a coterie of generals before whom, to the end, he had to play the strongman dedicated to his "military first" or *songun* policy.

Threats of "all-out confrontation," the launch of Taepodong-2, the second nuclear test, renunciation of the armistice on May 28—they all betrayed the failure and futility of Sunshine. Secretary of State Hillary Clinton, in Seoul in February to perpetuate her husband's legacy, offered diplomatic relations and a peace treaty in place of the Korean War armistice if only the North would live up to its agreements and abandon its nukes, but North Korea had no good faith. Danger worsened as the North raised the stakes for money and power.

Kim Dae Jung shed tears at the funeral on May 29, 2009, of his successor. Roh Moo Hyun, who had leapt off a cliff on a hiking trail six days earlier. DJ's appearance showed his gratitude to Roh, whose loyalty to Sunshine had culminated near the end of his presidency in the second inter-Korean summit with Kim Jong Il in Pyongyang on October 4, 2007. Roh in the days before his death faced the shame of a deepening investigation of bribes totalling $6 million, a trifling sum by presidential standards, proffered mainly to his wife by a businessman. For DJ, in a wheelchair, walking a few steps with a cane when he had to, his appearance at the funeral testified to his will to carry on. Six weeks later, he was hospitalized with pneumonia.

DJ might have been weeping for the death of Sunshine. Purchased in secrecy for billions, enough to finance a nuclear program while most of the North's 24 million people suffered in cruelly enforced silence, Sunshine had been a mirage. Now the United States, South Korea, China, Japan, and Russia, often at odds, drawn together in frustrating "talks," would have to pay a far higher price for a bankrupt policy. With DJ's passing on August 18, wife Lee Hee Ho and sons Hong Il, Hong Up and Hong Gul at his bedside at Seoul's Severance Hospital, hopes for Sunshine were born again. The "hard-line" President Lee ordered a state funeral, the second in Korea's history—the first since the funeral nearly 30 years earlier for DJ's arch-enemy, Park Chung Hee—before the National Assembly building where DJ had been inaugurated as president. A delegation from North Korea laid a wreath in his honor and, on the day of the funeral, Sunday, August 23, delivered an "oral" message from Kim Jong Il to Lee, whom the North's rhetoricians had been reviling as a "traitor" and American "lackey." From a firmament for the world's apostles of peace, Kim Dae Jung had to be smiling.

The Blue House said the message from Kim Jong Il spoke of "progress" in relations, nothing about nuclear weapons and missiles. Sunshine, having faded into oblivion, lived on as a device for funeral diplomacy. Two weeks before DJ died, a seemingly revived Kim Jong Il had posed for photographs with Bill Clinton, in Pyongyang on an "unofficial mission" to bring home two women from Al Gore's Current TV network who'd been picked up in March filming along the Tumen River border with China. Then, four days before DJ's death, the Dear Leader had sat again for a formal photo, this time with the Hyundai Asan chief, Hyun Jung Eun, hoping to revive projects to buttress the North's downward-spiraling economy. The nuclear program was never on the agenda. Kim Jong Il would stick to his guns, and nukes, while Kim Dae Jung's disciples clung to the dream of reconciliation—and, some day, reunification.

NOTES*

* A number of articles attributed to *The New York Times* appeared originally in the *International Herald Tribune* before the *Times* took complete control of the IHT in 2003. The *Times* in 2008 incorporated IHT articles on its Web site, www.nytimes.com, with credit to the *Times* after dropping the IHT Web site.

One   Man from Mokpo

1. The author visited Haui-do in 2004, twice in 2008 and again in March 2009.
2. *Kim Dae-jung: President The Republic of Korea: A Profile of Courage and Vision*, fifth revised edition, Korea Information Service, Seoul, 1998. The birthdate given here was when it was formally registered. Births of Koreans, particularly of older generations, generally were recorded some time after the actual date of birth. The reason often was that parents wanted to see if the baby would survive. To determine real age, Koreans sometimes ask the date of a person's birth "at home" as opposed to when the birth was registered.
3. Kim Young Un, editor, *With the History, with the Age*, compiled by NHK, Japan Broadcasting (In-Dong, 1999).
4. Conversation with the author, Haui-do, May 2004.
5. Inscription accompanying exhibit, Museum of the Peasants Movement in Haui 3 Islands.
6. This account was provided by the author at the local government office.
7. Kim Soo Young, *Kim Dae Jung: His Life and Politics* (Dongbang, Seoul, 1986); Lee Tae Ho, *Kim Dae Jung's Politics with Two Wings* (Saeroun sijak eul wihayeo, Seoul, 1995).
8. Kim Dae Jung, "An Endless Road: Politics and My life," *A New Beginning: A Collection of Essays*; George Oakley Totten III, editor; translated by Lee Young Jack, Kim Yong Mok, Center for Multiethnic and Transnational Studies, University of Southern California, Los Angeles, 1996; originally published by Saeroun sijak eul wihayeo, Seoul, 1993, p. 3.
9. Ibid., pp. 3–4.
10. Kim Young Un, *With the History, with the Age*.
11. Ibid.
12. Ibid. Testimony of Jeong Jin Tae, Mokpo Commercial High School schoolmate.
13. "Historical documents on Kim Dae-Jung's Childhood School Records" (Historical Documents Review Series 1 January 2006, Kim Dae Jung Presidential Library and Museum).
14. Ibid.

15. Kim Young Un, *With the History, with the Age.*
16. Ibid.
17. Kim Soo Young, *Kim Dae Jung,* Ibid.
18. Kim Young Un, *With the History, with the Age,* Ibid.
19. "Kim Dae Jung's Holograph Testimony, 1980," at his trial for treason in connection with the Gwangu Revolt, quoted in *Monthly Chosun,* March 2002.
20. Ibid.
21. *Monthly Chosun,* April 2002, summarized this analysis by the Korean Central Intelligence Agency.
22. Journalist Choe Sang Hun explained the Bodo Yeonmaeng's role.
23. *Monthly Chosun,* April 2002.
24. Ibid.
25. Andrei Lankov, historian, provided these estimates.
26. *Monthly Chosun,* March 2002.
27. *"Kim Dae Jung's* Holograph Testimony, 1980."
28. *Monthly Chosun,* March, April 2002.
29. Kim Young Un, *With the History, with the Age,* Ibid.
30. *Monthly Chosun,* April 2002 cites an interview with Kim Young Hun in Washington, DC, March 7, 2002. The magazine also cites an article by Shibada Minoru of the conservative Japanese daily, *Sankei Shimbun,* entitled, "What Is behind the Gwangju Accident," published in a Japanese magazine in July 1980.
31. *Monthly Chosun,* April 2002, from "Kim Dae Jung's Army History and His Ideology before and after the Korean War," published by Saechungchi Kukminhoeui, August 1997, quoting Woo Yong Taek, a member of the National Assembly, in interview with Song In Myung, New York, August 14, 1997.
32. Kim Young Un, *With the History, with the Age,* Ibid.

Two   People's Choice

1. *Monthly Chosun,* April 2002.
2. Kim Soo Young, *Kim Dae Jung,* Ibid.
3. Kim Young Un, *With the History, with the Age,* Ibid.
4. Norm Goldstein, *Kim Dae-Jung* (Chelsea House, Philadelphia, 1999), p. 33.
5. Kim Young Un, *With the History, with the Age,* Ibid.
6. Kim Dae Jung. *A New Beginning: A Collection of Essays,* edited by George Oakley Totten III, translated by Lee Young Jack, Kim Yong Mok, Center for Multiethnic and Transnational Studies. Los Angeles: University of Southern California, 1996. p. 137.
7. Kim Dae Jung, *Conscience in Action,* quoted in Goldstein, *Kim Dae-Jung,* pp. 36–37.
8. Kim Soo Young, *Kim Dae Jung,* Ibid.
9. Ibid.
10. Ibid.
11. Lee Hee Ho, *My Love, My Country,* translated by Rhee Tong Chin (Center for Multiethnic and Transnational Studies, University of Southern California, 1997), published in Seoul by Kim Dae Jung Peace Foundation for Asia-Pacific Region Press, pp. 1–9.
12. Ibid., p. 14
13. Ibid., p. 15.
14. United Methodist News Service, May 9, 2002. The campus of Scarritt College was converted to the Scarritt-Bennett Center, a Methodist retreat, after the college stopped giving degrees in 1988.

NOTES 219

15. "Longest Speaking Record in National Assembly, 5 Hours 19 Minutes, to prevent arrest of lawmaker Kim Yoon Yeon, Seoul, 20 April 1964," certificate, the Guinness Book of Records, signed by Peter Mathews and Norris McWhirter. (A note at the bottom states, "This certificate does not necessarily denote entry into the Guinness Book of Records.")
16. Quoted in Kim Soo Young, *Kim Dae Jung*.
17. *Monthly Chosun*, March 2002. Jung, arrested in 1968, was executed four years later.

Three   Matador Politics

1. Kim Soo Young, *Kim Dae Jung*.
2. Ibid.
3. Ibid.
4. "Historical documents on the Presidential Election of 1971—donated by Kim Dae Jung," Kim Dae Jung Presidential Library and Museum, Seoul, speech at Busan, October 25, 1970, and at Incheon, October 31, 1970.
5. Ibid., speech at Jeonju, November 21, 1970, and at Daejeon, October 24, 1970.
6. Korea National Election Commission.
7. C.I. Eugene Kim, "The Meaning of the 1971 Korean Elections: A Pattern of Political Development," *Asian Survey*, Vol. 12, No. 3 (March, 1972), pp. 213–224.
8. Donald Kirk, "Korea's CIA Role Seen as Dictatorial," *Chicago Tribune*, October 15, 1972. The author researched the KCIA while reporting on Korea in September and October 1972.
9. Quoted by Donald Gregg, "Park Chung Hee," Time 100, *Time*, August 23–30, Vo. 154, No. 7/8, 1999.
10. "South-North Joint Communique," Seoul and Pyongyang, July 4, 1972.
11. Don Oberdorfer, "First Red Cross Talks," included in *Korea Witness: 135 Years of War, Crisis and News in the Land of the Morning Calm*, Donald Kirk, Choe Sang Hun, editors (EunHaengNamu, Seoul), pp. 145–147.
12. The brochure is on display in the Kim Dae Jung Presidential Library and Museum, Seoul.
13. *Monthly Chosun*, March 2002.
14. Donald Kirk, "Korea's CIA Role Seen as Dictatorial," *Chicago Tribune*, October 15, 1972. The interview was conducted shortly before Kim Dae Jung's departure for Japan on October 11.
15. "Restoring Democracy in Korea, an interview with Kim Dae Jung," interviewed by communications missionaries of the United Church of Christ in Japan, New World Outlook, Board of Global Missionaries of the United Methodist Church in association with the United Presbyterian Church, New York, Vol. 33, No. 9, May 1973, p. 19.
16. Donald Kirk, "Martial Law in Korea Cripples Park's Foes," *Chicago Tribune*, October 24, 1972.
17. Ibid.
18. Stephen Cardinal Kim Suhan, statement, March 17, 1972.
19. Kim Dae Jung, "To My Beloved Young People," *A New Beginning: A Collection of Essays*, p. 142.
20. "Restoring Democracy in Korea," p. 19.
21. Kim Dae Jung Library, over display of brochures and pamphlets.
22. *Monthly Chosun*, March 2002.
23. Ibid.
24. Ibid.

25. "Collected Letters between Kim Dae Jung and Kim Jong Choong," Kim Dae Jung Presidential Library and Museum, Seoul. The letter, beginning "Dear Mr. Satou Numada," was dated December 21, 1975.
26. *New World Outlook*, May 1973, p. 20.
27. Lee Wan Bom, "Korea-Japan Conflicting Relationship under the U.S. Alliance in the 1970s: Kim Dae Jung Kidnapping Incident and the Assassination Attempt on Park Chung Hee," Woodrow Wilson International Center for Scholars, Washington, and University of North Korean Studies—Institute for Far Eastern Studies, Seoul, p. 97.
28. Kim Dae Jung, "You Will Find Me Tender-Hearted," *A New Beginning*, p. 136.
29. Ibid.
30. Lee Wan Bom, "Korea-Japan Conflicting Relationship under the U.S. Alliance in the 1970s," p. 96.
31. Victor Fic, communication from a former U.S. official who wished to remain anonymous, May 6, 2008.
32. Ibid.
33. Donald A. Ranard, "Kim Dae Jung's Close Call: A Tale of Three Dissidents," *Washington Post*, February 23, 2003.
34. Norm Goldstein, Kim Dae Jung, p. 57. This book may be accepted as the account that DJ wanted publicized. Donald A. Ranard, son of Donald L. Ranard, has cited his father as saying that Habib called on the prime minister, Kim Jong Pil.
35. Donald A. Ranard, "Kim Dae Jung's Close Call," *Washington Post*, February 23, 2003.
36. Donald Kirk, "Park as Bad as Reds, Dissident Says," *Chicago Tribune*, March 20, 1974, interview with the author.
37. Lee Hee Ho, *My Love, My Country*, pp. 47–49.
38. "Historical documents from Hanmintong's branch office in the US—donated by Keun-pal Lee," secretary-general of the office and secretary-general of the Korea Institute for Human Rights, Kim Dae Jung Presidential Library and Museum, Seoul.

Four Time of Violence

1. Donald Kirk, "Korea Aide Had Kidnap Role: Japan," *Chicago Tribune*, September 6, 1973.
2. Donald Kirk, "South Korea to Apologize to Japan in Kidnap Case," *Chicago Tribune*, November 2, 1973.
3. Donald Kirk, "S. Korea's Park Keeps Foes at Bay," *Chicago Tribune*, March 17, 1974, interviews with the author.
4. Ibid.
5. Donald Kirk, "Park as Bad as Reds, Dissident Says," *Chicago Tribune* March 20, 1974, interview with the author.
6. Richard Halloran, "Nightmare Come True," included in *Korea Witness: 135 Years of War, Crisis and News in the Land of the Morning Calm*, Donald Kirk, Choe Sang Hun, editors (EunHaengNamu, Seoul), pp. 156–160. Mun Se Gwang was executed four months later, in December 1974.
7. Namhee Lee, *The Making of Minjung: Democracy and the Politics of Representation in South Korea* (Cornell University Press, Ithaca, 2007), p. 94.
8. Donald Baker, "The International Christian Network for Korea's Democratization," chapter 7, *Democratic Movements and Korean Society: Historical Documents and Korean Studies*, Rhyu Sang Young, editor (Yonsei University Press, Seoul, 2007), p. 145.
9. Ibid., p. 146.
10. Paul Shin, "A Dark Chapter," *Korea Witness: 135 Years of War Crisis and News in the Land of the Morning Calm* (EunHaengNamu, Seoul, 2006), Donald Kirk and Choe Sang Hun, editors, p. 180.

11. "Declaration for Democracy and National Salvation," Seoul, March 1, 1976.
12. Senator Edward M. Kennedy, letter to "Mrs. Kim Dae Jung," March 23, 1976. The letter is on display in the Kim Dae Jung Library, Seoul. (Korean women retain their original surnames after marriage. Lee Hee Ho would normally be addressed as "Mrs. Lee" or "Ms. Lee," not "Mrs. Kim.")
13. Joint Communiqué Issued at the Conclusion of Meetings with President Park, July 1, 1979.
14. *Monthly Chosun*, March 2002.
15. Donald Kirk, "A Grieving South Korea Gives Park Hero's Burial," *Boston Globe*, November 4, 1979. The author attended the funeral.
16. Fuji Kamiya, "The Korean Peninsula After Park Chung Hee," *Asian Survey*, Vol. 20, No. 7, July 1980, p. 744.
17. The author attended the press conference on October 30, 1979.
18. The announcement is on display in the Kim Dae Jung Library.
19. Korean Overseas Information Service, "Nationwide Martial Law: Background and Necessity," brochure dated May 17, 1980. p. 9. The author witnessed the demonstrations.
20. Lee Hee Ho, *My Love, My Country*, pp. 145–146.
21. *Korea Herald*, "Martial Law Command: Kim Dae-jung Student Instigator," May 23, 1980, p. 1.
22. Kim Dae Jung, Foreword, *The Kwangju Uprising: Eyewitness Press Accounts of Korea's Tiananmen*, Henry Scott-Stokes and Lee Jae Eui, editors (M.E. Sharpe, Armonk, New York, 2000), pp xiii–xiv.
23. Ibid., p. xiv.
24. Kim Chung Keun, "Days and Nights on the Street," *The Kwangju Uprising*, pp. 7–8.
25. Kim Dae Jung, Foreword, *The Kwangju Uprising*, p. xiv–xv.

Five   On Trial for Democracy

1. Norman D. Levin and Han Yong Sup, "The South Korean Debate Over Policies Toward North Korea: Internal Dynamics," Rand Corporation, Santa Monica, March 2002.
2. Donald Kirk, "South Korea politician goes on trial," *Boston Globe*, August 15, 1980. Oh Ilson, Reuters, pool report, August 14, 1980. The dispatch was labeled as "censored," with the notation, "The following pages of Seoul lead Kim series have been subject to military censorship."
3. Kyodo News Agency, Tokyo, August 14, 1980, summary of indictment.
4. Patrick Minn, Agence France Presse, pool report, August 18, 1990. All the quotations cited were marked for deletions by Martial Law Command censors, who stamped the report after indicating portions not to be used.
5. Shim Jae Hoon, *New York Times*, and Shimamoto, *Yomiuri Shimbun*, pool report, August 18, 1980.
6. Paul Shin, United Press International, pool report, August 19, 1980. All quotations censored.
7. Kim Sang Hyeop, AP, and Andrew Nagorski, *Newsweek*, pool report, August 19, 1980.
8. Oh Ilson, pool report, August 19, 1980.
9. Edward Conley, Voice of America, pool report, August 20, 1980.
10. Patrick K. Minn, AFP, pool report, August 21, 1980. Kim Sang Hyun's denials, including the quotations, were censored.
11. Paul Shin, UPI, pool report, August 22, 1980. The quotations were censored.
12. Oh Ilson, Reuters, pool report, August 25, 1980. DJ's political speech was censored.

13. John Needham, UPI, pool report. August 25, 1980.
14. Ibid.
15. Ibid.
16. Norman Thorpe, *Asian Wall Street Journal*, and Lee Young Ho, pool report, August 26, 1980.
17. Ibid.
18. Hugh Sandeman, *Economist*, and Lee, *Nihon Keizai Shimbun*, pool report, August 27, 1980.
19. Patrick Minn, AFP, pool report, August 28, 2008.
20. Ibid.
21. Ibid.
22. K.C. Hwang, AP, pool report, August 29, 1980.
23. Ibid.
24. K.C. Hwang, AP, pool report, September 11, 1980.
25. Ibid.
26. Patrick Minn, AFP, pool report, September 11, 1980.
27. Ibid.
28. Norman Thorpe, AWSJ, and Kim Sang Hyeop, AP, pool report, September 12, 1980.
29. Ibid.
30. Ibid.
31. Ibid.
32. Ibid.
33. Ibid.
34. Ibid.
35. Thorpe and Kim, pool report, September 12, 1980.
36. Lee Young Ho, *Washington Post*, pool report, September 12, 1980.
37. Ibid.
38. Ibid.
39. *Wall Street Journal*, editorial, September 23, 1980.
40. Donald Kirk, "Kim ends trial with blast at Korean regime," *Boston Globe*, September 14, 1980; Kim Sang Hyeop, AP, pool report, September 13, 1980.
41. Ibid.
42. Ibid.
43. Donald Kirk, "Death for S. Korean Dissident," *Newsday*, September 17, 1980; Lee Young Ho, *Washington Post*, September 17, 1980.
44. Ibid.
45. Ken Kaliher, ABC Radio, and Patrick Minn, AFP, pool report, October 24, 2008.
46. Ibid.
47. Patrick Minn, AFP, pool report, October 24, 1980.
48. Norman Thorpe, AWSJ, Oh Ilson, Reuters, pool report, October 29, 1980.
49. K.C. Hwang, AP, pool report, October 29, 1950.
50. Ibid.
51. Paul Shin, UPI, pool report, October 30, 1980.
52. Lee Young Ho, *Washington Post/Newsweek*, pool report, October 30, 1980.
53. Lee Young Ho and Paul Shin, pool reports, January 23, 1981.

Six From Prison to Exile

1. State Department briefing, excerpted text, May 19, 1980
2. State Department report, news briefing, May 21, 1980.
3. "Historical documents on the Kim Dae-jung Case in 1980—Cherokee documents from the US State Department," Kim Dae Jung Presidential Library and Museum.

NOTES

4. Tim Shorrock, "Ex-Leaders Go on Trial in Seoul," *Journal of Commerce*, New York, February 27, 1996.
5. State Department statement, spokesman for the Department of State, May 22, 1980.
6. Oh Ilson, Reuters, August 14, 1980.
7. "Historical documents on the Kim Dae-jung Case in 1980—Cherokee documents from the US State Department," Kim Dae Jung Presidential Library and Museum. (NODIS is the acronym for "No Distribution," and Cherokee the code name for the system for transmitting messages within a select group of recipients in the State Department.)
8. "Historical documents on the Kim Dae-jung Case in 1980—Cherokee documents from the US State Department," from U.S. Embassy, Seoul, to the Department of State, August 21, 1980, Kim Dae Jung Presidential Library and Museum, Seoul.
9. Ibid., letter from Richard Holbrooke to W.H. Gleysteen, written "a few days" after the court imposed the death sentence.
10. Lee Hee Ho, letter to President and Mrs. Jimmy Carter, October 1, 1980. The letter is on display in the Kim Dae Jung Library. (The "National Defense law" to which she refers is the National Security Law. Chun during his presidency abolished the anticommunist law.)
11. "Historical documents on the Kim Dae-jung Case in 1980—Cherokee documents from the US State Department," from U.S. Embassy, Seoul, to the Department of State, November 21, 1980.
12. "Cloak and Dagger Games: Saving the Life of a Leader," by Stella Kim/Seoul. With reporting by Douglas Waller/Washington, *Time*, Vol. 151, No. 8, March 2, 1998.
13. Kyodo news agency, Tokyo, April 24, 1980.
14. "Historical documents on the Kim Dae-jung Case in 1980—Cherokee documents from the US State Department," from U.S. Embassy, Seoul, to the Department of State, December 31, 1980.
15. Don Oberdorfer, *The Two Koreas: A Contemporary History* (Addison-Wesley, Reading, Massachusetts, 1997), p. 136. Oberdorfer provides an authoritative account of Allen's mission, p. 135.
16. Donald Kirk, "Chun spares Kim; action may gain points in US," *Boston Globe*, January 24, 1981.
17. Donald Kirk, *Atlanta Constitution*, "S. Korea Martial Law Ends," January 24, 1981.
18. Ibid. This dispatch was disseminated as a sidebar to the dispatch on the State Department response.
19. Korea Press Service, January 24, 1981.
20. Kim Dae Jung, *Prison Writings*, translated by Choi Sung Il and David R. McCann, foreword by David R. McCann (University of California Press, 1987).
21. Ibid., "A Father's Guilt," November 24, 1980, p. 5.
22. Ibid., "Forgiving the Enemy," December 7, 1980, p. 7.
23. Ibid., "The Beginning of a Solitary Period," February 21, 1981, p. 25.
24. Lee Hee Ho. *Praying for Tomorrow: Letters to My Husband in Prison*. Translated by Rhee Tong Chin; edited by George Oakley Totten III. Revised ed. Los Angeles: University of Southern California Korea Project, University of Southern California, 1999, p.34.
25. Inscriptions inside the case explain the importance of each of the items on display.
26. Ibid., p. 36.
27. Kim Dae Jung, "The Road the Saints March," June 23, 1981, *Prison Writings*, p. 57.
28. Lee Hee Ho, July 3, 1981, *Praying for Tomorrow*, p. 149
29. Ibid., December 31, 1981, p. 338.
30. Kim Dae Jung, "For Moral Reconstruction," January 29, 1982, *Prison Writings*, pp. 122–123.
31. Ibid., "Does God Exist," April 26, 1982, *Prison Writings*, pp. 169–170.
32. Ibid., "Love That Gives and Love That Takes," June 25, 1982, *Prison Writings*, pp. 196–199.

33. Ibid., "The Origins of the Masses and the Nobility," July 27, 1982, *Prison Writings*, p. 252.
34. Ibid., "What Is This Called My Life," November 2, 1982, *Prison Writings*, pp. 278–279. (The letter as published is erroneously dated November 2, 1985, a typographical or editing error.)
35. Ibid., p. 283.
36. Ibid., p. 288.
37. Donald Kirk, "Democracy without Dissent in Korea," *New Leader*, Vol. 65, No. 5, March 8, 1982, pp. 5–6.
38. James Cramer, *The Harvard Crimson*, "Reischauer Confers with Ambassadors in Attempt to Release Korean Leader," November 29, 1973.
39. "Historical documents from Hanmintong's branch office in the US—donated by Keun-pal Lee," Kim Dae Jung Presidential Library and Museum.
40. Ibid.
41. Kim Dae Jung, preface, *Mass Participatory Economy: Korea's Road to World Economic Power*, revised and updated edition (Center for International Affairs, Harvard University, and University Press of America, Lanham, New York, London, 1996), p. ix.
42. Kim Dae Jung, "Preface to the First Edition," *Mass-Participatory Economy: Korea's Road to World Economic Power*, p. xi.
43. Ibid., pp. xii, xiii.

Seven   Birth of Democracy

1. *USA Today*, given the chance for an exclusive story, published only a few unsigned paragraphs, not preserved in the newspaper's library or the author's files.
2. Kim Dae Jung, "Why an Exile Wants to Go Home: South Korean Opposition Leader Risks Prison to Rejoin People," *Los Angeles Times*, p. E7, October 11, 1984. An italicized note beneath the article identified him as "a longtime South Korean opposition leader" who "lives in the Washington area" rather than as a fellow at Harvard.
3. Letter, Congress of the United States, House of Representatives, to His Excellency Chun Doo Hwan, president of the Republic of Korea, Blue House, Seoul, October 16, 1984. The letter is on display in the Kim Dae Jung Library.
4. Interview with Korean journalists, Washington, November 4, 1984, "Historical records on Kim Dae-jung's homecoming—donated by the Korea Institute for Human Rights (Chi-whan Kim and others)," Kim Dae Jung Presidential Library and Museum, Seoul.
5. Letter, Jimmy Carter to Kim Dae Jung, November 24, 1984. The letter is on display in the Kim Dae Jung Library.
6. Don Kirk, "2 Exiled Opposition Leaders Going Home: South Korean Dissident Could Be Jailed on Return," *USA Today*, January 21, 1985, interview with the author. (The other "opposition leader," as reported in a separate story under the same top headline, was Jovita Salonga, whom I had also interviewed. He returned to the Philippines from New York on the day of publication of my interview with DJ.)
7. The author attended the reception.
8. Don Kirk, "Korean Exile Returns/Battered Activist Expecting Arrest," *USA Today*, February 6, 1985.
9. *USA Today*, "U.S. Delegation Protests Kim's Treatment," February 11, 1985. Unsigned article was by the author.
10. Don Kirk, "Kim: The U.S.-Korean Equation," *USA Today*, February 12, 1985.
11. Ibid.
12. "Historical records on Kim Dae-jung's homecoming," Kim Dae Jung Presidential Library and Museum.

Notes

13. "Kim's Party Doubles Expectations," *USA Today*, February 13, 1985, unsigned article by the author.
14. Don Kirk, "Cover Story: Big Gamble for World Prestige," interview with the author, *USA Today*, April 25, 1985.
15. Ibid., interview with the author.
16. Ibid.
17. Don Kirk, "Student Riots Shake S. Korea," *USA Today*, April 17, 1987.
18. Ibid., interview with the author.
19. Don Kirk, Gannett News Service, April 18, 1987, interviews with the author.
20. Ibid., telephone interview with the author.
21. Ibid., June 11, telephone interview with the author.
22. Don Kirk, "S. Korea Riots Worst in 7 Years," *USA Today*, June 16, 1987.
23. Don Kirk, "Opposition Leader Gives an Ultimatum; Elections or Riots," *USA Today*, June 23, 1987, telephone interview with the author.
24. Kevin T. McGee and Don Kirk, "S Korean Warned to Keep Pledge," *USA Today*, June 30, 1987.
25. Don Kirk and Kevin T. McGee, "President Agrees to Reforms," *USA Today*, July 1, 1987. Lee Keun Pal telephone interview with Don Kirk.
26. Kevin T. McGee and Don Kirk, "S. Koreans Warned to Keep Pledge," *USA Today*, June 30, 1987.
27. Don Kirk, Gannett News Service, July 1, 1987, telephone interviews with the author.
28. Ibid.
29. Don Kirk, "S. Korea at the Polls: D-for-Democracy Day," *USA Today*, December 16, 1987.
30. Don Kirk, "Opponents Call Victory by Roh 'Null and Void,'" *USA Today*, December 18, 1987.
31. Don Kirk, *USA Today*, interview with the author.
32. Don Kirk, "Roh Vow: 'Stability' for Games," *USA Today*, December 19, 1987.
33. Don Kirk, "S. Korean Rivals Not Giving In," *USA Today*, December 23, 1987.

Eight   In Democratic Opposition

1. Kim Dae Jung, *Philosophy & Dialogues: Building Peace & Democracy*, Korean Independent Monitor (New York, 1987), cover material.
2. Ibid., p. 484.
3. The National Broadcasting Co. had the rights to coverage of the games. In one of the great scandals of Olympic history, judges who had been liberally entertained by Korean boxing promoters awarded victory to a Korean in a gold-medal match in which the American Roy Jones, later to become one of boxing's greats, clearly had the upper hand. The author witnessed the match.
4. Kim Choong Nam, *The Korean Presidents: Leadership for Nation Building* (Eastbridge, Norwalk, 2007), p. 227.
5. Ibid., p. 229.
6. Ibid., p. 240.
7. Kim Dae Jung, "On Declaring the Beginning of the People's Politics," speech before the National Assembly, January 30, 1991, included in *The New Democratic Party, in the Name of Justice and Peace: Main Speeches of Kim Dae Jung, M.P.*, president, New Democratic Party in 1991 (New Democratic Party, Seoul, 1991), pp. 17–18.
8. Ibid., Foreword.

9. Kim Dae Jung, "Realization of a Grand Democratic Alliance as against the Grand Alliance for Keeping the Old Order," statement at the Seoul Foreign Correspondents' Club, July 25, 1991.
10. Kim Dae Jung, "Press Conference in Commemoration of the 46th Anniversary of the Liberation Day," August 17, 1991, in *In the Name of Justice and Peace*, p. 116.
11. Cho Sung Gwan, "Kim Dae Jung's Unification Policy under Critical Scrutiny: 'A Critical Inquiry into Kim Dae Jung's Policy of National Unification,'" *Monthly Chosun*, July 1991, pp. 304–323, translated and published in *In the Name of Justice and Peace*, p. 65. Cho Gab Je had become editor-in-chief of *Monthly Chosun* several months earlier.
12. Ibid., p. 66.
13. Ibid., pp. 66–67.
14. Ibid., pp. 67–68.
15. Ibid., p. 68.
16. National Security Law, article 7, quoted in Department of State, "Republic of Korea Human Rights Practices," 1995.
17. Cho Sung Gwan, "Kim Dae Jung's Unification Policy under Critical Scrutiny: 'A Critical Inquiry into Kim Dae Jung's Policy of National Unification,'" p. 73.
18. Ibid.
19. Ibid., p. 76.
20. Kim Choong Nam, *The Korean Presidents*, p. 256.
21. Donald Kirk, *Korean Dynasty: Hyundai and Chung Ju Yung* (M.E. Sharpe, Armonk, and Asia 2000, Hong Kong, 1994), p. 326. The author attended rallies for all three candidates. Chung applied the term "stonehead idiot" and other epithets to Kim Young Sam but was less critical of Kim Dae Jung.
22. Central Election Management Committee, December 1992, cited in Kirk, *Korean Dynasty: Hyundai and Chung Ju Yung*, p. 327.
23. *Financial Times*, London, December 7, 1992. The author spent much of the evening watching returns at Chung Ju Yung's campaign headquarters.
24. Yonhap, December 19, 2002. The author witnessed the statements on TV screens at the government's election headquarters.
25. A former official with the National Intelligence Service, who wishes to remain anonymous, provided the author with this information.
26. Amnesty International, "Interfaith Activism: South Korea: Prisoners Held for National Security Offenses," www.amnestyusa.org/interfaith.
27. Human Rights Watch, Asia: South Korea, "Retreat from Reform," report, November 1, 1995.
28. Kim Dae Jung made the proposal in a speech at the National Press Club, Washington, May 12, 1994. The author attended the speech.
29. *Hankyoreh Sinmun*, June 26, 2000, quoted by Kim Choong Nam, *The Korean Presidents*, p. 283.
30. Korean Central News Agency, quoting foreign ministry spokesman, December 29, 1996.
31. Kim Dae Jung, "Is Culture Destiny: The Myth of Asia's Anti-Democratic Values," *Foreign Affairs*, November/December 1994.
32. *Washington Times*, July 19, 1995.
33. Kim Choong Nam, *The Korean Presidents*, pp. 290–292.
34. Kim Dae Jung, Foreword, *The Kwangju Uprising*, p. xv.
35. Ibid., pp. 292–293.
36. Donald Kirk, *Korean Crisis: Unraveling of the Miracle in the IMF Era* (St. Martin's, New York, 2000, Palgrave, 2002), p. 75.

Nine Dawn of Sunshine

1. Don Kirk, "The South Korean Spy Chief Who Paved the Way for Thaw with North," *International Herald Tribune*, p. 2, January 31, 2001.
2. *Korea Times*, May 22, 1998.
3. Yonhap, December 6, 1997.
4. The Korean media reported on the meeting on December 13, 1997.
5. Kim Choong Nam, to the author.
6. National Election Commission, Seoul.
7. The author compared Kim Dae Jung to both Walesa and Mandela in an article published the next day, December 19, 1997, on the editorial page of the *Asian Wall Street Journal*.
8. Korean Broadcasting System, "Conversation with Citizens," featuring Kim Dae Jung, January 18, 1998.
9. Donald Kirk, *Korean Crisis: Unraveling of the Miracle in the IMF Era* (St. Martin's Press, New York, 2000), p. 76. The author attended the inauguration.
10. Kim Dae Jung, inaugural address, February 25, 1998.
11. Ibid.
12. Gunnar Berge, chairman of the Norwegian Nobel Committee, repeated this oft-told explanation of the origin of the term in his speech at the ceremony at which Kim Dae Jung received the Nobel Peace Prize, October 10, 2000.
13. Yonhap, March 12, 1998.
14. Donald Macintyre, "The Blade in the Bible," *Time Asia*, April 6, 1998, Vol. 151, No. 13.
15. People's Solidarity for Participatory Democracy, statement, quoted by Choe Sang-hun, NYT, August 6, 2005.
16. Don Kirk, NYT, August 17, 1998.
17. Interview with the author, July 1999.
18. Federation of Korean Industries, statement, January 13, 1998.
19. Yonhap, February 9, 1998.
20. Lee Namhee, *The Making of Minjung: Democracy and the Politics of Representation in South Korea* (Cornell University Press, Ithaca, 2007). p. 302.
21. Don Kirk, NYT, May 23, 2000.
22. Yonhap, December 22, 1997.
23. The author witnessed the demonstrations and picked up the pamphlets.
24. The author covered the strike, the negotiations, and the final settlement in the Hyundai Motor office in Ulsan on August 24, 1998.
25. Yonhap, December 7, 1998.
26. Blue House press release, Kim Dae Jung's remarks to his cabinet, April 20, 1999.
27. Shim Yi Taek, promoted from executive vice president to president, announced the changes at a press conference attended by the author, April 22, 1999.
28. Korean Broadcasting System, August 15, 1999.
29. Yonhap, November 25, 1999.
30. Kim Dae Jung made this remark at a luncheon for foreign business people on January 28, 1999.
31. Donald Kirk, *Korean Crisis*, pp. 245–248.
32. Interviews with the author, Seoul, January 28 and May 6, 1999.
33. Interview with the author, Seoul, July 1, 2008.
34. Interview with the author, Seoul, February 1999.
35. Conversation with the author, Seoul Foreign Correspondents' Club, April 2008.
36. Yonhap, March 1, 1998.
37. Don Kirk, NYT, March 12, 1998.

38. Korean Central News Agency, April 29, 1998.
39. Don Kirk, NYT, April 30, 1998.
40. Korean Broadcasting System, June 22, 1998.
41. Don Kirk, NYT, March 9, 1999.
42. Ibid., June 17, 1999.

Ten   Sunshine at Its Zenith

1. Kyodo, September 13, 1999.
2. The author gathered information on Lim Dong Won's background from confidential sources in January 2001.
3. Kim Dae Jung, address, Free University of Berlin, March 9, 2000.
4. Don Kirk, "The South Korean Spy Chief Who Paved the Way for Thaw with North," IHT, January 31, 2001. "While the payoff remains unconfirmed," said the article, "it is believed that it was necessary in a society where bribery, often in the guise of gift-giving, is a long-standing tradition in both Koreas, North and South." Kim Myong Sik, assistant minister in charge of the Korean Overseas Information Service, wrote a lengthy protest to the IHT denying payment for the summit. The paper published the letter without apology or retraction. This article, which attracted much attention, appears on *The New York Times* website along with other IHT articles. It is attributed here to the IHT in view of the special interest of the IHT editor, David Ignatius, who requested it and later asked about the source or sources.
5. U.S. Department of State, Bureau of Democracy, Human Rights and Labor, "Korea, Republic of, International Religious Freedom Report 2003."
6. Yonhap, June 13, 2000. The author was at the Seoul Airport send-off. Chung Mong Hun, waiting to board, politely declined comment on the trip.
7. *Monthly Chosun*, July 2000, reporting on General Hwang's speech before the Korean Veterans' association.
8. Ibid.
9. North-South Joint Declaration, June 15, 2000.
10. Lim Dong Won, *Peacemaker: 20 Years of Inter-Korean Relations and North Korean Nuclear Issue* (JoongAng Books, 2008), quoted in *Hankyoreh Sinmun*, "Inter-Korean Hotline Preserved Summit Accord," June 10, 2008.
11. Han Sung Joo, interview with the author, June 2000.
12. Choi Won Ki (Brent Choi), interview with the author, June 2000.
13. *Chosun Ilbo*, June 16, 2000.
14. *JoongAng Ilbo*, June 16, 2000.
15. Korean Overseas Information Service, "An Analysis of the Outcome of the Inter-Korea Summit Talks," June 15, 2000.
16. Don Kirk, NYT, September 8, 2000.
17. Ibid., June 18, 2000.
18. Ministry of Unification, survey results, September 22, 2000.
19. *Chosun Ilbo*, quoted by Don Kirk, "The South Korean Spy Chief Who Paved the Way for Thaw with North," IHT, January 31, 2001.
20. Interview with the author, December 2003.
21. *Chosun Ilbo*, October 7, 2000; Yonhap, October 8, 2000.
22. Madeleine Albright, with Bill Woodward, *Memo to the President-Elect: How We Can Restore America's Reputation and Leadership* (HarperCollins, New York, 2008) pp. 185–186.
23. Scientists at the Space Research Center of the Korean Advanced Institute of Science and Technology told the author on April 7, 2009, they believed the "satellite" was a dummy after

the U.S. North American Aerospace Defense Command said it had failed to go into orbit before the missile plunged into the sea after going approximately 2,000 miles. Dr. Myung Noh Hoon, director of the center, told the author, "They did not build a satellite."
24. Albright made these comments in response to questions as she signed copies of two of her books at the launch of *Memo to the President-Elect in* Washington, DC, in January 2008.
25. Madeleine Albright, *Memo to the President-Elect*, pp. 187–188.

Eleven   Sunshine under Fire

1. Korean Central News Agency, Pyongyang, September 11, 2000.
2. *Japan Times*, August 29, 2000.
3. Andrew Wood, BBC, report, September 4, 2000.
4. Interview with the author, December 2000.
5. Quoted in Donald Kirk, "Kim Dae-jung and Sunshine: Polls, Popularity and Politics," *Korea Observer*, Vol. 32, No. 3, Autumn 2001, p. 413.
6. Kim Dae Jung, Nobel lecture, Oslo, December 10, 2000
7. Ibid.
8. Don Kirk, NYT, December 12, 2000. See also, "South Korea in 2000: A Summit and the Search for New Institutional Identity," Yong-Chool Ha, *Asian Survey*, Vol. 41, No. 1, A Survey of Asia in 2000 (January–February, 2001), pp. 30–39.
9. Ibid.
10. *Chosun Ilbo*, December 7, 2000. Kim Dae Joong's name is the same as that of Kim Dae Jung except for the spelling of the second given name in transliteration from Hangul.
11. *Dong A Ilbo*, December 7, 2000.
12. *Korea Herald*, February 13, 2001.
13. Han Sung Joo, telephone interview with the author, January 2001.
14. Quoted in Kirk, "Kim Dae-jung and Sunshine," pp. 416–417.
15. Ibid., p. 417.
16. Nobel Peace Prize Committee, announcement, Oslo, October 13, 2000.
17. Interview, Korean Broadcasting System (KBS), August 8, 2001.
18. Shim Jae Hoon, "The Moral Cost of Engagement," *Far Eastern Economic Review*, December 28–January 4, 2001.
19. Grand National Party official to the author, December 2000.
20. Hangil Research Company, survey, *Naeil Shinmun*, December 5, 2000.
21. *Munhwa Ilbo*, November 7, 2000.
22. Quoted in Don Kirk, NYT, December 12, 2000.
23. Quoted in Kirk, "Kim Dae-jung and Sunshine," p. 416.
24. Reporters without Borders, "Reporters without Borders Will Monitor Implementation of New Print Media Law Closely," *Asia Press Release*, July 27, 2005.
25. Don Kirk, NYT, May 30, 2001.
26. George W. Bush, "State of the Union Address," The White House, Washington, January 30, 2002.
27. "Remarks by President Bush and President Kim Dae-Jung in Press Availability—Seoul, Korea, The Blue House, Seoul, Republic of Korea," The White House, Washington, February 21, 2002. The author attended the press conference. Bush referred to Kim Jong Il as "president" though Kim does not hold that title, reserved for his late father, Kim IL Sung, as "eternal president."
28. The railroad tie is on display at Dorasan Station along with tablets of the words spoken by Presidents Bush and Kim Dae Jung.

29. The author sat on the last day of the games in a section behind the cheering women, shielded from questions by a stern-looking security matron.
30. Larry A. Niksch, "Korea: U.S.-Korean Relations—Issues for Congress," updated April 14, 2006, pp. 11–12.
31. Tong Kim, State Department interpreter accompanying Kelly, confirmed to the author in a conversation in October 2008 that Kang acknowledged the uranium program. North Korea has said that Kang spoke only of North Korea's right to conduct such a program.
32. "NRDC Nuclear Notebook: North Korea's nuclear program, 2005," Robert S. Norris and Hans M. Kristensen, Natural Resources Defense Council, *Bulletin of Atomic Scientists*, May–June 2005, Vol. 61, No. 3, p. 65.
33. Victor Fic provided this description of a scene also witnessed by the author.
34. The author monitored KBS, MBC, SBS, and YTN reports on the episode, June 29–30, 2002.
35. Korean Central News Agency, Pyongyang, July 10, 2002; Yonhap News Agency, Seoul, July 10, 2002.
36. Korean Central News Agency, Pyongyang, July 9, 2002, quoting commentary in *Minju Joson*, newspaper of the government of the Democratic People's Republic of Korea.
37. Don Kirk, NYT, December 10, 2002. The author covered the demonstrations on a nightly basis for several weeks.

Twelve Time of Corruption

1. Asia-Pacific Peace Committee, quoted by the Korean Central News Agency, Pyongyang, August 5, 2003.
2. Don Kirk, NYT, August 6, 2003.
3. Ibid.
4. Ibid.
5. Don Kirk, NYT, June 26, 2003.
6. YTN, Korea's 24-hour news cable channel, broadcast Song's remarks, in Korean, June 25, 2003.
7. Kim Dae Jung offered this explanation on February 14, 2003, as reported in the Korean media.
8. *Korea Herald*, July 4, 2003, reported Lim Dong Won's explanation as the trial began on July 3.
9. Don Kirk, NYT, June 24, 2003.
10. Yonhap, June 23, 2003.
11. Ibid., June 19, 2003.
12. Interview with the author, June 2003.
13. Yonhap, June 20, 2003.
14. Don Kirk, NYT, May 16, 2002.
15. Kim Dae Jung, television address on all Korean networks, June 21, 2003.
16. Yonhap, June 21, 2003.
17. Don Kirk, NYT, June 7, 2002.
18. Yonhap, July 17, 2003.
19. Larry A. Niksch, "Korea: U.S.-Korean Relations—Issues for Congress," updated April 14, 2006, pp. 13–14, summarizes some of the details.
20. *JoongAng Ilbo*, May 14, 2003.
21. Niksch, "Korea: U.S.-Korean Relations," p. 11.

22. *JoongAng Daily*, October 20, 2006. *JoongAng Daily*, the English-language subsidiary of *JoongAng Ilbo*, carried the story under the headline, "Scandal, Inc.: Government and Big Business have an Insidious Relationship." The article summarized the outcome of a number of different cases.
23. Korean Central News Agency, Pyongyang, April 1, 2004.
24. *JoongAng Daily*, November 13, 2004, cited remarks by Kim Dae Jung, visiting World Food Program in Rome, as quoted by Kim Han Jung, one of DJ's most trusted aides.
25. Yonhap, February 10, 2007.
26. *Future Korea Journal*, January 31, 2008.
27. Niksch, "Korea: U.S.-Korean Relations—Issues for Congress," Congressional Research Service, Updated April 14, 2006, p. 5.
28. Kim Ki Sam, Interview with the author, Fairfax, Virginia, November 2006.
29. Kim Ki Sam, "Ex-Spy Says He Has Evidence that the KCIA Had Plan to Have Kim Dae Jung Win the Nobel Prize," *Weekly Chosun*, May 5, 2008.
30. Ibid.
31. Kim Ki Sam, "Plastered Mask, Portrait of Devil," translation by Kim of article that he posted on-line in Korea before leaving for the United States.
32. Ibid.
33. *Dong A Ilbo*, March 26, 2003.
34. Therese Jebsen, executive director of the Rafto Foundation, discussed the prize in telephone conversation with the author, July 15, 2009.
35. Kim Ki Sam, "'Ex-Spy Says He Has Evidence that the KCIA Had Plan to Have Kim Dae Jung Win the Nobel Prize," *Weekly Chosun*, May 5, 2008.
36. Ibid.
37. Ibid.
38. Bishop Gunnar Stålsett emailed the author on July 18, 2009 in response to email and telephone messages. Michael Sohlman responded in a telephone call to his home in Stockholm on July 14. Nobel officials in Oslo and Stockholm were reached by telephone on July 13.
39. Song Seung Ho. "Two Years of Tracing: the Lobby of Kim Dae Jung's Nobel Peace Prize and the Role of the National Intelligence Service," *Monthly Chosun*, October 2004.
40. Ibid.
41. Kim Ki Sam, "Plastered Mask, Portrait of Devil."

Epilogue   Nobel *Oblige*

1. *JoongAng Ilbo*, "An Ethical Divide," February 18, 2008. Park Jie Won, vindicated at last, won but Kim Hong Up lost in the National Assembly elections.
2. Kim Dae Jung, "The Pursuit of Human Rights and Social Justice in Asia," speech, University of San Francisco, Center for the Pacific Rim, April 26, 2005.
3. Donald Kirk, "Consumed by Divisions," *Kyoto Journal*, No. 60, 2005, pp. 17–19. The author inspected the display and attended demonstrations during the assembly debate, January 2005.
4. CBS News correspondent Allen Pizzey, on his first visit to Korea, conducted the interview with Kim Dae Jung on October 14, 2006. The author, representing CBS Radio, was present but was told not to participate, thus having no chance to question DJ's assertions.
5. David Hawk, *The Hidden Gulag: Exposing North Korea's Prison Camps*. Washington, DC: U.S. Committee for Human Rights in North Korea, 2003, p. 24.

6. Kim Dae Jung, "Speech at Harvard Kennedy School," published in *The Sunshine Policy, The Road to Success, Kim Dae Jung Peace Center*, Seoul, 2008. The author attended the talks at both the Kennedy School and Tufts' Fletcher School, April 22 and 23, 2008.
7. Kim Dae Jung made these remarks in response to questions at a luncheon at the Fletcher School on April 23, 2008. The quotes are from the author's notes. Stephen Bosworth, Fletcher dean, hosted the luncheon. Bosworth, as ambassador to Korea from 1997 to 2000, had seen DJ in the Blue House while Bill and Hillary Clinton were in the White House. Hillary Clinton, as secretary of state, named Bosworth special envoy on Korea during her visit to Seoul on February 20, 2009.
8. *Weekly Chosun*. "Ex-Spy Says He Has Evidence That the KCIA Had Plan to Have Kim Dae Jung Win the Nobel Prize," May 5, 2008.
9. Kim Dae Jung, "The Obama Administration and the Korean Peninsula," speech, Seoul Foreign Correspondents' Club, January 15, 2009. The author attended the speech, the last time he met DJ, who arrived in a wheelchair, walked to the head table and then left by wheelchair. DJ's wife, Lee Hee Ho, and aides Lim Dong Won and Park Jie Won, were seated together at a separate table.

BIBLIOGRAPHY

Albright, Madeleine, with Bill Woodward. *Madam Secretary*. New York: Hyperion, 2003.
———. *Memo to the President-Elect: How We Can Restore America's Reputation and Leadership*. New York: HarperCollins, 2008.
Amnesty International. *South Korea: Prisoners Held for National Security Reasons*. New York: Amnesty International, 1991.
Asia Watch. "A Stern, Steady Crackdown: Legal Process and Human Rights in South Korea." Washington, D.C.: Asia Watch, 1987.
Bechtol, Bruce E. Jr. *Red Rogue: The Persistent Challenge of North Korea*. Washington, DC: Potomac Books, 2007.
Cho Gab Je. "An In-Depth Interview of Kim Dae Jung, Chairman, Inaugural Committee for the National Congress for New Politics (NCNP)," translated from *Wolgan Chosun [Monthly Chosun]*, September 1995, pp. 204–228, published in *Kim Dae Jung: The Man and His Times, His Ideas and Place in Korea's Turbulent Politics*. Seoul: National Congress for New Politics, 1996, pp. 21–60.
Cho Gab Je. *Kim Dae Jung Eui Jung Chae* (True Identity of Kim Dae Jung). Seoul, 2006: chogabje.com.
Creekmore, Marion, Jr. *A Moment of Crisis: Jimmy Carter, the Power of a Peacemaker, and North Korea's Nuclear Ambitions*. New York: Public Affairs, 2006.
Cumings, Bruce. *Korea's Place in the Sun: A Modern History*. New York: W.W. Norton, 1998.
———. *The Origins of the Korean War: Liberation and the Emergence of Separate Regimes 1945–1947*. Princeton: Princeton University Press, 1989.
Eberstadt, Nicholas. *The End of North Korea*. Washington, DC: AEI Press, 1999.
Gleysteen, William H. Jr. *Massive Entanglement, Marginal Influence: Carter and Korea in Crisis*. Washington: Brookings Institution Press, Washington, DC, 1999.
Goldstein, Norm. *Kim Dae-Jung*. Philadelphia: Chealsea House, 1999; Hangul translation, *Segyeui Jidoja (World's Leader)*, Seoul: Uhmungak, 2000.
Hanley, Charles J., Sang-Hun Choe, and Martha Mendozo. *The Bridge at No Gun Ri: A Hidden Nightmare from the Korean War*. New York: Henry Holt, 2001.
Hawk, David. *The Hidden Gulag: Exposing North Korea's Prison Camps*. Washington, DC: U.S. Committee for Human Rights in North Korea, 2003.
Huer, John. *Marching Orders: The Role of the Military in South Korea's "Economic Miracle," 1961–1971*. Westport: Greenwood Press, 1989.
Kim Choong Nam. *The Korean Presidents: Leadership for Nation Building*. Norwalk: Eastbridge, 2007.
———. "State and Nation Building in South Korea: A Comparative Historical Perspective." Paper, Honolulu: East-West Center, 2008.

Bibliography

Kim Dae Jung. Address, Free University of Berlin, March 9, 2000.

Kim Dae Jung. *Conscience in Action*, with co-author Choi Woon Gang, foreign policy adviser to Party for Peace and Democracy, and Hahm Hwa Gap, vice chairman, international relations committee, Party for Peace and Democracy, vice chairman. Seoul: Chung Do, 1988.

———. "A Glimmer of Peace on the Korean Peninsula." Speech, National Press Club, Washington, DC, September 18, 2007.

———. *In the Name of Justice and Peace, Main Speeches of Kim Dae Jung, President, New Democratic Party, 1991.* Seoul: New Democratic Party, 1991.

———. "Is Culture Destiny? The Myth of Asia's Anti-Democratic Values," pp. 234–241, *The New Shape of World Politics: Contending Paradigms in International Relations*. New York and London: W.W. Norton, 1999, appeared originally in *Foreign Affairs*, November/December 1994.

Kim Dae Jung—Jib Kwon Bisa (Kim Dae Jung—The Story Behind). Hankyoreh Sinmunsa. Seoul: 1998.

Kim Dae Jung. *Kim Dae Jung's "Three-Stage" Approach to Korean Reunification: Focusing on the South-North Confederal Stage*, translated by Rhee Tong Chin. Los Angeles: Center for Multiethnic and Transnational Studies, University of Southern California, 1997.

———. *Korea and Asia, a Collection of Essays, Speeches and Discussions with Kim Dae Jung*. Seoul: Kim Dae Jung Peace Foundation Press, 1994.

———. *The Korean Problem: Nuclear Crisis, Democracy and Reunification, a Collection of Essays, Speeches and Discussions*. Seoul: Kim Dae Jung Peace Foundation Press, Chung Do, 1994.

———. *Korean Reunification*, Cambridge, Clare Hall, University of Cambridge, Lectures during the research period in Cambridge, January–June 1993.

———. *Mass Participatory Economy: Korea's Road to World Economic Power*, University Press of America, 1996, revised edition of *Mass Participatory Economy: A Democratic Alternative for Korea*, University Press of America, 1985; Hangul translation, *Segye Kyungje Palganguro Ganun Gil (The Way to World Number Eight in Economy)*. Seoul: Chungdo, 1992.

———. *Naui Gil, Naui Sasang (My Way, My Ideology)*. Seoul: Hangilsa, third edition, 2000.

———. *A New Beginning: A Collection of Essays*, edited by George Oakley Totten III, translated by Lee Young Jack, Kim Yong Mok, Center for Multiethnic and Transnational Studies. Los Angeles: University of Southern California, 1996; originally published by Saeroun sijak eul wihayeo, Seoul, 1993.

———. Nobel Lecture, Norwegian Nobel Institute. Oslo, December 10, 2000.

———. "The Obama Administration and the Korean Peninsula." Speech, Seoul Foreign Correspondents' Club, January 15, 2009.

———. *Philosophy & Dialogues: Building Peace & Democracy*. New York: Korean Independent Monitor, August 1987.

———. *Prison Writings.* translated by Choi Sung Il and David R. McCann, foreword by David R. McCann, Berkeley: University of California Press, 1987; Hangul translation, *Okjung Seoshin (Prison Letters)*. Hanul, Seoul, 2004.

———. "The Pursuit of Human Rights and Social Justice in Asia." Speech. University of San Francisco, Center for the Pacific Rim, April 2005.

———. "Realization of a Grand Democratic Alliance as against the Grand Alliance for Keeping the Old Order." Statement, Seoul Foreign Correspondents' Club, July 25, 1991.

———. *Seroun Sijakul Wehayoe (For the New Beginning)*. Seoul: Kim Young Sa, 1993.

———. *The 21st Century and the Korean People: Selected Speeches of Kim Dae Jung, 1998–2004.* Seoul: Hakgojae, 2004.

———. *Unification of South and North Korea, Philosophy of Kim Dae Jung*, president of New Democratic Party in Seoul, 1991.

BIBLIOGRAPHY

———. "President Kim Dae-jung's Press Conference on the Economy: We Can Surely Overcome the Economic Crisis." Seoul Foreign Correspondents' Club, September 28, 1998.

Kim Dae Jung Peace Center, "Road to Peace on the Korean Peninsula: Lectures and Press Interviews." Seoul: December 2006.

———. "Special Lectures in Search of Peace on the Korean Peninsula." Seoul: December 2008.

———. "13-Day Journey to the U.S. In Search of Peace on the Korean Peninsula." Seoul: 2008.

———. "The Sunshine Policy, the Road to Success." Seoul: 2008.

Kim Dae Jung Presidential Library and Museum. "Collected Letters between Kim Dae-jung and Kim Jong-choong." Historical Documents Review Series 7. Seoul: Yonsei University, January 2007.

———. "Historical documents on the Presidential Election of 1971." Historical Documents Review Series 2. Seoul: Yonsei University, January 2007.

———. "Historical documents on the Kim Dae-jung Case in 1980—Cherokee documents from the U.S. State Department." Historical Documents Review Series 6. Seoul: Yonsei University, January 2006.

———. "Historical documents on the first exile of Kim Dae-jung to the U.S." Historical Documents Review Series 3. Seoul: Yonsei University, January 2006.

———. "Historical documents from Hanmintong's branch office in the US." Historical Documents Review Series 4. Seoul: Yonsei University, January 2007.

———. "Historical records on Kim Dae-jung's homecoming." Historical Documents Review Series 5. Seoul: Yonsei University January 2007.

———. "Historical documents on Kim Dae-jung's childhood school records." Historical Documents Review Series 1. Seoul: Yonsei University, January 2006.

Kim, Dong Choon. "Forgotten War, Forgotten Massacres—The Korean War (1950–1953) as Licensed Mass Killings." *Journal of Genocide Research*, December 2004, pp. 523–544.

Kim Ki Sam. "Chronological Summary of the NP [Nobel Prize] Project." Unpublished, 2008.

———. "Dongwon Lim's Connection with North Korea," Unpublished, February 15, 2003

———. "Plastered Mask, Portrait of Devil." Also, in slightly different version, "DJ Kim's Nobel Prize Scandal and Payoff to Kim Jong-il." Unpublished manuscripts, January 30, 2003.

———. "Weapons Purchase Corruption in YS and DJ Regime." Unpublished, May 18, 2004.

———. "Wiretapping Practice in the NIS." Unpublished, March 24, 2003.

Kim, Pyong Guk. *Kim Dae Jung: Hero of the Masses, Conscience in Action*. Seoul: Ilweolseogak, 1992.

Kim Soo Young. *Kim Dae Jung: Gui Inseng Kwa Jungchi (Kim Dae Jung: His Life and Politics)*. Seoul: Dongbang, 1986.

Kim Young Un, editor. *With the History, with the Age*, compiled by NHK, Japan Broadcasting, In-Dong, 1999.

Kirk, Don. "The South Korean Spy Chief Who Paved the Way for Thaw with North." *International Herald Tribune*, January 31, 2001, p. 2.

Kirk, Donald. "America's Friend in Korea: National Unity by Force." *Worldview*, February 1975.

———. "Consumed by Divisions." *Kyoto Journal*, No. 60, 2005, pp. 17–19.

———. "The Bold Words of Kim [Kim Chi Ha]; In Korea, Officials Curse, Intellectuals Cheer." *New York Times Magazine*, January 7, 1973.

Kirk, Donald. "The Death of the Sunshine Policy." *Far Eastern Economic Review*, Vol. 172, No. 5, June 2009, pp. 33–36.

———. "Kim Dae Jung." Biographical article, *Encyclopedia of Human Rights*, Vol. 3. New York: Oxford University Press, 2009.

———. "Democracy without Dissent in Korea." *New Leader*, Vol. 65, No. 5, March 8, 1982, pp. 5–6.

———. "Kim Dae-jung and Sunshine: Polls, Popularity and Politics." *Korea Observer*, Vol. 32, No. 3, Autumn 2001, pp. 409–429.

———. "Korean Crisis: Pride and Identity in the IMF Era." *The Journal of East Asian Affairs*. Vol. 13, No, 2, Fall/Winter 1999, pp. 335–360.

———. *Korean Crisis: Unraveling of the Miracle in the IMF Era*. New York: St. Martin's Press, 2000.

———. *Korean Dynasty: Hyundai and Chung Ju Yung*. Armonk: M.E. Sharpe, Asia 2000, 1994.

———. "Sunshine Policy." Chapter in *Korea Confronts the Future*, edited by John Barry Kotch and Frank-Jurgen Richter. Singapore: Marshall Cavendish International, 2005.

———. "North Korea." Article in *Encyclopedia of Human Rights*, Vol. 3. New York: Oxford University Press, 2009.

———."South Korea." Article in *Encyclopedia of Human Rights*, Vol. 3. New York: Oxford University Press, 2009.

———. "The U.S. and South Korea: From 'Sunshine' to 'Pragmatism.'" *Korea Policy Review*, John F. Kennedy School of Government, Harvard University, Vol. 3, 2008, pp. 9–17.

Kirk, Donald and Choe Sang Hun, editors. *Korea Witness: 135 Years of War, Crisis and News in the Land of the Morning Calm*. Seoul: EunHaeng NaMu, 2006.

Koh, Byung Chul, editor. *The Korean Peninsula in Transition: the Summit and Its Aftermath*. Seoul: Institute for Far Eastern Studies, Kyungnam University Press, 2002.

Korean Information Service. *Kim Dae-jung: President The Republic of Korea: A Profile of Courage and Vision*, fifth revised edition. Seoul: 1998.

Korean Overseas Information Service. "Nationwide Martial Law—Background and Necessity." Seoul: May 17, 1980.

———. "Report on the Investigation of Kim Dae-jung." Seoul: July 1980.

Kotch, John Barry and Frank-Jurgen Richter, editors. *Korea Confronts the Future*. Singapore: Marshall Cavendish International, 2005.

Lee Hee Ho. *My Love, My Country*, translated by Rhee Tong Chin. Los Angeles: Center for Multiethnic and Transnational Studies, University of Southern California, 1997; Seoul: Kim Dae Jung Peace Foundation for Asia-Pacific Region Press.

Lee Hee Ho. *Praying for Tomorrow: Letters to My Husband in Prison*, translated by Rhee Tong Chin; edited by George Oakley Totten III. Los Angeles: University of Southern California Korea Project, revised edition, 1999.

Lee Hyun Hee, Park Sung Soo, and Yoon Nae-hyun. *New History of Korea*, translated by Center for Information on Korean Culture the Academy of Korean Studies. Seoul: Jinmoondang, 2005.

Lee Jae Eui and Henry Scott-Stokes, editors. *Kwangju Uprising: Eyewitness Press Accounts of Korea's Tiananmen*. Armonk, NY: M.E. Sharpe, 2000.

Lee Ki Baik. *A New History of Korea*, translated by Edward W. Wagner with Edward J. Shultz. Seoul: Ilchokak, 1984.

Lee Namhee. *The Making of Minjung: Democracy and the Politics of Representation in South Korea*. Ithaca: Cornell University Press, 2007.

Lee Tae Ho. *Kim Dae Jung's Politics with Two Wings*. Seoul: Saeroun sijak eul wihayeo, 1995.

Bibliography

Lee Wan Bom. "Korea-Japan Conflicting Relationship under the U.S. Alliance in the 1970s: Kim Dae Jung Kidnapping Incident and the Assassination Attempt on Park Chung Hee." Woodrow Wilson International Center for Scholars, Washington, and University of North Korean Studies—Institute for Far Eastern Studies, Seoul, August 2007.

Lim Dong Won. "Inter-Korean Relations Oriented Toward Reconciliation and Cooperation," Chapter in *Korea Under Roh Tae-Woo: Democratisation, Northern Policy and Inter-Korean Relations*, edited by James Cotton. Canberra: Allen & Unwin in association with Department of International Relations, Australia National University, 1993.

Lim Dong Won. *Piseu Meikeo* (Peacemaker). Seoul: JoongAng Books, 2008.

Martin, Bradley K. *Under the Loving Care of the Fatherly Leader: North Korea and the Kim Dynasty.* New York: St. Martin's Press, 2004.

Monthly Chosun (Wolgan Chosun). April 2002, March 2002, October 2002, March 2003, October 2004.

Moon Chung In and David Steinberg, editors. *Korea in Transition: Three Years under the Kim Dae Jung Government.* Seoul: Yonsei University Press, 2002.

Niksch, Larry A. "Korea: U.S.-Korean Relations—Issues for Congress." Washington, DC: Congressional Research Service, updated April 14, 2006.

Norris, Robert S. and Hans M. Kristensen, "NRDC Nuclear Notebook: North Korea's Nuclear Program, 2005." *Bulletin of Atomic Scientists*, May–June 2005, Vol. 61, No. 3.

Oberdorfer, Don. *The Two Koreas: A Contemporary History.* Reading, MA: Addison-Wesley, 1997.

Ogle, George W. *South Korea: Dissent within the Economic Miracle.* London, Atlantic Highlands, Zed Books, London and Atlantic Highlands, 1990.

Oh Se Young. *Dae Jung Eun Salaitda* (Dae Jung Is Alive). Seoul: Parangse, 1987.

Paik, Sun Yup. *From Pusan to Panmunjom: War-Time Memoirs of the Republic of Korea's First Four-Star General.* Dulles,Virginia: Potomac Books, 1999.

Park Kyung Ae and Kim Dal Choong, editors. *Korean Security Dynamics in Transition.* New York: Palgrave Macmillan, 2001.

Rhyu Sang Young, editor. *Democratic Movements and Korean Society: Historical Documents and Korean Studies.* Seoul: Yonsei University Press, 2007.

Seoul Foreign Correspondents' Club. Trial of Kim Dae Jung, pool reports. Ahn Moo Hoon (AP), Edward Conley (VOA), K.C. Hwang (AP), Ken Kaliher (ABC), J.H. "Jimmy" Kim (UPI), Kim Sang Hyeop (AP), Lee Young Ho (*Washington Post*), Patrick K. Minn (AFP), Andrew Nagorski (*Newsweek*), John Needham (UPI), Lee (*Nihon Keizai Shimbun*), Oh Ilson (Reuters), Ron Richardson (*Far Eastern Economic Review*), Hugh Sandeman (*Economist*), Shim Jae Hoon (*New York Times*), Paul Shin (UPI), Henry Scott-Stokes (*New York Times*), Norman Thorpe (*Asian Wall Street Journal*). Seoul: August 14, 1980–June 23, 1981.

Shorrock, Tim. "Ex-Leaders Go on Trial in Seoul." *Journal of Commerce*, February 27, 1996.

Sohn, Hak Kyu. *Authoritarianism and Opposition in South Korea.* London and New York: Routledge, 1989.

Sohn Jae Shik. *Peace and Unification of Korea.* Seoul: Seoul Computer Press, 1991.

Society for Northeast Asian Peace Studies. *The Kim Dae Jung Government: The Sunshine Policy.* Seoul, Korea: Millennium Books, 1999.

Song Seung Ho. "Two Years of Tracing: The Lobby of Kim Dae Jung's Nobel Peace Prize and the Role of the National Intelligence Service." *Monthly Chosun*, October 2004.

Stueck, William. *The Korean War: An International History.* Princeton: Princeton University Press, 1995.

U.S. Congress, House Foreign Affairs Committee. "Human Rights in South Korea: Implications for U.S. Policy." Washington, DC: U.S. Government Printing Office, 1974.

U.S. Congress. "Political Developments and Human Rights in the Republic of Korea," House Committee on Foreign Affairs, Subcommittee on Human Rights and International Organizations. Washington, DC: U.S. Government Printing Office, 1986.

U.S. Department of State. "Republic of Korea Human Rights Practices." 1995.

Weekly Chosun (Joogan Chosun). "Ex-Spy Says He Has Evidence that the KCIA Had Plan to Have Kim Dae Jung Win the Nobel Prize." May 5, 2008.

Wickham, John A. *Korea on the Brink: A Memoir of Political Intrigue and Military Crisis*, foreword by Richard Holbrooke. Dulles, Virginia: Potomac Books, 2000.

INDEX

Abrams, Elliott, 103
Aesop's Fable, Sunshine, 127, 141
Agreement on Reconciliation,
    Non-Aggression, Exchanges
    and Cooperation, 127, 157
Albright, Madeleine, 167–168,
    170–172, 178
Allen, Richard, 89
American Federation of Labor-Congress
    of Industrial Organizations
    (AFL-CIO), 119
Andaman Sea, 126
Anti-Communist Law, 76, 89
Aquino, Benigno, 106, 107
Arirang TV, 183
Article Four, *see* National Security Law
Asan, village, North Korea, 191
Asan Bay, 5
Asia-Pacific Economic Cooperation
    group (APEC), 155
Asia-Pacific Peace Committee (North
    Korea), 137, 157, 170, 191, 193,
    197, 202
Asia-Pacific Peace Foundation, 99, 100,
    157, 177, 197
Asian Games, 186, 195
Asian Wall Street Journal, 78
Association of Southeast Asian Nations
    (ASEAN), 167
Auckland, 155
Aung San Suu Kyi, 206
Australia, 156

Baekje kingdom, 5
Baker, Donald, 55
Banco Delta Asia, 200, 211
Bangkok, 167
Bank of China, 200
Beijing, 38, 39, 156, 157, 159, 160,
    161, 162
Bergen, Norway, 206
Berlin, 155
"Berlin Declaration," 157
Berlin Wall, 126, 127
"Big Three" newspapers, *Chosun Ilbo,
    Dong A Ilbo, JoongAng Ilbo*, 182–183
Blue House, 43, 120. 122, 131, 135,
    148, 151, 157, 159, 174, 184,
    185, 188, 196–197, 203, 205,
    207, 210
    raid, 30, 31, 34
Bodo Yeonmaeng (National Guidance
    Alliance), 11
Bondevik, Kjell Magne, 207
Bosworth, Stephen, 168
Breen, Michael, 177
Brown, Harold, 89
Bukgyo Elementary School, 6
Burma, 126
Busan, ix, 5, 12, 14–15, 17, 24, 34, 35,
    48, 63, 79, 95, 129, 182, 186, 195
Bush, George W., Bush administration,
    169, 172, 178, 179, 184–185, 189,
    211, 212
    "axis-of-evil" speech, 184–185, 213

Bush, George W., Bush administration—*Continued*
  Kim Dae Jung, summits, 178, 179, 185, 211, 212
Byrne, Thomas J., 149–150

Cambodia, 104
Cambridge University, 130
Camp Casey, 188
Carter, Hodding, 85, 86, 87, 107
Carter, Jimmy, 57–58, 86, 87, 88, 89, 105–106, 107, 131, 179
Catholic, Catholicism, 20, 42, 46, 93–94, 107
Central Intelligence Agency, U.S., 21, 47, 52
Civil Air Transport, 21
Cha Bo Ryun, father-in-law, 10, 13
Cha Chi Chul, 59
Cha Yong Ae, 7, 12, 21, 22, 25, 26
chaebol (conglomerates), 55, 94, 97, 110, 113, 138, 143, 144, 145, 149, 182, 192, 198, 199, 203
  Top five, Samsung, Hyundai, LG, SK, and Daewoo, 145
Chang Chung Sik, 180
Chang Ki Taek, x
Chang Myun, 20, 22, 23
Chang Sang, 198–199
Chang Sung Eun, x
Chang Sung Hee, x
Cheongju Prison, 91–94, 97
Chiang Kai-shek, 161
China
  Chinese rule, 5
  Communist revolution, 9, 161
  Korean War, 17, 20, 95, 159, 189
  Nationalist Chinese, 9, 161–163
  negotiations, 18, 35, 213, 216
  North Korea, 57, 95, 128, 152, 163
  U.S. relations, 38–39, 104, 152, 212
Cho Choong Hoon, 148
Cho Gab Je, ix, 40, 170
Cho Sung Woo, 76
Cho Yang Ho, 148

Choe Sang Hun, x
Choi Gyu Baek, 202
Choi Jang Jip, 174
Choi Kyu Hah, Prime Minister, 59, 60, 62, 68, 71, 73, 75, 85, 87
Choi Kyu Sun, 196, 197
Choi Kyung Hwan, 205
Choi Won Ki, ix, 166
Cholla, Cholla region, 2, 7, 8, 18, 19, 20, 21, 22, 23, 28, 29, 31, 34, 35, 52, 64, 65, 96, 103, 115, 116, 117. 122, 123, 129, 134, 139, 140, 143, 182, 195, 209
Chosun dynasty, *see* Yi dynasty
Chosun Ilbo, 40, 166, 170, 175, 182–183, 198
Chou En Lai, 39
Christians, Christian missionaries, 55, 72, 75, 78, 88, 92, 93–94, 114, 156
Chun Doo Hwan, 42–43, 60
  abuses, corruption, trial, amnesty, 120, 121, 128, 135, 140, 146, 156, 197, 198
  Burma bombing, 126
  Decree Number Ten, Martial Law Command, martial law, 62, 63, 64, 65, 68, 70, 73, 74, 75, 77, 85, 90, 94, 95, 97, 106, 113, 114, 182
  democracy constitution, presidential election, 112–115, 119
  mini-coup, "12/12," 60–61, 135
  Olympics, 109
  "palace coup," 62
  protest, demonstrations, 61, 62, 63, 78, 110–113, 121
  Reagan summit, 89–91
  Return of Kim Dae Jung, 103, 104, 105, 107, 145
  Trial of Kim Dae Jung, 67–85
  U.S. pressure, 87–88, 89, 97–98, 99, 100
Chun Kyung Hwan, 120
Chung Ju Yung, 37, 128, 129, 151, 157, 191–192, 200, 201,202, 204
Chung Mong Hun, 157, 164, 191–195, 196, 200–202, 203, 204, 205

INDEX

Chung Mong Joon, 192
Chung Mong Koo, 192–193
Chung Seung Hwa, 59, 60–61
Chungcheong region, provinces (North and South), 29, 34, 139
Clinton, Bill, Clinton administration, 131, 133, 152, 155, 169, 170, 178–179, 184, 211, 214, 216
Clinton, Hillary, 215
Coalition for Economic Justice, 175
Coe, David, 175
Cohen, Jerome A., 99
Cohen, William, 170
Communist Youth League, 11
Communists, Communist, communism, 8, 11, 13, 18, 19, 23, 24, 29, 35, 36, 39, 42, 52, 53, 54, 55, 56, 73, 74, 77, 81, 82, 95, 126, 127, 130, 143
Cuba, 104
Current TV, 216

Daedong River, 131
Daejeon, ix, 12, 29, 36, 93, 139
Daegu, ix, 12, 23, 34, 62, 81, 129, 156, 182
  riots, 10
Daewoo Group, 37, 148
  Daewoo Electronics, 147
  Daewoo Motors, 147, 148
Declaration of Democracy, 56
Decree Number Ten, 62
Delta Air Lines, 148
Demilitarized Zone (DMZ), 21, 39, 53, 61, 63, 66, 126, 129, 156, 160, 162, 163, 179, 180, 185, 187
democracy constitution, presidential election, 112–115
Democratic Justice Party, 109, 111, 116, 121
Democratic Labor Party, 158
Democratic Liberal Party, 121. 122, 123, 128
Democratic Party (Korea), *see* Minju-dang

Democratic Party (U.S.), 40, 56, 106, 178
Democratic Youth League, 10
Derian, Patricia, 107, 108
Dong A Ilbo, 64, 73, 175, 182–183
Donghae, 152, 201
Doosan's OB Brewery, 149
Dora Station, Dorasan, 185, 187
DPRK, Democratic People's Republic of Korea, *see* North Korea

East Timor, 206
Eisenhower, Dwight D., 17, 40
Eliasson, Jan, 207
Euh Kyong Taek, 175–176
European Union, 184
Ewha Girls' School, 24
Ewha Woman's University, 24, 198

Federation of Korean Industries (FKI), 144
Federation of Korean Residents, Japan, 40, 44, 57, 74, 81, 99
Federation of Korean Trade Unions, 146–147
Feighan, Edward, 107, 108
Fic, Victor, x
Financial Supervisory Commission, 144, 176
Financial Times, 129
Fletcher School of Law and Diplomacy, Tufts University, 213
Florida recount, 178
Foglietta, Thomas, 107, 108, 205
Ford, Gerald, 57
Foreign Affairs, 133–134
Foreign Correspondents' Club of Japan, 72
France, 208
Fraternity for Democratic Constitutional Rule, 63
Free University of Berlin, 157
Freidrich-Naumann-Stiftung, 177
From Prison to President, 206
Fulbright, J. William, 40
Full Gospel Church, 183

Gallucci, Robert, 132
General Motors (GM), 148
Geneva, four-party talks (U.S., China, N., S. Korea), 150–151
Geneva framework agreement, 132, 152, 161, 166, 172, 186, 187, 190, 209
George Meany-Lane Kirkland Human Rights Award, 119
Germany, East, West, 126–127
Gimhae, 5
Gleysteen, William H. Jr, 86–89
Golden Dragon, 47, 48
Gorbachev, Mikhail, 127, 212
Gore, Al, 178, 216
Grand National Party, 138, 158, 167, 170, 171, 174, 180, 195, 197, 198
Grand Palace Hotel, Tokyo, 46
Gregg, Donald, 47, 52, 89
Guinness Book of Records, 27
Gunkukjunbi, the Committee for Founding the New Government, 8
Gwangju, 1, 5, 37, 116, 139–140
  Gwangju revolt, ix, 62–66, 85–88, 106, 110, 111, 115, 120, 129, 135, 140, 182, 210
  Trial of Kim Dae Jung, 67–85

Habib, Philip, 47–48
Habitat for Humanity, 179
Halloran, Richard, 54
Han River, 168
Han Sung Hon, 73, 75
Han Sung Joo, 132, 166, 176
Han Wan Sang, 73, 78, 131
Hanbo group, 136
Hangil Research, 181
Hanjin Group, 147–148
Hankuk Minju-dang (Korea Democratic Party), 10
Hankuk Political and Research Institute, 63
Hankyoreh Shinmun, 183
Hanmintong, *Hankuk Minju Hoebok Tongil Chokjin Kukmin Hoei*, literally "Korea National Committee to Restore Democracy and Promote Reunification," also "Korean Congress for Democracy and Unification," 40–41, 43–44, 49, 58, 61, 68, 69, 70, 71, 74, 75, 79, 81, 82, 88, 99
Hanmintong Newsletter, 49
Harrisburg, Pennsylvania, 205
Harvard, 45, 98–99, 100, 103, 106, 144, 213
Harvey, Pharis; wife, Jane, 55, 110, 116
Haui-do, Haui Island, 1, 3, 4, 5, 45, 209
Hawk, David, x
Hill, Christopher, 214
Holbrooke, Richard, 88, 89
Hong Kong, 163, 200
Hong Seok Hyun, 142, 182
Honshu, island, 151
Hue, Vietnam 31
Huh Kyung Man, 74, 75
Human Rights Watch, 131
Hwang Ha Soo, 171
Hwang Won Duk, 164–165
Hyun Jung Eun, 201, 216
Hyundai Group, 36, 67, 128, 129, 151, 152, 161, 181, 191, 194, 195, 200
Hyundai Asan, 157, 191–194, 200, 202, 204, 208, 213
Hyundai Automotive, Hyundai Motor, 146–147, 192–193, 195
Hyundai Electronics (Hynix), 200, 201
Hyundai Engineering and Construction, 62, 192, 200, 201, 214
Hyundai Heavy Industries, 192, 195
Hyundai Merchant Marine, 192, 200, 201
Hyundai Securities, 195, 200, 203

Ilsan, 197
Im Su Kyong, 121, 128, 130, 158
Incheon, Inchon, ix, 13, 36, 55, 133, 189
Inje County, 20–22, 23, 26

INDEX

Inouye, Daniel, 189
Institute of Foreign Affairs and National Security, 156
International Atomic Energy Agency (IAEA), 131, 132, 186, 212
International Monetary Fund (IMF), "IMF Crisis," 138–139, 140–142, 146, 175, 205
Iran, 184–185, 211
Iraq, 185
Israel, 178, 214

Jackson, Michael, 140–141, 206
Jang Song Hyon, x, 195
Jang Su Geum, mother, 3–4
Japan, 27, 30, 35, 40, 41, 42, 43, 44, 45, 47, 48, 51, 53, 54, 55, 58, 68, 69, 74, 75, 81, 88, 90, 98, 99, 104, 121, 127, 132, 151–152, 155, 158, 162, 163, 164, 195, 204, 213, 216
  Japanese colonial rule, 1, 2, 4–10, 23, 25, 27, 28, 36, 56, 59, 61, 95, 110, 114, 123, 143, 159, 204
  Korea-Japan Treaty, 27
Jayu-Dang (Liberal Party), 19–20
Jeju Island, 133, 170, 210
Jeong Jin Tae, 6
Jeong Woo Il, 197
Jeonju, 36
Jinro Coors, 149
Jo Myong Rok, 170–171
Johnson, Lyndon Baines, 31
Joint Declaration, June 15, 2000, 159, 164, 165, 167, 168
JoongAng Ilbo, 142, 166–167, 182, 209
Jung Tae Muk, 11, 29, 74

Kaesong, x, 5, 11, 179, 187, 193, 208, 213
Kamiya, Fuji, 60
Kang Sok Ju, 132, 186
Kangwon Province, 20, 129
Kartman, Charles, 150–151, 152, 155
Kazakhstan, 208

Keio Plaza Hotel, 44
Kelly, James, 186, 209
Kennedy, Edward M., 40, 56
Khan, Abdul Qadeer, 186
Khe Sanh, 31
Kia Motor, 147
Kim Bo Hyun, 156, 157
Kim Chi Ha, 37, 99
Kim Chol Gyu, Rev., 20
Kim Chong Wan, 75
Kim Choong Nam, x. 122, 128, 135, 139
Kim Chung Keun, 64
Kim Dae Joong, 175
Kim Dae Jung (DJ)
  anti-corruption campaign, 144
  baptism, 20
  birthplace, 1–5
  childhood, 1–4
  city, provincial elections, 1991, 123
  city, provincial elections, 1995, 134
  confederation, North-South federation, 58, 72, 96, 123–125, 129, 137, 165
  democracy protests, 1987, 110–115
  dissent, dissidence, 56, 58, 60, 61, 63–66, 210
  economy, economic crisis, ix, 100–101, 112, 114–115, 138–142, 144–150, 175–176
  education, 1, 5–7
  electronic eavesdropping, 142–143, 210
  family reunions, 161, 165, 179–180, 184, 207, 212–213
  Foreign Affairs article, 133–134
  four powers, U.S., China, Japan Russia, 95–96
  human rights, North Korea, 150, 172, 173, 187
  illness, death, funeral, 210–211, 216
  imprisonment, 56, 60, 63, 64, 68, 80, 90–98, 103, 106
  inauguration, 140–141

243

Kim Dae Jung (DJ)—*Continued*
　inter-Korean summit, ix, 90, 131,
　　151, 153, 155, 156–167, 173, 178,
　　179, 183–184, 191–195, 201, 202,
　　204, 209, 212, 215
　Japan, 27, 28, 40–41
　kidnapping, 45–49, 51, 52–53, 68, 88
　Korean War activities, 11, 12, 14
　labor, tripartite commission, 146–147
　motor vehicle accident, 37
　Nobel Peace Prize, ceremony,
　　controversy, 173–177, 181, 191,
　　204–208, 209, 211, 213
　North Korea, 39–40, 42, 58, 66, 100,
　　119, 131, 138, 139, 141, 150–151,
　　183–184, 212, 214–215
　North-South hotline, 165–166
　Office of External Cooperation, 205
　Olympics, 109, 114
　Park Chung Hee, 28, 29–30, 31, 40,
　　41, 43, 56, 145
　polls, popularity, 175–176, 182
　presidential election, campaign, 1971,
　　34–37, 70, 72, 78
　presidential election, campaign, 1987,
　　113–117, 120, 121
　presidential election, campaign, 1992,
　　122, 128–130, 135
　presidential election, campaign, 1997,
　　ix, 134–140, 142, 203
　presidential election, campaign, 2002,
　　190, 199
　"prisoners of conscience," long-term
　　prisoners, 143–144, 173
　reforms, 209–210
　responses to West Sea skirmish and
　　deaths of two schoolgirls, 2002,
　　187–190
　return from U.S., 103–108
　politics, early career, 9–11, 17–27
　scandals of sons, 196–200, 210
　Sunshine policy, engagement,
　　reconciliation, 40, 123–125, 127,
　　131, 134, 137, 141, 149–153,
　　155–170, 175–176, 178, 184–185,
　　186, 187, 189–190, 191–194, 201,
　　204, 208, 209–216
　trial, sentencing, 67–85 121
　Vietnam, 27–28, 212
Kim Dae Jung Peace Foundation for
　Asia and the Pacific, 137, 197, 211
Kim Dae Jung Presidential Library and
　Museum, Kim Dae Jung Library,
　44, 86, 88, 92–93, 197, 211
Kim Dong Shin, 189, 198
"Kim Dongmu," 74
Kim Han Jung, 158, 205, 206
Kim Hong Gul (third son), 27, 91–92,
　196, 198, 199, 206, 216
Kim Hong Il (first son), 63, 92–93, 199,
　203, 216
Kim Hong Up (second son), 12, 78,
　91–93, 196–197, 199, 209, 216
Kim Hyun Chul, 136, 144, 203
Kim Il Sung, 8, 9, 31, 39, 72, 82, 100,
　121, 124, 125, 131–132, 137, 152,
　164, 177, 179, 214
Kim Jae Kyu, 59, 63
Kim Jong Nam
Kim, Jimmy, 115
Kim Jong Choong, 45
Kim Jong Il, 132, 137, 141, 151, 152,
　153, 156, 157, 158, 159, 160,
　162–171, 173–175, 178, 179,
　180, 183–184, 189, 195, 202,
　204, 205, 208, 212, 215
Kim Jong Pil (JP), ix, 34, 35, 45, 51, 52,
　61, 62, 63, 74, 116, 120, 121, 139,
　145, 158
Kim Jong Un, 215
Kim Ki Sam, ix, 204–205, 206, 207,
　208, 213
Kim Kye Gwan, 151, 155
Kim Kyung Jae, 120
Kim Sang Chul, 134
Kim Sang Hyun, 70–71, 72–73, 78
Kim Seung Kyu, 143
Kim Stephen Cardinal, Sou Hwan, 42
Kim Woo Choong, 37, 148
Kim Yeong Wan, 202

Kim Yong Ju, 39
Kim Yoon Kyu, 202
Kim Yong Nam, 159, 171, 207
Kim Yong Sun, 137, 170
Kim Yoon Sik, 73.
Kim Young Sam (YS), ix, 33, 54, 60, 61, 62, 63, 67, 68, 74, 109, 111, 112, 115, 116, 120, 121, 122, 128–130, 131, 132, 133, 134–136, 138–140, 142, 143, 144, 203, 205
Kim Yun Sik, father, 2, 3, 5–7
Kim Zohng Chill, 110
Kimpo Airport, 107
King Kojong, 5
Kissinger, Henry, 38–39, 45, 212
Ko Un Tae, 76
Kong Un Young, 142
Kongwha-dang (Republican Party), 35, 37, 68
Kookmin Ilbo, 183
Korea Development Bank, 194, 200, 202
Korea Electric Power Corporation (KEPCO), 132
Korea Herald, 176
Korea Military Academy, 61, 156
Korea National Tourist Organization, 110
Korea Railroad (KORAIL), 147
Korea Research Center, 176
Korea University, 54, 68, 70, 72, 121, 174
Korea-Japan Treaty, 27
Korean Air, 126, 147
  crashes, 147–148
Korean Broadcasting System (KBS), 140, 151, 181
Korean Central Intelligence Agency (KCIA), 10, 34, 35, 38, 39, 40–41, 43, 45, 47, 48, 51, 52, 53, 54, 56, 59, 61, 62, 63–64, 68, 72, 76, 79, 92, 99, 109, 139, 142, 199, 205, 211, 213
Korean Confederation of Trade Unions, 128, 146–147, 210
Korean Institute for Human Rights, 99, 110

Korean Peninsula Energy Development Organization (KEDO), 132, 152
Korean War, 9, 11, 12–14, 17–18, 19, 20, 24, 30, 31, 34, 37–38, 55, 57, 95, 104, 124, 126, 133, 150, 151, 156, 159, 165, 177, 178, 179, 188, 189, 190, 194, 210, 214
Korean Young Women's Group, 24
Kotch, John Barry, x
Kreibel, Wes, 48
Kumchangri, 152–153
Kumho, 132, 172, 190
Kumho Group, 203
Kumkang, Mount, x, 20, 151, 152, 161, 179, 180, 191, 193, 201, 204, 208, 212, 213
Kuomintang, 9, 161
Kuwait, 62
Kwangju, *see* Gwangju
"Kwangju Democratization Movement," 63
Kwangwhamun, 59
Kwon Chul Hyun, 174
Kwon Roh Kap, 202
Kwon Young Hae. 142, 203
Kyongbok Palace, 59
Kyongsang region, provinces (North and South), 23, 34, 35, 46, 62, 122, 129, 182
Kyunggi Province, 139
Kyunghyang Shinmun, 175

Lambuth College, Jackson, Tennessee, 24
Laos, 31, 55, 104
Le Duc Tho, 45, 212
League of Democratic Youth associations, 63
Lee Bu Young, 144
Lee Byung Chul, 37
Lee Chang Choon, x
Lee Hae Chan, 76, 82
Lee Hae Dong, 77
Lee Hak Soo, 142
Lee Han Dong, 145

246 Index

Lee Hee Ho, 15, 24–27, 48–49, 55, 56, 62, 80, 83, 88–89, 91, 97, 98, 196, 210, 213, 216
Lee Ho Chul, 73, 78
Lee Hoi Chang, 138–139, 142, 144, 190
Lee Hu Rak, 39, 47, 52
Lee Hun Jai, 144–145
Lee Ik Chi, 203
Lee Jong Chan, 205, 206, 207
Lee Keun Pal, 110, 113
Lee Keun Young, 194, 202
Lee Ki Ho, 195, 201–202
Lee Kuan Yew, 133–134
Lee Kun Hee, 142, 182
Lee Kwang Pyo, 90–91
Lee Kyu Sung, 145
Lee Mun Yong, 68, 70, 72
Lee, Myung Bak, 214
Lee Nam Bok, x
Lee Nam Hee, 145
Lee Shin Bom, 76, 111
Lee Sok Pyo, 75–76
Lee Taek Dong, 73, 78
Lee Wan Bom, 47
Lee Young Ho, 80, 83
Lee Young Sup, 83
Liberal Democratic Party (Japan), 121
Liberty Medal, 205, 206
Lenin, Vladimir, 9
Lim Chang Yuel, 138
Lim Dong Won, 137, 153, 155, 156, 157, 165–166, 169–170, 193–194, 197, 201, 202, 203
  background, 156–157
Loh Shin Yong, 109
Los Angeles, 109, 196
Los Angeles Times, 103–104

Macao, 200
MacArthur, Douglas, 13, 189
Madison Square Garden, 107
Maehyang-ri, 168
Manchoukuo, 7
Manchuria, 7, 23
Mandela, Nelson, 140, 175, 177, 181, 205

Manila, 106
Mao Zedong, 39, 161
Mapo District, Mapo-Gu, Seoul, ix, 41, 42, 43, 48–49, 53, 107
Marcos, Ferdinand, 106
Masan, 59, 79, 129
matador politics, 33
Matthews, Gene, 109
May First Stadium, 171
Mayflower Hotel, Washington, 61
McCune-Reischauer transliteration system, ix, 98
media reform, 182–183
Meinardus, Ronald, 177
Methodism, Methodist church, 24, 55, 93, 109, 116
Mikulski, Barbara A., 105
Millennium Democratic Party, 158, 180, 181, 196
Minjoksibo, 45
Minju-Dang (Democratic Party), 10, 20, 21, 22, 27, 29, 30, 45, 72, 73
Mokpo, 1, 5, 7, 10, 12, 13, 14, 18, 20, 23, 24, 25, 26, 27, 29, 30, 37, 44, 74, 197
Mokpo Commercial Public High School, 6
Mokpo Ilbo, 14
Mokpo marine league (Mokpo-haesang-dan), 11
Mokpo Youth League, 8
Monthly Chosun, ix, 18, 40, 44, 124–126, 207, 208
Moody's Investor Service, 149–150
Moon Ik Hwan, Rev., 68, 69, 71–72, 74, 77, 82, 115, 121, 130
Moon Jae In, 195
Moon Kyu Hyun, Rev., 158
Moon Sun Myung, Rev., 134
More, Thomas, 20
Moscow, 127, 128, 179
Muan County, 209
Mun Se Gwang, 54
Mun Ung Shi, 80
Munhwa Ilbo, 181

Museum of the Peasants Movement in Haui 3 Islands, 3
Muskie, Edmund, 87
Musudan-ri, 151, 155
Myanmar, 206
Myongdong Cathedral, 56, 111, 146

Naeil Shinmun, 181
Namdaemun (South Gate), 61
Nampo, 133
Namro-Dang (South Workers' Party), 9, 74
National Assembly, 17, 26, 27, 28,29, 34, 35, 37, 38, 45, 54, 61, 70, 73, 76, 116, 121, 122, 129, 176, 177, 180, 198, 199, 205, 210
   election of Rhee Syngman, 15
   elections, 1954, 19–20
   elections, 1957–1959, 20–21
   elections, 1960, 1961, 22, 23
   elections, 1963, 26–27
   elections, 1967–1968, 30, 45, 74
   elections, 1971, 37
   elections, 1981, 90
   elections, 1985, 108–109
   elections, 1988, 120
   elections, 1996, 135
   elections, 2000, 158, 204
   elections, 2008, 209, 213
National Conference for Unification, 91
National Congress for New Politics, 138, 145
National Constitution Center, 205
National Council for Unification, 41
National Defense Law, *see* National Security Law
National Human Rights Commission, 210
National Intelligence Service (NIS, formerly KCIA, NSPA), 42, 43, 130, 142–143, 155–156, 159, 165, 169–170, 194, 200, 202, 204, 205, 206, 207, 208
National Police, 43
National Press Club, Washington, 90

National Security Law, 36, 38, 42, 54, 72, 76, 81, 89, 125–126, 130, 182, 201, 210
National Security Planning Agency (formerly KCIA), 130, 137–138, 141–142
National Seoul, 63
National Theater, 53–54
NBC News, 108, 121
New Democratic Party, 122
New Korea Corporation, 2
New Korea Democratic Party, 108
New York Times, 54
Nigeria, 156
Nixon Doctrine, 34
Nixon, Richard, 34, 38, 39, 57, 212
Nobel Foundation, 207
Nobel Peace Prize, ix, 119, 123, 130, 137, 150, 158, 171, 173–177, 181, 191, 200, 211
   Lobbying for Nobel, 204–209, 213
   Nobel Peace Prize Committee, 207
Nodis Cherokee, 87–88
Nordpolitik, 127
North Cholla Province, 36, 129, 139
North Korea (DPRK), ix, 6, 17, 18, 29, 30, 31, 34–35, 36, 38, 42, 53, 54, 57, 58, 66, 69, 72, 80, 81, 82, 94, 95, 100, 111, 115, 116, 124–126, 127–129, 130, 132, 150–153
   Bureau 39, 200, 204
   DPRK Red Cross Society, 173
   economy, famine, 160–161, 162, 213
   gulag system, human rights abuses, 126–127, 187, 204, 212
   inter-Korean summit, 90, 131, 151, 153, 155, 156–167, 173, 178, 179, 183–184, 191–195, 201, 202, 204, 209, 212, 215–216
   missiles, 151, 155, 160, 163, 171–172, 178
   National Defense Commission, 171, 172, 174
   North-South agreements, 127–128, 137, 157

North Korea (DPRK)—*Continued*
  nuclear program, 127, 131, 132–133, 160, 163, 178, 186–188, 204, 207, 208, 214–215
  nuclear tests, 172, 209, 211, 212
  sanctions, 160, 211
  submarine incidents, 132–133, 151
  Supreme People's Assembly, 152, 159, 163, 171, 207, 215
  "terrorist" label, 160, 214
North Korean residents, Japan, *see* Federation of Korean Residents, Japan
North Koreans, 11, 12, 13, 39, 74, 121
Northern Limit Line (NLL), 153, 188
"northern wind" conspiracy, 138, 141–142, 203
Norway, 174, 175, 206
Numada, Satou, 45

Obama, Barack, 214
Oberdorfer, Don, 39
Obuchi, Keizo, 155
Ogle, George, 55
Olympic Games, 1988, 105, 109–111, 114, 115–116, 120–121
Olympic Stadium, Seoul, 206
Oriental Development Company, 2
Oslo Center for Peace and Human Rights, 207
Oslo Church of Norway, 207
Oslo, Norway, 174, 175, 207

Paek Nam Sun, 167
Paekhwawon guesthouse, 164.
Paekje, *see* Baekje
Pakistan, 186, 208
Palos Verde, 196
Panmunjom, 17, 39, 121, 131, 156, 159, 193
  Joint Security Area, 57, 135
Paris peace talks, Accord, 31
Park Chung Hee
  abuses, torture, 42, 85, 128, 199, 210
  assassination, 59, 78, 81, 90, 135
  assassination of wife, Yook Young Soo, 53–54
  Communist background, 24
  coup, 1961, 22–23, 34
  economic policies, 28, 55, 56, 58–60, 96–97, 100–101
  election, 1963, 26
  election, 1967, 29
  election, 1971, 34–37
  Emergency Declaration, Decree Number Nine, decrees, 38, 41, 43, 52, 54
  funeral, 59
  Japanese army, 23–24
  Kim Dae Jung, 29–30, 35, 40, 42, 43, 45, 47, 48, 51–53, 56, 57, 58, 60, 69, 94, 95, 100, 122, 142, 146
  labor, 58–59
  martial law, 41, 106
  North Korea, 39–40, 42, 100
  Korean War, 24
  politics, 34, 35, 55–56, 57, 62, 68, 109, 120, 122, 123, 130, 139
  U.S. relations, 57–58, 86
Park Jie Won, 119–120, 157, 160, 193–195, 201, 202, 209, 213
Park Tae Joon, 145, 193
Party for Peace and Democracy, 121–122
payoff to North Korea for inter-Korean summit, 157–158, 164, 192–195, 200–205, 207–208, 213, 216
Peace Corps, 55
"peace regime," 160
People's Revolutionary Party, 54, 55
People's Solidarity for Participatory Democracy, 143
Peres, Shimon, 205
perestroika, 127
Perry, William, "Perry Review," 152–153, 155, 157
Persson, Goran
Peter, Paul and Mary, 107
Philadelphia, 205, 206
Philippines, 106, 204
Philosophy & Dialogues, 119, 120

Index

Piper, Hal, x
Pohang Iron and Steel (POSCO), 145, 170, 198
Poitras, Edward, 116
Poland, 140
Powell, Colin, 178
Presbyterian, 68
Princeton Theological Seminary, 199
Princeton University, 199
Pueblo, U.S.S., 30, 31, 47
Pusan, *see* Busan
Putin, Vladimir, 179
Pyongyang, 8, 36, 39, 81, 121, 127, 131, 133, 135, 137, 150, 153, 156, 157, 159, 163, 165, 171, 178, 179, 180, 183, 184, 189, 203, 212, 215

Rafto Foundation, 206
Rafto, Thoroff, 206
Ramos-Horta, Jose, 206
Ranard, Donald A., 48
Ranard, Donald L., 48
Rangoon, 126
Reagan, Ronald; Reagan administration, 89, 91, 98, 99, 105, 107, 115, 116, 212
Red Cross, South, 180
Red Cross talks, North-South, 1972, 39, 73, 100, 160
Reischauer, Edwin O., 98, 99, 107
Renault, 148
Research Institute of Korean Politics and Culture, 70
Revolutionary Wars and anti-Communist Strategy, 156
Rhee In Je, 139
Rhee Syngman, 8, 14–15, 17–18, 19, 20, 21, 22, 23, 25, 40, 42, 48, 72, 95, 96, 104, 123, 124
 student revolution, 21, 70, 78, 95, 134
Rice, Condoleezza, 214
Roh Moo Hyun, 146, 172, 190, 192–195, 203, 215
Roh Shin Young, 89

Roh Tae Woo, 61, 62, 109, 110, 111, 112, 113, 114, 115–116, 121, 122, 123, 127–128, 130, 139, 156, 215
 corruption, trial, amnesty, 120, 135, 140, 197
ROK, Republic of Korea, *see* South Korea
Rooney, James, 149
Russia, 162, 163, 164, 204, 208, 213, 216
Russo-Japanese War, 6

Saddam Hussein, 185
Saemaul movement, 120
Samsung Group, 37, 142, 182
 Samsung Electronics, 147
 Samsung Motors, 147, 148
Saudi Arabia, 62
Scarritt College for Christian Workers, Nashville, 24, 26, 116
Secret Garden, 191
Sejong-ro, 59
Seoul Airport, K-16 base, 116
Seoul National University, 24, 76, 97, 204
Seoul Olympic Organizing Committee, 109
Seoul protests 61–63, 70, 73, 110–113, 116, 121
"Seoul Spring," 61
Seoul Station, 61
Shanghai, 160
Shanghai Communique, 39
Sherman, Wendy, 171
Shim Jae Joon, x
Shin Kwang Soo, 173
Shin, Paul, 56, 83
Shinmin-dang (New Democratic Party), 9, 34, 37, 68, 122
Shultz, George, 108
Shorrock, Tim, 86–87
Sigur, Gaston, 111, 113
Silla kingdom, 5
Singapore, 133, 157–158, 200
Sinnott, James, 55

six-party talks, 213, 214, 216
SK Group, 145, 203
SK Telecom, 149
Sohlman, Michael, 207
Sokcho, 151
Song Doo Hwan, 193–194
Song Ki Won, 75
Song Kun Ho, 73
Soros, George, 140
South Africa, 140
South Cholla Province, 1, 24, 116, 120, 129, 139–140
South Chungcheong Province, 29
South Korea (ROK), ix, 31, 38, 39, 41, 53, 56, 57, 69, 78, 81, 82, 85, 103, 104, 106, 132
    agreements, North Korea, 127–128, 133, 157
    armed forces, special forces, 85–88
    prisoners, fishermen, soldiers in North Korea, 173–174, 180
    Unification ministry, survey, 168–169
Soviet Union, 8, 30, 35, 127, 128, 162, 212
Springfield, Virginia, 99
Stålsett, Gunnar, bishop, 207
Stasi, 126
Stevens, Ted, 189
Stevenson, Adlai, 17
Stockholm, 207
Stueck, William, x
Sul Hoon, 77
Sunan Airport, 163
Supreme Court, Korea, 21, 82, 90, 138, 195, 203
Sweden, 206
Syria, 214

Tadaaki, Hara, 173
Taegu, *see* Daegu
Taejon, *see* Daejeon
Taepodong, Taepodong-2, missile, 151, 155, 171–172, 214
Taft-Katsura memorandum, 204
Taipei, 106

Taiwan, 161, 162–163
Tanaka, Kakuei, Prime Minister, 40
Templeton Investment Trust, 149
Thorpe, Norman, 78
"386 generation," 145
"three Kims," ix, 61, 120, 123
Tiger Division, Vietnam, 27
Tiger Management, 149
Tiger Pools International, 196
"TK Mafia," 62
Toffler, Alvin, 93
Tong Kim, 186
Tonghak revolt, 5
Tongil (unification) group, 134
Tran Duc Luong, 212
Travers, Mary, 107
Truman, Harry S., 17
Truth and Reconciliation Commission, 210
Tumen River, 216

Ulsan, 67, 128, 129, 146
Unification Church, 134
United Liberal Democrats, 145, 158
United Nations, 57
    North and South Korea, 95, 127
United Nations Command, 17, 86, 95, 188
United Press International, 115
United States, 8, 18, 35, 43, 55, 162
    armed forces, bases, 13, 30, 34, 47, 52, 56, 57, 95, 106, 111, 112, 115, 126, 131, 133, 151, 153, 160, 162, 165, 166–167, 168, 179, 187–190
    axe murder incident, 57
    deaths of two schoolgirls, 187–190
    House of Representatives, 105
    National Security Council, 89
    North Korea, peace treaty, sanctions, "terrorist" label, 160–161, 163, 214–215
    nuclear negotiations, 132, 133, 152–153, 155, 213, 215, 216
    Pentagon, 40, 57

Senate Foreign Relations
  Committee, 40
State Department, 48, 57, 80, 85,
  86, 87–88, 89, 103, 107, 108,
  171–172, 204, 214
Status of Forces Agreement (SOFA),
  189
U.S. Command, 23, 86, 87
U.S. Information Service, 86
U.S.-Korea alliance, 30, 31, 52, 56,
  57, 81, 86, 95, 110, 113,
  164–168
White House, 40, 89–91, 178
University of San Francisco, 209–210
University of Southern California, 196
Urban Industrial Mission, 55
USA Today, 103
U.S. Freedom of Information Act, 86

Vienna, 200
Viet Cong, 30
Viet Cong factions, 44–45
Vietnam, South, 27–28, 30, 31, 34, 38,
  40, 44, 45, 56, 212
  Tet 1968 offensive, 30–31
Vietnam War, 56, 57, 212
Vietnam, Vietnamese, North, 30–31,
  38, 45, 57, 104, 212
Vietnamization, 38

Walesa, Lech, 140, 205
Walker, Richard L., 108
Wall Street Journal, 78
Washington, 40, 43, 61, 99–100, 103,
  106, 108, 110, 142, 178, 179, 183,
  184–185
Washington Post, 39, 80
Washington Times, 134
"We Shall Overcome," 79

West Sea, 1, 133
  naval battle, 1999, 153
  naval battle, 2002, 188–189, 196, 198
Westin Chosun Hotel, 142
White Horse Division, Vietnam, 27
White, Robert E., 107
Wi Pyoung Ryang , 175
Wickham, John A., 86–87
Wolmido, 13
Wonsan, 191
Woo Lae Oak, 107
Workers' Party, North, 74, 124,
  170–171, 174, 180, 200
Workers' Party, South, *see*
  Namro-dang
World Bank, 145
World Cup, 2002, 187, 195, 196
World War II, 7, 17, 162

Ye Choon Ho, 70, 76–77
Yellow Sea, *see* West Sea
Yi dynasty, 3, 5, 20, 24, 36, 59, 91, 95,
  190
Yong Sun Mok, 181
Yongbyon, nuclear complex, 127, 131,
  132, 152, 186, 209, 214
Yongsan base, 168
Yonsei University, 92, 121, 197
Yoo In Ho, 73
Yoo Sang Boo, 198
Yook Young Soo, 54
Young Men's Christian Association
  (YMCA), 73
Young Women's Christian Association
  (YWCA), 24–25
YTN, cable TV network, 183
Yushin Constitution, 41, 43, 54, 60, 70,
  71, 72, 73, 78, 79, 90, 91
Yun Po Sun, 23, 26, 27, 29, 37

GPSR Compliance
The European Union's (EU) General Product Safety Regulation (GPSR) is a set of rules that requires consumer products to be safe and our obligations to ensure this.

If you have any concerns about our products, you can contact us on

ProductSafety@springernature.com

In case Publisher is established outside the EU, the EU authorized representative is:

Springer Nature Customer Service Center GmbH
Europaplatz 3
69115 Heidelberg, Germany

www.ingramcontent.com/pod-product-compliance
Lightning Source LLC
LaVergne TN
LVHW091535060526
838200LV00036B/617